# HOLIDAY WALKS
# in
# THE LOIRE VALLEY

Judy Smith

**Published by** Sigma Leisure – an imprint of
Sigma Press, 1 South Oak Lane, Wilmslow, Cheshire SK9 6AR, England.

**British Library Cataloguing in Publication Data**
A CIP record for this book is available from the British Library.

**ISBN:** 1-85058-772-8

**Typesetting and Design by:** Sigma Press, Wilmslow, Cheshire.

**Cover design by:** The Agency, Macclesfield, Cheshire

**Printed by:** MFP Design & Print

**Cover Photographs:** main cover picture - Château de Chenonceau; smaller pictures, from left, Château de Montsoreau beside the Loire - sunflowers in Touraine - Pont de La Valla and priory, Pommiers

**Photographs:** the author

**Maps:** Michael Gilbert

**Thanks:** to the very helpful staff of Offices de Tourisme all over the Loire Valley

## DISCLAIMER

# Preface

The Loire Valley is one of the most popular holiday destinations in Europe. Each year, around six million visitors descend on the region, attracted by the magnificent châteaux, diversity of wines and cuisine, wealth of history, excellent climate and at the heart of it all, the blue, sandy-banked, summery Loire itself. Perhaps surprisingly, the region also has a first-class network of footpaths – and there is so much more to be gained from a visit to the Loire Valley if you can explore a little on foot.

The 32 walks in this book are scattered throughout the region and set out to cater for all tastes and abilities. For the casual walker and those with a young family, there are many short rambles – wanders beside the river-bank or around a lake, ambles through wild flower woods or along a canal towpath. For the more regular walker, there are all-day hikes on terrain that may be a little more demanding – longer treks through the forests and well-marked trails over ranges of hills you may never have thought of. There are also suggestions for covering long (and short) sections of the GR3, the long-distance footpath running the length of the Loire Valley. Alongside each walk, there are ideas for several more routes in the same area – enough to keep you busy all holiday.

This book contains an extra theme, 'From the Source to the Sea', a special series of 12 walks spaced along the whole length of the river.

In conclusion, my sincere thanks go to my husband Eric, for his companionship on all these walks. We had visited the Loire Valley many times before, but we greatly enjoyed the opportunity to explore its byways so thoroughly this year. The book also provided us with a reason to seek the source of the river and to wander among the curious but incredibly beautiful volcanic peaks of the Cévennes. The Loire Valley leaves us with many memories – mountain pansies covering the slopes of the Mézenc in springtime, the shining red leaves of autumn vines in the Layon Valley and a first glimpse of the glorious Château of Chenonceau, mirrored in the calm waters of the Cher, caught in the long rays of evening sun. I hope that you will gain as much pleasure as we have had from rambling in the Loire Valley. So now read on – and find out more about the holiday walks that await you. Good luck on your journey!

*Judy Smith*

# Contents

## The Loire Valley



## The Upper Reaches



## Orléanais and Blésois (the *départements* of Loiret and Loir-et-Cher)

***Note: Walk nos. 1, 2, 3, 4, 5, 6, 7, 8, 11, 18, 26, 30 and 32 form the series 'From the Source to the Sea'.***

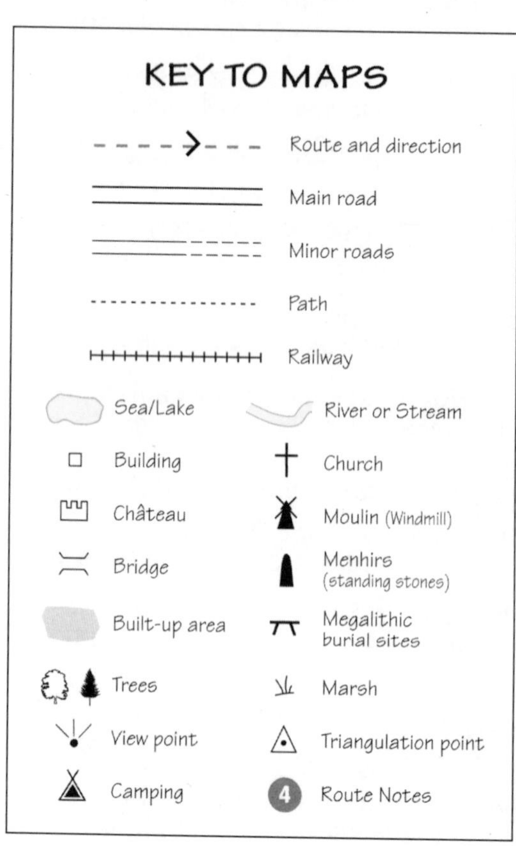

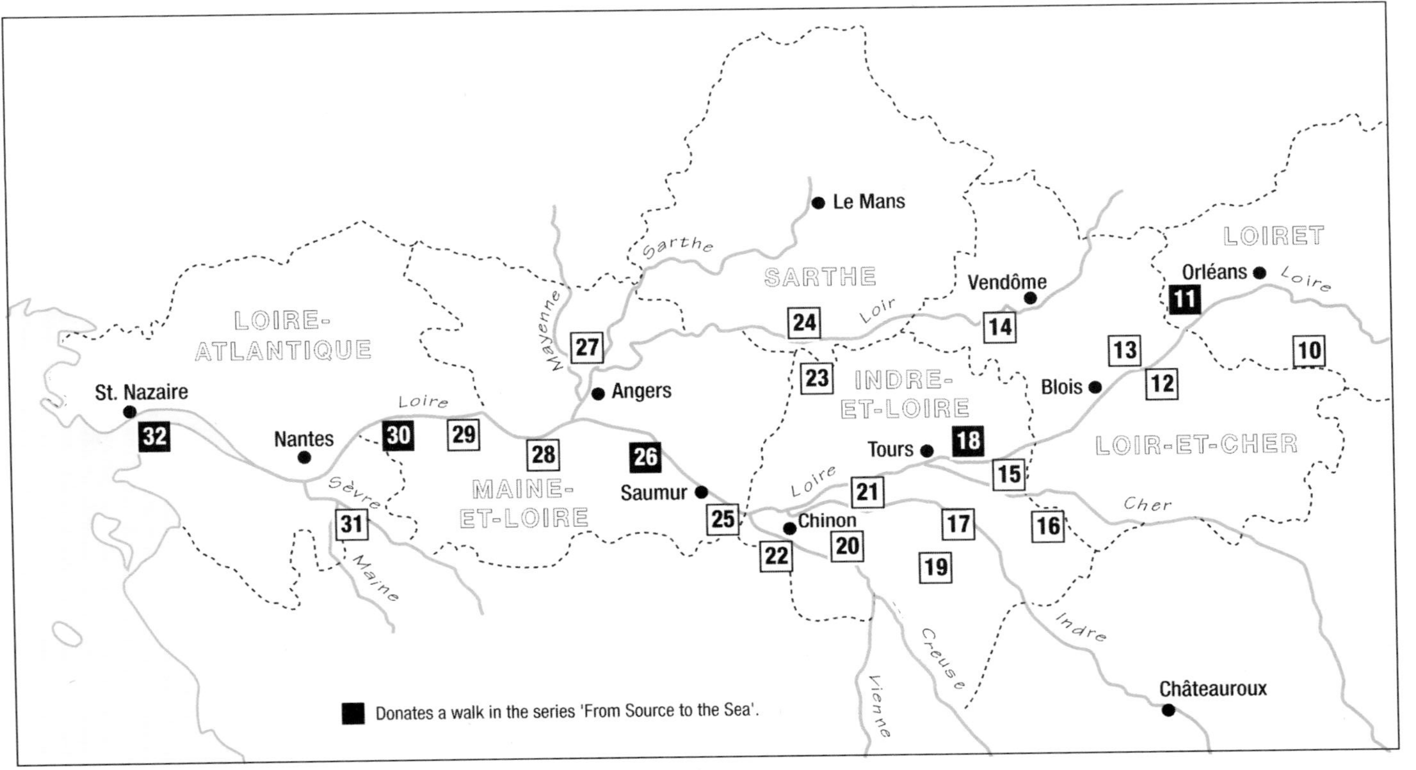


Location Map 1

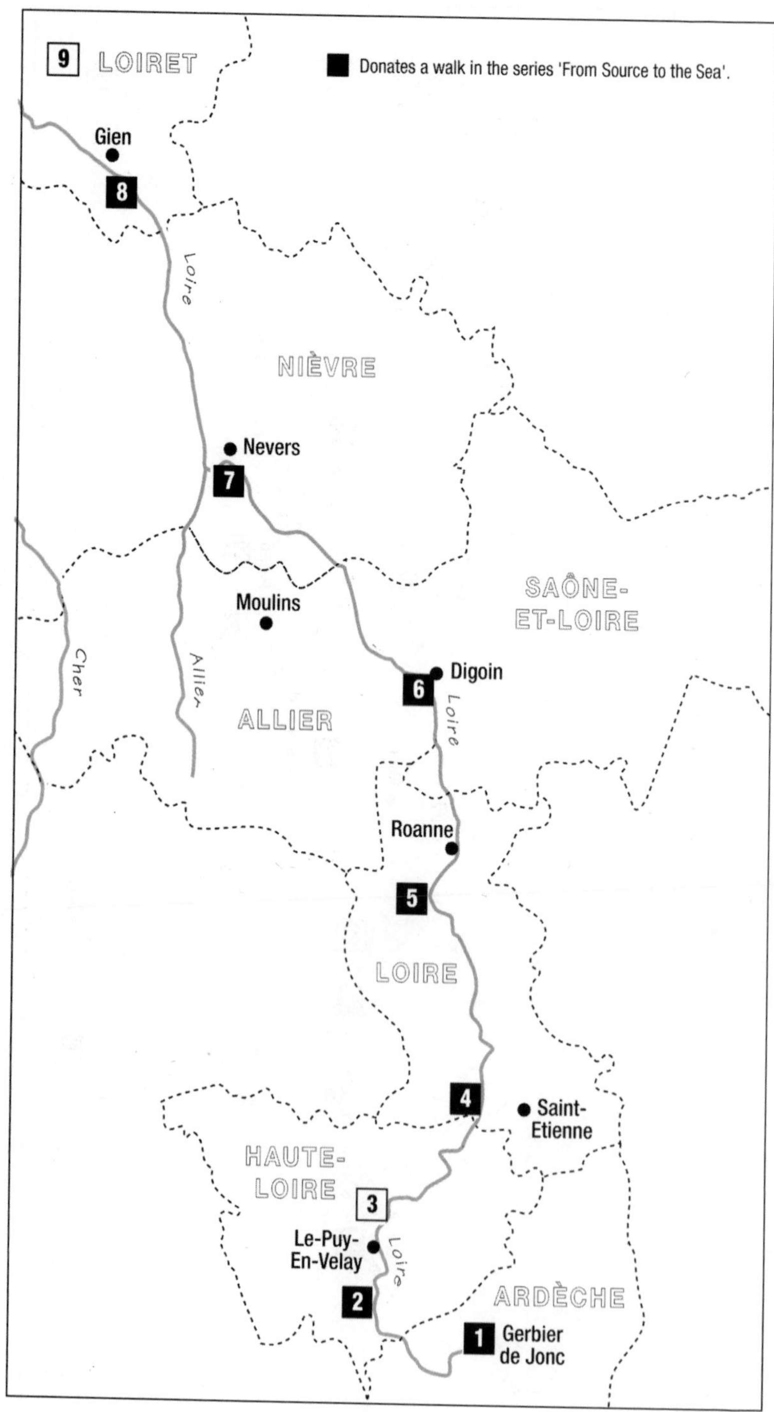


Location Map 2

# The Loire Valley

The Royal River, the last wild river of Europe, the Valley of Kings and the Garden of France — the Loire and its valley have earned a string of epithets. Here, in summer at least, the shallow languorous river slips between banks of golden sand and tree-topped islands, under cliffs of creamy-yellow tufa, past fairy-tale and fortress-like châteaux, between vineyards producing some of the finest wines in France. The Loire Valley is a favourite holiday destination for the entire world. The British love it – the Loire is about as far south as you can drive in a day – and they contribute some two hundred thousand visitors every year. The climate is mild, warmed from the south but tempered by the Atlantic – spring comes early, autumn lasts long and there are only few days in summer when the walking must be done in the morning before the sun is high in the sky.

Many of you reading this will have visited the Loire Valley before and may be very well-acquainted with its attractions. Even so, this book can offer you something quite different. When walking, you will have time to take in the landscape around you and enjoy the panorama from viewpoints that are accessible to no-one but you. You will pass ancient churches, châteaux and cave dwellings that are not on the tourist trail, stop for drinks in villages well away from the crowds, and enjoy the delights of the vineyards at first-hand. Walking brings you closer to the land and to its people and you will find that farmers and wine-growers smile at you, and that local folk are far more ready to exchange a few words with those on foot. And to enjoy this, there really is no need for sophisticated equipment – anyone can take a walk!

The walks in this book are scattered throughout the region and are intended to cater for all ranges of ability and inclination. They vary in length between 2 and 10½ miles – but even then, there are suggested short cuts or extensions to most of them. Almost all the routes are circular, so that you will have no problems with transport – there are only two where an easy bus ride will take you to the starting point, leaving you to follow a linear path home. With each walk, there are suggestions for others in the area nearby. But before you set out, here are just a few words about the varied countryside you will find on foot in the Loire Valley.

The Loire rises in the Cévennes, on the northern slopes of the Massif Central, and flows around 1020km to its mouth on the Bay of Biscay. Nevertheless, most guidebooks of 'The Loire Valley' confine themselves to that stretch of the river between Gien and Nantes, with the occasional one continuing the journey to the coast. Rarely, outlying areas such as Sarthe or Berry are included. In this way, at least, most of the châteaux are taken into account, and that is what most of the visitors are here for. But this is a walking book, and the Loire Valley is taken literally, following the river all the way from its source on the Gerbier de Jonc to the sea. The book therefore includes not only a little of the Loire-Atlantique, but also something of the remote mountains and spectacular gorges in which the river spends its early days. Those peripheral regions are discussed in the section 'From the Source to the Sea', to be found on page 3. But, for the meantime, let us concentrate on that part of the Loire Valley that is the most popular holiday destination, and in which most of the walks are situated.

The Loire Valley is a region of diverse natural beauty and enormous historical interest – and the walks here reflect just that. First there are the woodlands. In the east is the vast oak and pine Forest of Orléans, at the heart of which the osprey nests – and, across the river, the beautiful forest of the Sologne, a land of lakes, birch and purple heather, a favourite haunt of deer and wild boar. Farther west, between the Loire and 'le Loir', is the scattered heath and woodland of the *gâtine tourangelle*, while south of the Loire, in the oak and holly woods around Gennes, lies a wealth of prehistoric megaliths amid the gorse and bracken. The vineyards are a complete contrast, in places stretching across the rolling landscape as far as the eye can see. Their open aspect gives distant views – around Saumur, along the length of the Loire Valley and back to the misty hills of Burgundy. Farther west, the Corniche Angevine is prime walking country, a range of vine-clad hills between the Loire and the Layon with splendid views into both valleys. These beautiful vineyards are a patchwork of red and gold in autumn – and the sweet wine of the Coteaux du Layon is as rich as the landscape itself. South of Nantes, around the pretty valleys of the Sèvre and the Maine, are the vineyards of the Muscadet region, where the hills are topped by windmills, each again with a magnificent view.

Linking these is the Loire itself, rushing, wild, and wide in winter, slipping calmly between islands and banks of sand in summer. Along the length of the river runs the Grande Randonnée 3; it would be wonderful to walk it all,but the routes do cover some of the most scenic stretches. You can follow the river past the nature reserves of Châtillon and the tufa cliffs and caves of Rochecorbon, learn the story of the Vendéen War as you walk the banks at St Florent, and at Champtoceaux, come across the unique ruins of an old toll booth on the river. The Loire's tributaries, the Cher and the Indre, each have their own Grande Randonnée – and the valleys of the Mayenne and Sarthe north of Angers offer more walks in a watery landscape, with superb wild flowers in springtime. Châteaux are omnipresent. You can arrive on foot at Saumur, Pléssis-Bourré, Montpoupon, Chambord and the magnificent Chenonceau, and lesser-known ones make their appearance on almost every walk.

Choosing routes in this varied country has not been easy. To include as many good walks as possible, a section of 'More Walks' has been provided with each route described. If you are planning to stay in an area, you should find that by taking advantage of these, you will have plenty of scope for your whole holiday. The maps and leaflets referred to can all be found in the local Office de Tourisme – and if you need any help with the French, just a little light might be shed by the 'Dictionary of Walking Words' on page 9 . Even so, in almost all cases, the combination of an excellent map and good waymarking on the ground will get you around without recourse to the text, so do not be afraid to try these extra suggestions. By the same token, do not hesitate to ask advice from any Office de Tourisme. They seem far more geared to the needs of walkers than in England, and often (particularly in rural locations) are acquainted with details of the walks as well as being able to provide bus timetables and help in finding a taxi. They also stock a wealth of regional literature. In the 'Places of Interest' section I have offered just a small selection that might appeal to walkers, but within the scope of this book it is not possible to mention even a fraction of all that is on offer in the Loire Valley.

I must make reference to two questions that are frequently asked about walking in France. The first is about the dangers and restrictions of *la chasse* – hunting. Hunting in France can mean an excursion with horses and hounds (as at Cheverny), but more often means a group of men accompanied by dogs of all shapes and sizes, ranging through the forest and firing at anything that moves. *La Chasse* normally takes place in the winter months and on designated days of the week (particularly weekends). On a summer ramble through the woods you would be most unlikely to have problems. The second question is that of dogs. France is undoubtedly a nation of dog lovers. In the villages it can seem that just about every household owns one – or several. Dogs on farms will bark at you but generally remain on their own territory – it is just the odd wanderer that causes the concern. There may well be dogs of malignant intent among these, but we have never met one. And although we don't carry a stick, a 'dog dazer' or any other defensive device, we have not yet been more than sniffed at in thirty-odd years of rambling. Someone once told us not to look the dog in the eye (this is apparently taking up its challenge) but rather to ignore it – it seems to work.

## From the Source to the Sea

The slopes of a volcanic mountain, the curious peaks of le Puy-en-Velay, the steep flower-banked gorges, the lakes of Grangent and Villerest, the plains of Forez, the canals of Digoin, the mouth of the Allier and Eiffel's famous canal bridge at Briare all come before what guide books have been known to refer to as the 'Loire proper'. And the other side of guide book territory, the Loire-Atlantique, is no less enticing – the windmills and vineyards of the Muscadet region, the atmospheric wetlands of the Brière, the salt marshes of the Guérande and the pretty coastal harbours of Pornic and le Croisic. If you have the time, this journey from source to the sea is one not to be missed.

I cannot claim the idea here is original. It came initially from a couple with a small motorhome whom we met on a campsite at Josselin in Brittany in the spring of 2000. They told us they liked to have a project for their holiday – and that, the previous year, they had followed the Loire from the Cévennes to the Bay of Biscay. Thank you – that was an excellent idea. We followed suit, and what is offered here evolved from that journey – a suggested route of around 650 miles (of course you can divert as you please), and twelve walks to take on the way. None of the walks is too difficult, and for those on the longer side, there is always a short cut. Each walk has a section beside the river and relates to some special point of interest – from the scaly volcanic peak where it is born to the strange fishing huts on the estuary where it meets the sea. You will find the routes that comprise this series marked in the list of walks, and the text of each has a special section telling you about the next stage of the journey. The only advice offered is to allow as much time as you can afford for this voyage – and I don't want to make any recommendations. For a start, it's not going to be easy to drag yourselves away from the splendours of the mountains. And when you do, the Loire Valley is scarcely short of places worth visiting as you go by. At the end of the day, completing the walks and reaching the sea is an achievement – and the Loire Valley can offer an excellent choice of wines for the celebration!

## Walking in France

France is almost certainly the best country for walking in Europe. The scenery is widely varied, the tracks are well-maintained and well-waymarked and every Office du Tourisme can offer you an assortment of routes and inexpensive maps of the area.

The excellence of the footpaths of France is due almost entirely to the Féderation Française de la Randonnée Pédestre – The FFRP – who over the last half century have waymarked and described routes of all kinds throughout France. Many of the walks in this book are based on their routes, and you will be grateful for some of their waymarking as you follow them. Their long distance paths, the Grandes Randonnées (GR), are the best waymarked paths imaginable, and will invariably lead you past all the most interesting features and best viewpoints in an area. If there is something worth seeing, the Grande Randonnée will take you there. Next there are the Grandes Randonnées du Pays (GRP), round tours of an area or region which may take anything from a couple of days to a week or more. They aim to show you the best a region has to offer. Finally there are the Petites Randonnées (PR), the equivalent of our short circular walks, and these are sprinkled generously over the whole country. Each of these route types has its own waymarks, painted on trees, rocks, telegraph poles, or any other convenient surface – the Grandes Randonnées are marked white on red, the Grandes Randonnées du Pays yellow on red and the Petites Randonnées, yellow. You will meet all of them on the walks in this book, so here is all you need to know:

Path  Wrong  Left turn  Right turn

Thus you are warned of every turn before you reach it, and halted by a cross if you have missed it. Nothing could be simpler! In fairness, it must be said that although Grandes Randonnées are invariably superbly waymarked, the state of a Petite Randonnée may reflect the level of enthusiasm of the local tourist board or walking group. Even so, most are excellent. To accompany these fine routes, the FFRP produces a series of Topoguides, which offer all the relevant information from flora and fauna to history, geology and details of available refreshment. The pity is that only very few have been translated into English, and, oddly, these are generally of the long distance routes. For the rest, at least a working knowledge of French is needed. If you decide to tackle these – or any other described routes – a vocabulary of 'walking words in French' has been included in this book to help out.

Another excellent feature of walking in France is that most paths are open to you – only those marked 'Privé' deny you access. It is accepted that you will not wander on crops or gardens and that you will not leave litter or pick flowers. It should be mentioned that in winter, some forest paths are temporarily closed for the period of 'la chasse' – the hunting season – generally from November to February, but these paths will again be marked. In France, farmers and landowners seem much more in tune with walkers than in England and will generally greet you cheerfully. If you can manage just a 'Bonjour' in return it is certain to go down well.

The footpaths of France await you – and they are guaranteed to be addictive. Take one short stretch of a Grande Randonnée and you may well be hooked for life! It remains only to wish you 'Bonne route!'

## *A Little History to Set The Scene*

### In the beginning

The River Loire began life in the Tertiary era, when great upheavals of the earth's crust created the Alps and the Massif Central. At first the river flowed north to join the valley of the Seine – but later movements and the sinking of the land caused it to divert to the west and take its present almost right-angled course to the Atlantic. After its long journey from the mountains, alluvial silt was deposited on the banks, making the soil particularly fertile. This and the underlying limestone and tufa attracted human settlement – the very earliest evidence of occupation consists of the flint tools of Neanderthal man, dating from some 50,000 years BC. A giant leap in time takes us to the megalithic period. The area south of the river around Saumur is particularly rich in prehistoric remains. Here, one of the largest dolmens in Europe, dating from around 5000 BC, is curiously tucked away in the garden of a bar in the suburbs. Not too far away at Gennes stands the impressive Dolmen de la Madeleine and there are many, many other dolmens and menhirs clustered in a relatively small area.

### Gauls, Romans, Franks and Vikings

When the Romans first came to the Loire Valley in the 1st century BC they found the area occupied by warlike Gallic tribes, of which the most powerful were the Carnutes. One of their strongholds was north of the river on the present day site of Orléans. In an epic battle in 52 BC, it was razed to the ground – and then rebuilt with the forum, baths and villas of a Roman town. Tours and Angers were similarly established at that time and connecting roads were built. Extensive Roman sites have been excavated and are on view today in the valley of le Loir at Cherré and at Gennes beside the Loire itself. The Romans were to remain for around 500 years and it was they who established the first vineyards in the Loire Valley. By the 4th century Christianity was arriving in the area – St Martin, the great Bishop of Tours, was a Roman legionary who was famously converted after giving half his cloak to a beggar. He went on to found the first monastery in Gaul. Meanwhile the threat of attack from outside was growing ever greater, and many towns, originally on Gallic sites, were further fortified by the building of outside walls. When finally the Romans withdrew to attend to affairs at home, the invaders moved in. Franks and Visigoths vied to claim territory in the Loire Valley. The Franks were the victors – and their ruler, Clovis, became converted to Christianity, encouraging the building of monasteries along the banks of the river. Nevertheless, the ensuing years saw many quarrels as his successors fought for power. In the 9th century more trouble arrived in the form of the Vikings, who each summer sailed their high-prowed boats up the river, and set up camps on its islands. From these they raided the monasteries for their treasures, and plundered and pillaged in the surrounding lands. The solution came in 911 with the Treaty of St Clair-sur-Epte, when one of their number was wisely offered the Duchy of Normandy by the uncharitably named Charles the Simple. The one important legacy the Vikings left to the Loire Valley was their technique of boat building – the flat-bottomed *gabares* that later plied the river were based on Viking design.

## Foulques Nerra, Count of Anjou

Early in the 10th century the lands around the Loire were in turmoil, as Feudal lords fought for territory. Among these were the Counts of Anjou, who took as their title Fouques (falcon) – now sometimes corrupted to Fulk. It was the Red Falcon (Foulques le Roux) who first came to power. Years on down the line, Foulques Nerra (the Black Falcon) and his equally acquisitive son Geoffrey took all Touraine from the rival Counts of Blois, and to protect their domain, built fortresses throughout the region. The keeps at Langeais and Loches are survivors from this period.

## The Plantagenets – and some auspicious marriages

At the death of William the Conqueror, his son Henry inherited the kingdom of England and the duchy of Normandy. Sadly, Henry's two sons were drowned in a shipwreck off the Normandy coast – leaving him only one daughter, Matilda. Henry thoughtfully arranged her marriage to Geoffrey, Count of Anjou, also known as Plantagenet from the sprig of broom (*genêt*) worn in his cap. Their son was also Henry – and although the succession was far from straightforward, he became Henry, Duke of Normandy and then in 1154, Henry II of England. His own marriage to Eleanor of Aquitaine ensured he ruled all the territory between 'the Arctic Ocean and the Pyrenees'. All would have been well, but for his very different sons. The first of these, Richard the Lionheart, wrested power from his own father's hands – and when Richard died 1199, brother John (known as Lackland) promptly lost all his lands (including Anjou and Touraine) to King Philippe-Auguste. In a twist of fate, those warring Plantagenets now lie together in peace in Fontevraud Abbey; in the hallowed light of its nave are the recumbent effigies of Henry II, Richard the Lionheart, Eleanor of Aquitaine and Isabella of Angoulême, the second wife of John Lackland.

## The Hundred Years War and Joan of Arc

In 1337, Edward III turned his sights on France and so began a war that was to last more than a hundred years. There were famous English victories at Crécy in 1346, at Poitiers in 1356 and again at Agincourt in 1415. At the beginning of 1429, the English were besieging Orléans when Joan (the French Jeanne), a seventeen-year-old farmer's daughter from Domrémy in the east of France, claimed to have heard voices from heaven telling her she could oust the English from France. Joan was escorted to Chinon where she was granted an audience with the Dauphin – and confirmed her divine inspiration by recognising him disguised among the courtiers. A tableau of the event can be seen in the Château de Chinon, although of the room where the meeting took place there remains only the fireplace. Joan was given an army with which she managed to enter Orléans by the Porte de Bourgogne. Two weeks later the English had fled. Joan went on to win other battles at Jargeau and Beaugency and then accompanied the dauphin Charles VII to his coronation in Reims. Eventually she was captured, tried by English sympathisers, and convicted of witchcraft and heresy. Joan was burnt at the stake in Rouen in 1431.

Although the war dragged on for another twenty years, there is no doubt that her brief campaign was its turning point.

### The Renaissance

With the retreat of the English in the middle of the $15^{th}$ century, a period of relative calm and prosperity settled on the Loire Valley. River trade began to increase, facilitated by new towpaths, and marked channels reducing the dangers of the shallows. Boats were made of wood – the simplest were carried downstream with the current and then broken up on arrival; those with sails could navigate both ways. A Guild controlled movement on the river and objections were raised to the many toll-booths that had sprung up to tax the passing goods (just one of these remains – at Champtoceaux). Along the banks and inland, the austere fortified keeps of earlier years began to be modified to include a little more comfort – living rooms were larger and windows let in more light, the outer walls were crenellated and the bare round towers crowned with pepper-pot turrets.

Around the turn of the $16^{th}$ century, life was becoming more cultured with greater focus on beauty, poetry and music. The great satirist Rabelais was born near Chinon in 1483. Early in the $16^{th}$ century, seven poets from the Loire Valley founded the group known as the Pléiade, headed by Ronsard and Joachim du Bellay. Recent unsuccessful military campaigns in Italy had brought Charles VIII – and subsequently Louis XII and François I – into contact with Italian architecture. The châteaux at Amboise and Blois were embellished with Italianate gardens and Chambord was built in the most flamboyant of styles. The king's ministers too bought themselves country mansions – and transformed them into the most sumptuous dwellings. The $16^{th}$ century saw the heyday of extravagance in the Loire Valley, with nobility throwing lavish parties and entertaining friends with hunting trips in the forests. But the Renaissance also brought new thinking on a religious front. A wave of Protestantism was sweeping through Europe and in France met with repression. In 1560, hundreds of Protestants were drowned in the Loire. Two years later the Huguenots retaliated by destroying Catholic churches and the Wars of Religion had begun in earnest. The struggle became a three-cornered fight between the Protestant Huguenots, the Catholic monarchy and an organisation known as the Catholic League. Orléans was a Huguenot stronghold (Calvin himself had been at university there) and the St Bartholomew's Day massacres, extending from Paris down the Loire, left hundreds dead in Orléans alone. In the end it was the conflict with the Catholic League that ended the affair – Henry III had its leader assassinated, and suffered the same fate himself a year later. With the accession of his cousin, the Protestant Henry IV, the Edict of Nantes (1598) gave freedom of worship – and, although Louis XIV later revoked it, peace returned again to the region.

### River trade in the $17^{th}$ and $18^{th}$ centuries

By the beginning of the $17^{th}$ century, the kings and their entourages had left the Loire Valley, and grand châteaux such as Chambord became nothing more than hunting lodges. River trade was increasing at this time, helped by the creation of canals. With the opening of the Briare canal in 1642, goods could be transported from the Loire (and so from the coast) to Paris. By the $18^{th}$ century the river was alive with boats carrying cargoes of wine, stone, wood, lime, cotton, salt, sugar, spices and more. Textile factories grew up at Tours and Angers among other places and imported sugar on its way to refineries at Orléans was responsible for the growth of the confectionery industry along the banks of the river. Receiving wine that had 'turned', Orléans also began the production of vinegar.

## The French Revolution (1789) and the Vendée Uprising

Associations with the monarchy and the Catholic Church in the Loire Valley meant that the Revolution was less welcomed here than in other parts of the country. Its main support came from the towns rather than the rural communities. The nobility fled or were killed and the great châteaux were abandoned. A few, such as Chenonceau, survived intact because their owners were well respected among the local population. With the subsequent Reign of Terror, the assassination of Louis XVI, the persecution of the Catholic priests and the call for conscription, the western Loire turned against the Republicans and in 1793 a peasant mob gathered at St Florent le-Vieil beside the Loire. Over the next months, Angers and Saumur were taken by the rebel 'whites' – but the Republicans (blues) were victorious at Cholet and thousands of Vendéen refugees crossed the Loire in the hope of escaping retribution. The subsequent massacres were terrible, leaving the Vendée a wasteland depleted of its people.

When Napoleon brought a relative peace to France, the Loire Valley thrived again. On the river, the first steam boats arrived (1822) and although at first they were far from safe, they were popular on account of the greatly reduced journey times. The first railway came to the Loire Valley in the middle of the 19th century and from then on, the livelihood of the river boatmen was threatened. Inevitably the railways triumphed, and commercial traffic on the Loire is now almost, but not quite, at an end.

## World War and progress

Perhaps the most significant event of the Second World War to take place in the region was the meeting of Maréchal Pétain and Hitler at the station of Montoire-sur-le-Loir in October 1940. Under tight security they discussed the partitioning of France – Vichy France was subsequently divided from occupied territory by a line running along the River Cher. The Resistance workers of the Loire Valley were some of the most heroic in France. Allied forces liberated the region in the September of 1944.

At the end of the war, St Nazaire, Nantes and many other towns in the region were in ruins, but rebuilding began immediately. With an eye to the future, three nuclear power stations were built on the river in the 1960s. Today the Loire Valley is still important for its abundance of cereals, fruit and vegetables, and for the Champignons de Paris (button mushrooms) that are cultivated in the tufa caves near Saumur. The economy has particularly thrived with the increasing popularity of wine and the enormous boom in tourism. Fast TGV links with Paris have improved the region's commerce. The Loire Valley welcomes an increasing number of visitors, around 6 million of them now arriving in the region annually. The châteaux are undoubtedly the biggest attraction – but the gentle climate, sandy-beached river and fine regional cuisine and wine play their part. In recent years the tourist boards have promoted eco-friendly tourism in the form of cycling and walking. A well-marked network of trails now awaits you in the Loire Valley.

# Dictionary of Walking Words

| | |
|---|---|
| anse | a cove, a small bay |
| atteindre | to reach |
| balisage | waymarking |
| bifurquer | to fork |
| blanc (blanche) | white |
| bleu(e) | blue |
| bois | a wood |
| bosquet | a spinney, a copse |
| chemin | a way, a path |
| colline | a hill |
| contourner | to go around, to skirt |
| creux | sunken or hollowed out |
| dessous | under |
| dessus | above |
| droit (tout droit) | straight ahead |
| droite | right |
| église | church |
| empierré | stony or metalled (as in road) |
| emprunter | to take (as in direction) |
| étang | a pond, a pool |
| en face | opposite |
| fourche | a fork |
| franchir | to clear, to cross |
| gauche | left |
| goudronnée | tarmacked |
| grimper | to climb |
| hameau | hamlet |
| jaune | yellow |
| jusqu'à | as far as |
| longer | to skirt |
| mener | to lead |
| monter | to climb |
| niveau | a level |
| patte d'oie | multiple path or road junction |
| pente | slope |
| prairie | a meadow |
| rouge | red |
| route | a road |
| ruisseau | a stream |
| sentier | a footpath, a track |
| sous-bois | undergrowth |
| suivre | to follow |
| talus | a slope or bank |
| tourner | to turn |
| traverser | to cross |
| variante | alternative route |
| vert(e) | green |
| virer | to bend or turn |

## Offices de Tourisme and other useful addresses

The Loire Valley is above all a holiday region and every place of any size has an Office de Tourisme. In the larger towns they are open all year – elsewhere it may be the summer months, or, in some villages, just July and August. Out of season the stock of the Office de Tourisme is usually transferred to the Mairie – and they won't mind you asking for it. The list below comprises the Offices de Tourisme referred to in each walk in this book. Every tourist office is happy to send you information on its region, and, where leaflets of walks are free, to include these if you request them. And whether writing or telephoning, in this holiday region there is almost always someone who can understand if you would prefer to use English. Strangely, it has always seemed to me that the smaller and more rural the Office de Tourisme, the more helpful and well-stocked it is.

| Walk | Location | Address |
|---|---|---|
| 1 | Les Estables | Le Bourg, 43150 Les Estables; Tel. 04 71 08 31 08 |
| 2/3 | Le Puy-en-Velay | Place du Breuil, 43000 Le Puy-en-Velay, Tel. 04 71 09 38 41<br>*Also, for more information:*<br>Comité Départemental de la Randonnée, Pédestre en Haute-Loire<br>La Croisée Des Chemins, 23, Rue Boucherie Basse BP 198, 43005 Le Puy-en-Velay; Tel. 04 71 04 15 95 |
| 4 | St Just-St Rambert | 7, Place de la Paix, 42170 St-Just-St-Rambert; Tel. 04 77 52 05 14 |
| 5 | Roanne | 1, Cours de la République, 42300 Roanne. Tel. 04 77 71 51 77 |
| 6 | Digoin | 8, Rue Guilleminot, 71160 Digoin. Tel. 03 85 53 00 81 |
| 7 | Nevers | Palais Ducal<br>entrée Rue Sabatier, 58008 Nevers. Tel. 03 86 68 46 00<br>*Also, for more information:*<br>Randonièvre, 3, Rue du Sort, 58000 Nevers. Tel. 03 86 36 92 98 |
| 8 | Briare-le-Canal | 1, Place Charles de Gaulle, 45250 Briare-le-Canal. Tel. 02 38 31 24 51 |
| 9 | Châteauneuf-sur-Loire | 3, Place Aristide Briand, 45110 Châteauneuf-sur-Loire. Tel. 02 38 58 44 79 |
| 10 | La Ferté-Saint-Aubin | Rue des Jardins, 45240 La Ferté-Saint-Aubin. Tel. 02 38 64 67 93 |
| 11 | Beaugency | 3, Place Dr. Hyvernaud, BP 44, 45190 Beaugency. Tel. 02 38 44 54 42 |
| 12 | Blois | 3, Avenue Jean Laigret, 41000 Blois. Tel. 02 54 90 41 41 |
| 13 | Suèvres | Place de la Mairie, 41500 Suèvres. Tel. 02 54 87 85 27 |
| 14 | Montoire-sur-le-Loir | 16, Place Clémenceau, 41800 Montoire-sur-le-Loir. Tel. 02 54 85 23 30 |
| 15 | Chenonceaux | 1, Rue Bretonneau, 37150 Chenonceaux. Tel. 02 47 23 94 45 |

| | | |
|---|---|---|
| **16** | Bléré | 8, Rue Jean-Jacques Rousseau, 37150 Bléré. Tel. 02 47 57 93 00 |
| **17** | Loches | Office de Tourisme, 37600 Loches. Tel. 02 47 91 82 82 |
| **18** | Rochecorbon | 2, Place du Croissant, 37210 Rochecorbon. Tel. 02 47 52 80 22 |
| **19** | Ste Maure-de-Touraine | Le Château, 37800 Ste-Maure-de-Touraine. Tel. 02 47 65 66 20 |
| **20** | Azay-le-Rideau | 5, Place de l'Europe, 37190 Azay-le-Rideau. Tel. 02 47 45 44 40 |
| **21** | Villandry | Le Potager, 37510 Villandry. Tel. 02 47 50 12 66 |
| **22** | Chinon | Place Hofheim, 37500 Chinon. Tel. 02 47 93 17 85 |
| **23** | Château-la-Vallière | Mairie, 37330 Château-la-Vallière. Tel. 02 47 24 00 21 |
| **24** | Le Lude | Office de Tourisme, 72800 Le Lude. Tel. 02 43 94 62 20 |
| **25** | Saumur | Place de la Bilange, 49418 Saumur. Tel. 02 41 40 20 60 |
| **26** | Gennes | Square de l'Europe, 49350 Gennes. Tel. 02 41 51 84 14 |
| **27** | Briollay | Place O'Kelly, 49125 Briollay. Tel.02 41 42 50 28 |
| **28** | Chalonnes-sur-Loire | Place de l'Hôtel de Ville, 49290 Chalonnes-Sur-Loire. Tel. 02 41 78 26 21 |
| **29** | St Florent-le-Vieil | Rue de Rénéville BP 54, 49410 Saint-Florent-le-Vieil. Tel. 02 41 72 62 32 |
| **30** | Champtoceaux | Maison de Champalud, 49270 Champtoceaux. Tel.02 40 83 57 49 |
| **31** | Clisson | Place du Minage, 44190 Clisson. Tel. 02 40 54 02 95 |
| **32** | St Brévin-les-Pins | 10, Rue de l'Église BP 10, 44250 Saint-Brévin-les-Pins. Tel. 02 40 27 24 32 |

## Map Supplies

| | | |
|---|---|---|
| **1** | Fédération Francaise de la Randonée Pédestre (FFRP) | 14, Rue Riquet<br>75019 Paris |
| **2** | Stanfords (for maps) | 12-14 Long Acre<br>London WC2E 9LP |
| **3** | The Map Shop | 15 High Street<br>Upton-upon-Severn<br>Worcestershire WR8 0HJ |

## Recommended Publications

*Michelin Tourist Guide – Auvergne, Rhone Valley*. ISBN 2-06-130402-8
*Michelin Green Guide – Château of the Loire*. ISBN 2-06-000123-4
*DK Eyewitness Travel Guide – Loire Valley*. ISBN 0-7513-0252-X
*Michelin in your Pocket Guide – The Loire Valley*. ISBN 2-06-630701-7
*Lonely Planet – The Loire, Nicola Williams*. ISBN 1-86450-097-2
*Loire Valley Insight Pocket Guide*. ISBN 9-81234528-0

## *The Loire Valley on the Internet*

Here are just a few websites you might find useful:

www.ffrp.ass.fr

This is the website of the French rambling association, the Fédération Française de la Randonnée Pédestre. Along with other information (in French), the site lists and describes the major Topoguides and gives information on ordering direct – a cheaper option than buying in the UK.

www.brittany-ferries.com

The website of Brittany Ferries giving sailing schedules, prices, online reservations and details of holiday properties all over France (including many in the Loire Valley)

www.poef.com/poef

The website of P and O European Ferries, with sailings from Portsmouth to Cherbourg and le Havre. Gives schedules, prices and opportunity for reservations.

www.posl.com

The website of P and O Stena Line, an independent company offering half-hourly super-ferries between Dover and Calais. Prices and reservations are available on the site.

www.eurotunel.co.uk

Eurotunnel would seem the preferred mode of travel if you are in a hurry, seasick, or have pets with you. This site offers schedules, fares and online booking.

www.eurostar.com

The website of Eurostar, giving timetables, fares and online booking. Waterloo – Paris is a journey of approximately 3 hours.

www.voyages-sncf.com

The site of the French railway system, offering train timetables and reservations. There are mainline and TGV services from Paris to Tours, TGV only to Nantes

www.gites-de-france.fr

A website giving details of thousands of holiday properties all over France. Choose and book online – or, to allow yourself more time for consideration, order the regional brochure.

www.loirevalleytourism.com

This appears to be the most useful website of the Loire Valley – and it is also accessible in English. Brochures can be ordered and there are details of a wide variety of holidays. This helpful website encourages you to 'ask for the moon' – i.e. just fill in a few details and they will send you information on anything. Unfortunately the site deals only with those départements in the region Centre – it does not include Anjou or Loire-Atlantique.

# The Upper Reaches

*Waters from the Gerbier de Jonc join to form the Loire*

# 1. At the source of the Loire

Every French schoolchild knows that the Loire arises on the slopes of the Gerbier de Jonc – and it's as curious a volcanic pile as you could ever wish to meet. Here are three walks to mix and match – an easy stroll around the sources, a short but energetic climb up the mountain and a long discovery trail through the valley below.

**Grade:** The route around the sources is easy. Climbing to the peak of the mountain itself is definitely strenuous, and the discovery trail involves a sustained strenuous uphill section.

**Distance:** Gerbier de Jonc – about 1km, but distance is irrelevant. Sources – 3km (2 miles); Discovery trail – 12.7km (8 miles).

**Time:** Gerbier de Jonc – 1 hour (allowing time to take in the views); Sources – ¾ hour; Discovery trail – 4½ hours.

**Map:** The best map of the area is IGN 83025 (*Massif du Mézenc, Gerbier de Jonc*), from the *Culture et Environnement* series with a scale of 1:33,333. It can be obtained from bookshops and some Offices de Tourisme, or from *La Croisée des Chemins* in le Puy-en-Velay (see below).

**Start and finish:** The bar/restaurant at the foot of the Gerbier de Jonc.

**How to get there:** From le Puy-en-Velay, head south-east through le Monastier-sur-Gazeille and les Estables. From here the mountain itself is signposted, and you follow the D378 all the way. The bar/restaurant is on the left-hand side as you come up to the rocky peak – farther around is a hotel, and (in summer) some wayside stalls.

**Refreshment:** The *Bar Restaurant du Gerbier de Jonc* will provide you with all you need. There is no other possibility for refreshment en route.

**Notes:** All these walks are on well-marked paths and could be tackled in good trainers in summertime. But the terrain is very different – grassy paths and quiet roads around the sources, a scramble up rock for the peak, and forest roads followed by a climb on narrower tracks for the discovery trail. On this latter you should equip yourself with plenty of fluid, particularly if the weather is hot. All the routes are at least partially exposed so take appropriate precautions if the day is sunny. Leaflets describing the features of the discovery trail (*La Montagne Ardéchoise – Sentier de Découverte*) can be obtained from nearby Offices de Tourisme in Ste-Eulalie and St-Martial.

**Waymarking:** The 'path' up and down the Gerbier de Jonc is waymarked in blue, as is the route around the sources. The discovery trail is marked with flashes of white on yellow and white on blue and ends by following a Grande Randonnée (waymarked white on red).

---

## Introduction

High in the Ardèche, the scaly hump of the Gerbier de Jonc provides a memorable setting for the source of France's longest river. The mountain (1551m.) is the most spectacular of the region's many 'sucs', peaks formed when thick molten lava, escaping through fissures in the earth's surface, cooled quickly when in contact with the air. The line of volcanic peaks here forms the watershed between the Mediterranean and the Atlantic. From the south-west face of the Gerbier de Jonc the waters flow

*Source of the Loire - l'Authentique*

to the Atlantic and here, on these slopes, the Loire is born. Water circulates freely between the sheets of volcanic rock and escapes to the surface at various points. The river has not one, but many sources. At least four of them are clearly identified – and guarantee confusion with names such as the 'authentic source' and the 'veritable source'. The short walk here will take you past them all and it could not be in more splendid countryside. Slopes of wild flowers, bright yellow broom, scattered pines and babbling streams are all dominated by the peculiar shaly peak of the Gerbier de Jonc.

For anyone with a head for heights and enthusiasm for a little rock climbing, there is a clearly marked route both up and down the Gerbier de Jonc. It's a climb to be tackled on all fours, but is not really dangerous and whole families from junior to grandmother seem to be having a go. Ropes have been fastened to the rocks at the trickiest points. The view from the top well repays all the effort. Volcanic peaks stretch around in all directions – to the north-west is the distinctively flat-topped Mézenc, at 1753m. the highest summit in the area and the third highest in the Massif Central. Closer and to the right of it is the conical Suc de Sara. Looking east on a clear day you can see beyond the local ranges to the Alps, faraway across the Rhone valley.

When you descend, you could call at the auberge before continuing – the gentle path around the sources waits, and you can decide whether to go on to take the long hike into the deep valley below the mountain. If you do, remember the old adage – or at least, its converse – 'that which goes down must come up'. Walking gently downhill for a couple of hours is very pleasant, but eventually the route turns, and the uphill climb is shorter and steeper. There are of course rewards – this is beautiful wild country, densely wooded with cascading streams, rocky outcrops and abundant wild flowers. In the depths is the tiny stone village of le Pradal –

from where you climb the tree-clad slopes to regain your former height. The path back is across high open country, typically the habitat of the marmots that have been reintroduced here – they are active by day and night, and you may be lucky enough to spot one. This whole route is now a *Circuit de Découverte* with various marked points of interest, and it is worth trying to get hold of the accompanying leaflet (try any of the local Offices de Tourisme in Ardèche for this – tourist information rarely seems to cross the departmental borders). But leaflet or not, if you have the stamina for a fairly demanding hike, don't miss out on the opportunity to explore this glorious remote countryside.

## *The Walk*

### For the Gerbier de Jonc

From the bar/restaurant, cross the springy turf below the mountain parallel to the road – you will soon pick up blue arrows directing you. Facing the mountain, the way up is on the right-hand side and that down is on the left – you probably wouldn't want to pass anyone else on your path. Although the way up is steep with lots of loose rock it is very clearly waymarked and you should reach the summit in half an hour or so. A similarly vertiginous path – provided with several rope handholds – brings you down to the bar restaurant again.

### For the path around the sources

1. Cross the road beside the bar restaurant to where a wooden fingerpost directs you to the left of a tumbling stream. This attractive path soon weaves in and out of woodland and then comes down to a road (the D116 to Ste-Eulalie). Cross straight over and go on to meet a gravelled track. Turning left on this you now have rough moorland beside you with many tiny springs rising from the boggy ground.

   Blue paint on the ground soon tells you that you are at Source 3, *la Prairie Tourbeuse* (the Peaty Meadow). Continuing along the gravely track you pass many more streamlets on their way to make their contribution to the great river.

2. After crossing a bridge over a rather larger stream, turn left and follow the track running through the woods beside it. This track climbs gently and soon you come to open fields. Continue on the bank above the stream until you can see a blue waymark on a post in a field high on the opposite bank. Choose a suitable place to cross over and follow the waymarks across the field. Soon you reach Source 4, *La Véritable*, with the painted inscription *'Ici commence ma course vers l'océan'*. Now climb to the road beside an auberge and turn left. In a few minutes you reach a road junction with the Gerbier de Jonc directly ahead.

3. If you are going to take the discovery trail, turn right here(but you may want to see the remaining sources first). To complete the 'Sources' walk, continue along the road ahead, passing the road junction on the left. Near the hotel and summertime wayside stalls, an arch over water tumbling beside the road announces *La Loire* – this source is *l'Authentique*! And if you cross the road and go down into the shed opposite, a spout from the wall delivers water to a trough below – the

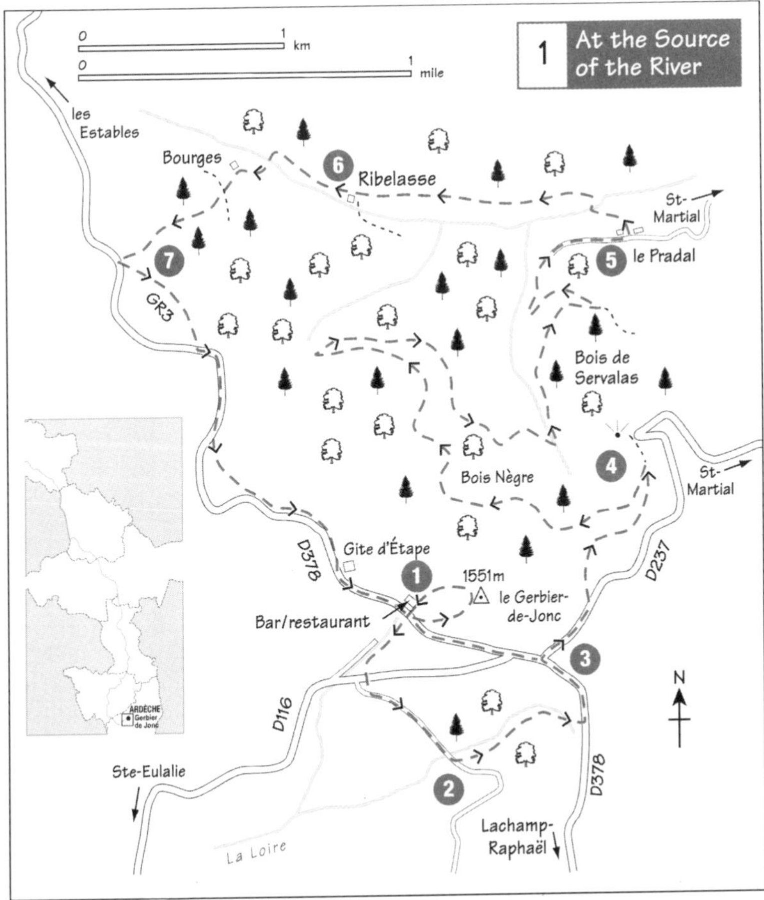


final source. Continue just a few more paces along the road to return to the bar restaurant.

## For the Discovery Trail

Walk along the main road from the bar/restaurant or follow the 'Sources' walk to the road junction at Point 3 on the map. From here take the D237 in the direction of St Martial. Leave the road almost immediately and take a grassy track running alongside the fence on the left – there is a white on yellow waymark on a post. The track becomes more obvious as you go and winds around the hill with some fine views ahead. Points 10 and 11 of the Circuit de Découverte are passed before you eventually reach a junction with a broad gravely forest road.

4. Turn left here (there is a viewpoint on the St-Martial road just a few metres to the right). The track now winds on down the side of the hill, always descending into the valley below. There are good views of the Gerbier de Jonc high above you and of the flat-topped twin-peaked Mézenc to the north-west. From viewpoints beside the path you look out over the Bois Nègre, the dark woods in the valley below. The white on yellow waymarks now seem to have been joined by white on blue – from hereon it seems you can follow any combination of the colours. After nearly an hour's walking (from Point 3), the track takes

a particularly sharp hairpin to the right and continues descending. After a further 20 minutes or so, two streams are crossed in quick succession and the track becomes steeper and more stony, now going through the Bois de Servelas. After a sharp bend to the left, soon followed by another to the right, you arrive at a stony road. Continue ahead into the hamlet of le Pradal.

5. Beside stone farm buildings, a post tells you that you are now at the starting point on the Circuit de Découverte – they obviously decided to take the climbing part first! If you haven't so far taken much notice of the altitudes given on these posts, you probably will from now on – at this point you are some 500 metres below the start. There are just a few more downhill steps to take – follow the little cobbled path down beside the stone building and at the cross, bear right and then left on a path to the river. After crossing the bridge the broad track now climbs steeply along the side of the valley with splendid views. Eventually you reach Ribelasse – an attractive huddle of stone habitations tucked in a fold in the hill.

6. As you enter Ribelasse, turn around the little outbuilding on the right to climb on a narrow track through woods above a babbling stream. The track soon turns and fords not only that stream but also another close by – there are no bridges. Now the climbing begins in earnest, as a narrow track takes you sharply uphill to the ruined stone buildings of Bourges. After passing these away on your right, a broad cross track is reached. Continue across it, maintaining your direction and still climbing steeply. At the fork in about 20 metres, keep left on the main uphill track beside the stone wall. A further burst of energy is required for the last few hundred metres to the top where you are greeted with a lovely grassy plateau before the road. A sign informs you that you are at the watershed between the Loire and the Rhône.

7. Turn left and follow the direction of the Grande Randonnée across the turf towards the pine trees. On reaching the wood, the GR goes off to the left, but you continue ahead following yellow waymarks through the trees (although it really doesn't make much difference which route you take as both arrive at the same point alongside the road again). At the road, turn left and walk beside it for about 300 metres, to where the GR is signed off on the left once more. The white-on-red waymarks lead uphill beside more pine trees and then return to the road again. But you need not walk on tarmac – the Grande Randonnée has its own grassy track which now parallels the road almost all the way back to the bar restaurant at the foot of the Gerbier de Jonc.

## More Walks in the Area

There is one other short circuit in the vicinity which should not be missed if you can afford the time to linger in this area – the climb to the top of Mézenc. Rest assured, this is not as steep as the Gerbier de Jonc and the path up is through pleasant woodland. From les Estables the whole route takes about 3 hours, but you can halve that time by starting at either the Croix de Peccata in the north or the Croix de Boutières in the south. The Office de Tourisme in les Estables will readily provide you with a photocopied route – but if you have acquired the recommended map for this region (IGN 83025) you can pick it out for yourselves. On the mountain top are two *tables d'orientations* and the claim is that it is possible to see a quarter of France – on the clearest of days, of course.

The IGN map mentioned above will give you access to all the major paths in the area. The Grandes Randonnées (3, 7, 73) are well waymarked and make splendid routes to follow if you have two cars, or can arrange to be picked up at the end. The GR3, the Grande Randonnée of the Loire Valley, starts near the Gerbier de Jonc and the section from there to the Lac d'Issarlès is about 20km (12½ miles) – a full and magnificent day's walk. Using also the GR du Pays *Tour du Mézenc – Gerbier*, one or two circular routes are possible. Starting from le Béage (west of the Gerbier de Jonc), you could head south-east (either by the D122 or a lesser road), join the GR3 to head north past the Suc de Montfol and the Suc de la Lauzière and return west along the Tour de Mézenc – Gerbier above the valley of the Gage. It is also possible to climb the Suc de Montfol, from which there is a fine view, using the paths shown on the map.

For other short circuits, the Comité Départemental de Tourisme publishes a series of leaflets *Itineraires Pédestres en Haute-Loire*. There are plenty to choose from, but if you want to incorporate a swim in your day's activities, try the 14km Circuit du Lac de Saint-Frond (north of the Gerbier de Jonc). Both wooded and open, this route has some fine views of the mountains. The best place for finding both maps and leaflets – and personal helpful advice – is *La Croisée des Chemins* in Le Puy-en-Velay (from the Office de Tourisme, turn right on the Bd. Mal Fayolle, left on the Rue P. d'Avignon, and right on the Rue Chèvrerie – *La Croisée* is on the left). A tiny but well-stocked establishment, it is devoted entirely to *la randonnée* in all its forms.

## Places of Interest Nearby

In this region all the attractions are natural – volcanic peaks and ridges, basalt flows, cascading waterfalls and clear lakes in the craters of one-time volcanoes. The most amazing display of all changes with the seasons – the flora of the Mézenc area are a botanist's dream. On the top of the mountain grows a rare form of groundsel, found elsewhere only on one mountain in the Pyrenees. Other species to be found are the insectivorous sundew, arnica and gentian. But you need no knowledge of botany whatsoever to appreciate the wide scattering of wild daffodils and mountain pansies, at their best on the slopes below the Mézenc in late spring. In July every year the village of Ste-Eulalie holds a 'Violet Fair' where medicinal herbs are sold.

The area is also a Mecca for geologists, being home to many different volcanic types. The Gerbier de Jonc is a 'phonolith', its name referring to the thick slabs of dark resonant lava that have spilled down its sides. Stromboli-type volcanoes have craters, and the region has several whose craters now hold lakes of the clearest blue water. Just 9 precipitous kilometres from the Gerbier de Jonc is the pretty village of St-Martial where there is a beautiful lake with a bathing beach. Better known – and very popular – is the Lac d'Issarlès to the west along the valley of the Loire. This natural lake is perfectly round with crystal clear waters. There are sandy bathing beaches, opportunities for boating, a campsite and a pleasant 3km walk around its shores.

The most spectacular waterfall in the area is Ray-Pic – head south-east to Lachamp-Raphaël and turn right just through the village. After driving around many hairpin bends deep into a ravine, you take a further 20 minutes or so 'stroll' down seemingly endless steps to the depths of the densely wooded valley. Here the waters of the Bourges hurtle over a precipice of volcanic basalt amid showers of white spray. It's a long climb back, but the effort is worthwhile.

## From the Source to the Sea

This is the first walk of the series – and you may well be wondering how you are going to tear yourself away from this exciting area to do the rest.

Thinking firstly of accommodation, there is plenty throughout the year in the area around the Gerbier de Jonc – the villages double as ski resorts in winter. Campsites, however, are generally not open until June and close again in September. For earlier or later visits, the nearest is probably the very pleasant site beside the Loire at Brives-Charensac just outside le Puy-en-Velay.

It may not be far from the Gerbier de Jonc to the second walk at Arlempdes, but given the odd stop or two, it is a journey that will take a whole day. From the Gerbier de Jonc, first take the road south to Ste-Eulalie. After about 3km, after you pass a stone cottage on the left, look back – there is a fine view of mingling waters, while far away the old scaly mountain looks down on the river to which it has given birth. A kilometre or so further on, the road passes (on the left) the first of very many bridges over La Loire.

Continuing south from Ste-Eulalie, the D116 closely follows the river but climbs again to reach the village of Usclades-et-Rieutard. Leaving by the D160 you arrive at La Palisse and its lake – created by the first dam on the river. From here the road crosses the valley of the Gage in a series of hairpin bend and finally descends beside the beautiful blue Lac d'Issarlès (see above). Below the village, turn left and continue high above the valley of the Loire. In Soubrey, turn left and take the D500, a road that crosses the river with some splendid views. Turn right on the D54 to enter Arlempdes alongside the Loire with classic views of the ancient château high above. Arlempdes is the starting place of the second walk in the series from Source to the Sea.

# 2. A château on the rocks at Arlempdes

The little village of Arlempdes boasts the first château of the Loire – an 11th-century ruin, perched on a basalt cliff high above the river. This walk offers fine views of river, gorge, château and distant mountains – and the abundance of wild flowers are an added bonus.

**Grade:** Moderate – but taking the short cut takes out the hardest climbing

**Distance:** 9.5km (6 miles) for complete route. Short circuit 6km (3¾ miles)

**Time:** Whole route 3¼ hours. Short circuit 2 hours.

**Map:** IGN Série Bleue 2736 E

**Start and finish:** Arlempdes. There is a small car park almost opposite the château.

**How to get there:** From le Puy-en-Velay, take the N88 south for 22km to the village of Costaros. Turn left where sign-posted to Arlempdes – a further 8km away. Arlempdes can also be reached from Issarlès – see 'From the Source to the Sea', Walk 1.

**Refreshments:** The Hotel du Manoir beside the château in Arlempdes can provide everything from a simple drink to a five-course meal.

**Notes:** It is possible to undertake this walk in trainers in fine weather, although for the longer route you would probably be happier in walking boots. The climb up to the plateau is short and not too steep, but the longer route then involves some more sustained climbing. If you want to delay your choice of route, you can see something of the ascent ahead from the junction. A fair proportion of the route is exposed, so take appropriate precautions in hot weather, and include lots to drink. In summer it is possible to swim in the river from the little beach at Arlempdes (although it is not supervised) – an extra you may appreciate on a hot day.

**Waymarking:** The main route is waymarked in yellow throughout.

---

## Introduction

Most guide books of the Loire Valley infer that 'château-country' begins in the neighbourhood of Gien. That simply isn't true, as you will find out from the next few walks – and it is the ancient village of Arlempdes, some 300 miles upstream from Gien, that justly claims the distinction of having 'le premier château de la Loire'.

The château of Arlempdes was built by the Montlaur family way back in the 11th century. There have been lots of additions and alterations since, but today it is only a skeleton of a château that remains. Its fame largely lies in its position – clinging to the summit of a bizarrely shaped basalt outcrop high above the river. A little chapel of red volcanic rock is its most prominent feature. In summer there are guided tours of the ruin – but it's more fun if you visit out of season. Then you can collect the château keys from the auberge below its gates and let yourself in. There's a lengthy English text to explain it all, but it's worth the entry fee just to enjoy the splendid views along the river valley. And when you come out, you can admire the cobbled village street with its 11th-century gateway and the elaborate wayside cross in front of the old church.

*Arlempdes with its château*

After all that, it's time to set out on the walk. The narrow path soon takes you up to a fine viewpoint where you can look down on all you have already seen – the little village and the château above the winding river deep in its gorge. The easy short route then takes you across a few quiet lanes to yet another viewpoint on a plateau strewn with glorious wildflowers. A prairie of early purple orchids is quite a sight in itself. Those with more energy to expend can attain the same flower-decked viewpoint by a route that climbs high in the hills behind. On the way down there is a splendid distant view, with the Mézenc and all the peaks of the Velay spread out before you. A pleasant woodland path takes you down into the valley below the château as you return to Arlempdes.

## The Walk

1. Leaving the little car park, head downhill on the road towards the river. Just after the first hairpin bend, take a track on the right heading uphill. At this point you are on the GR3 and can follow white on red waymarks along with the yellow. The track passes a wayside cross overlooking the valley and is then joined by a track from the left before curving to the right. At the top of the hill the track forks – bear right following the signpost for *La Roche des Bonnes Dames*. There is a superb view over the gorges of the Loire and Arlempdes with its château. Continue along the broad track, which climbs and then descends before reaching a farm. Pass in front of the farm and continue ahead on a wide track between fields.

2. The track meets a tarmacked road, and you have a choice of routes.

   **For the short circuit:** Turn right here and walk ahead to meet the D54. Follow this to the left, through the hamlet of Freycenet, and take the first small road on the right, sign-posted to Masclaux (approxi-

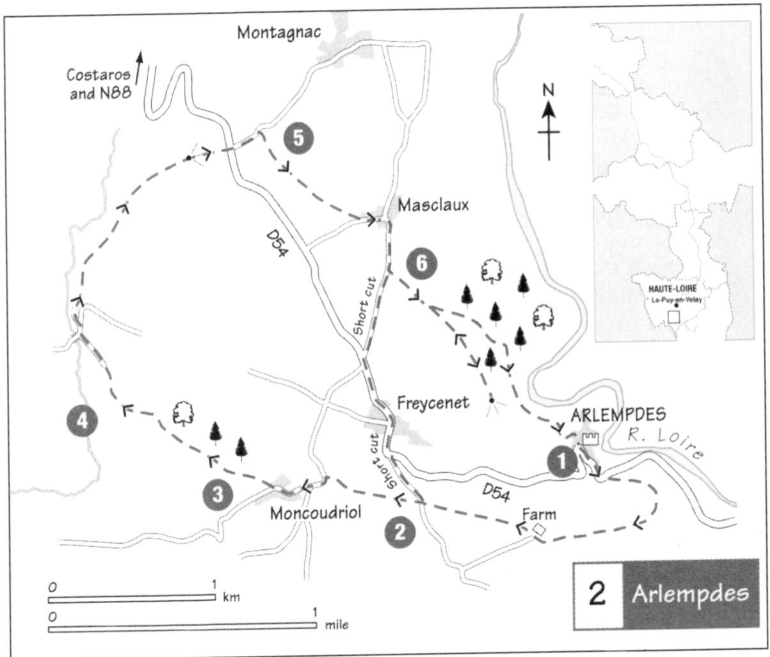


mately 1km from Point 2). In about 300 metres, you arrive at a narrow road to a house on the right – Point 6 on the map.

**For the full route:** Cross the road directly and continue on the rough track opposite. Climbing up the hill, you have views behind you into the mountains – the highest peak you can see is the Mézenc. Coming to another road, you turn left into the village of Moncoudriol. Ignore a road on the left and keep ahead through the village.

3. At the end of the village, opposite a farm, take the earth track on the right, again heading uphill. On reaching the top, pass through the fence (a section can be lifted aside) and bear left to walk between the line of pines. At its end you are in a well-fenced corner of a field with a wood in front of you. Step over the fence on your left and walk ahead with the fenced woodland on your right. You are on a track heading into the trees when you again come upon yellow waymarks (it seems the route must once have gone through the wood, but this has now been fenced off). The track becomes quite obvious and descends. At the edge of the wood, take a track on the left running downhill along the edge of a field (hedge on left). At the bottom of the field you emerge on another broad track with a pretty valley ahead.

4. Turn right on this track. At the farm, turn left on the tarmacked road and follow it downhill. Just before the bridge over the stream, turn right on another earthen track. This immediately forks, and you take the left-hand option – again you are on a Grande Randonnée with the white on red waymarks. The track winds on around the hill and soon there is a fine view to the north-east where all the peaks of the Velay adorn the horizon. The highest of all, the Mézenc at 1753m, is at a narrow angle to the right of the path. Coming down to the D54, cross straight over in the direction of Montagnac

5. After 100 metres or so, take the track on the right (leaving the GR). This eventually passes to the right of some farm buildings and comes down to a tarmacked road. Turn left here and continue into the village of Masclaux. At the T-junction in front of a splendidly restored farm house, turn right and follow the road for about 200m to the next intersection.

6. Turn left along the tarmacked road to a house (Those arriving on the short circuit will need to turn right). After the house the track becomes unsurfaced and in about 100m a track is seen descending through the woods on the left. This is the way back to Arlempdes – but first you might like to continue ahead to reach the plateau viewpoint (8 minutes approx.). From a field sprinkled with wild flowers and ringed with broom and heather you have a splendid view over Arlempdes in its gorge far below.

   Retracing your steps, take the track you passed earlier (it is marked as a Grande Randonnée), and descend through the pines. The path winds along the side of the gorge and there are more views of the château ahead. After crossing the stream by a little waterfall at the bottom of the hill, there's a final uphill stretch to reach the gateway to the château.

## More Walks in the Area

The other local walk is the 13km circuit through the Bois d'Arlempdes – you saw it sign-posted to the left at the top of the first climb. This route again crosses the contours, with many viewpoints as you follow the course of the little River Méjeanne. The route (along with this one) can be found in a booklet entitled *Le Pays de Pradelles*, which contains not only 12 walks, but 2 discovery trails and a mountain-bike route in the area. Any nearby Office de Tourisme – or La Croisée des Chemins at le Puy-en-Velay (see Walk 1) – should be able to find it for you.

This is fine walking country and the *Comité Départemental de la Randonnée* has produced a series of folders entitled *Itineraires Pédestres en Haute- Loire*. Each folder contains leaflets of several circular walks in that particular area. The maps in these leaflets are very good and quite easy to follow; the quite lengthy text is, as usual, only in French. But walking is very important to the tourist industry in these parts, and the waymarking on all circuits is well-maintained. Among so many routes it is difficult to make a recommendation, but if you are following the Loire, in about 17km you will arrive at the attractive town of Solignac-sur-Loire. Here starts the 10km *Circuit de la Cascade de la Beaume* (described in the folder *Autour du Puy-en-Velay)*, which leads you into a deep wooded valley where the Beaume (a tributary of the Loire) tumbles 27 metres over a spur of volcanic rock amid much noise and spray.

One of the most interesting places nearby (see below) is the village of Le Monastier-sur-Gazeille. From a walking point of view, it is on the route of two Grandes Randonnées (with bus connections) and five classified Petites Randonnées (short circuits) as well as several others. Moreover it was the point from which Robert Louis Stevenson set out on his famous 'Travels with a Donkey'. That well-documented journey lasted merely 12 days (it would have been much quicker without the donkey!), but nearly 150 years on, it still generates much interest in these parts. The very well-stocked and helpful Office de Tourisme in Le Monastier can give you an English translation of Stevenson's route – it has recently been waymarked for walkers. The total length is around a hundred miles and, donkeyless, should easily be managed in a week. But if you do fancy the companionship of a donkey, an organisation by the name of *Gentiane* in Castagnols (farther south) can arrange for a one or two day's hike or even the whole Stevenson trail – ask at the Office de Tourisme in le Monastier for details.

And finally, also with access from le Monastier, there is the *Transcévenole*. In the 19th century a railway was planned across the Cévennes. It was a mammoth undertaking with many spectacular viaducts on the way. Suddenly, with all except the rails in place, the whole project was scrapped – the war had intervened and afterwards the automobile had taken over. For years the route lay unused (except for bungee jumpers), but now it has been opened up for walkers, mountain bikers and equestrians. It is possible to walk the 25km from Peyrard to Presailles, but a simple circular walk (9km.) can be taken from le Monastier, joining the track near the College Laurent Eynac on the road to Les Estables. Cross the spectacular Recoumène Viaduct and continue to the village of Avouac, returning to Le Monastier along the quiet road. If you haven't time for a walk but would just like to see this impressive viaduct, it crosses the valley just 1.5km from Le Monastier, on the road to Les Estables.

## Places of Interest Nearby

Le Monastier-sur-Gazeille has been mentioned in the More Walks section. A long drawn out village it overhangs the valley of the Gazeille with some splendid views. A Benedictine monastery was founded here in the 7th century and became very powerful before its decline some 1000 years later. Now the abbey buildings (an 18th-century version) house the *Mairie*, but beside it, the old abbey church (11th century onwards) is worth a visit. And at the other end of town, the recently restored Église Saint-Jean (the original dating from the 9th century) commands splendid views over the river valley below.

St Michel rock and chapel

You could not possibly leave this area without visiting le Puy-en-Velay – even if its traffic problems do not endear it to the walker. It is a town built in the crater of a volcano and from a distance two strange spikes of volcanic rock can be seen rising from among the houses. The first is the St Michel rock – and, being France, it is topped with a chapel. The Chapelle de St

Michel d'Aiguilhe seems literally to have grown from the rock – a mere 268 steps up its side will give you a magnificent view. The second peak, the Rocher Corneille, is crowned with a glowing statue of Our Lady. Made from molten gun metal (from the cannons of Sebastopol) it is hollow and those who wish may venture inside as far as the neck – for more views. Beside the statue is the Cathedral, accessed via the steep cobbled Rue des Tables flanked by lace-makers plying their trade. Behind are the famous cloisters and the alley leading on to the statue of Notre Dame. All and more are on a waymarked town trail, of which you can get details from the Office de Tourisme. Le Puy-en-Velay has another claim to fame – it was the starting point for one of the four Chemins de St Jacques, the ancient pilgrim routes across France to Santiago de Compostela in Spain, where the body of the apostle St James was buried. In the Middle Ages many thousands of pilgrims a year made the journey (around 1500km.). Today there is a revival of interest, particularly in this, the *Via Podiensis*, which is the best preserved of the four routes. A Pilgrim Centre (*Accueil Saint-Jacques*) beside the cathedral is happy to welcome not only pilgrims but anyone interested in the trail.

## From the Source to the Sea

Following on down river, you reach Goudet, where another château looks down from its height across the river. Just beyond, there is a fine view down the Loire from the D49 above St Martin-de-Fugères. At Solignac, the road is high above the river, but you can soon descend to Volhac and keep to the river bank all the way to Brives-Charensac on the outskirts of le Puy-en-Velay. The river avoids Le Puy, running north and plunging into the gorges of Peyredeyre – the road is beside it all the way. Note the fine château across the bridge at Lavoute-sur-Loire. Carrying on downstream, the journey is very picturesque with the road crossing from bank to bank. There are many, many excellent walks in these gorges – some suggestions are included under Walk 3. At Roche-en-Régnier (turn left where signed) there is a splendid view of the mountains of the Velay and Forez from the old tower on the hilltop. Further on is Retournac, a *Station Verte* keen to welcome visitors, and offering them no fewer than four *tables d'orientations* at viewpoints in the hills and plateau above. After Retournac, the road briefly leaves the river and you might consider a diversion to Bas-en-Basset (there's a fine view from the Château de Rochebaron), or yet again cross the river to visit Monistrol-sur-Loire, a town with an old bishop's palace and lots of medieval character. At Aurec you reach the start of the Lac de Grangent, created by the Grangent dam several miles downstream. The road crosses the lake and climbs on the left bank with some splendid views. Turn off to reach the medieval village of Chambles for Walk 4 (the third in the series *From the Source to the Sea*).

# 3. In the Gorges de Peyredeyre

North of Le Puy-en-Velay, the Loire plunges into attractive wooded gorges. One of the prettiest spots is Lavoûte-sur-Loire, from where this walk leads you up the slopes for some impressive views of the meandering river and the fortress-like château of Lavoûte-Polignac.

**Grade:** Moderate

**Distance:** 10km (6¼ miles)

**Time:** 3 hours

**Map:** IGN Série Bleue 2735 E

**Start and finish:** Car park on the left bank of the river, Lavoûte-sur-Loire.

**How to get there:** Lavoûte-sur-Loire is about 14km north of Le Puy-en-Velay on the D103. The car park is at the north end of the town, just across the river bridge.

**Refreshment:** There is a bar/restaurant just beside the car park, and plenty of others in Lavoûte-sur-Loire. There are no refreshment possibilities en route.

**Notes:** This walk is almost entirely on tracks winding along the wooded sides of the gorge. At the outset, there is a steady climb for around half an hour – after which there is no real exertion. The tracks are at times rough and stony and you may benefit from walking boots. The woodland gives good shade on a hot day, but nevertheless, you should carry plenty of fluid. And you might like to take binoculars for the superb views down the river.

**Waymarking:** The route is waymarked in yellow throughout.

## Introduction

Near Le Puy-en-Velay the Loire is a wide calm river. Entering the Gorges of Peyredeyre it becomes wild again, rushing through narrow channels and bounding and tumbling over boulders in its bed. The granite slopes are also wild – clad in oak and beech they are at their most splendid in autumn. In spring the broom is prominent – bright yellow splashes of it along every path. At your feet there are wild flowers in profusion, but the most striking of all are the rock plants. In late spring the granite outcrops are spectacularly covered in a pink campion (*silene armeria*).

Getting to the top of these slopes is quite hard going, but there are some excellent views down the river by way of reward. At the top, the picturesque stone hamlet of la Roche welcomes you with a wandering posse of farm goats and a couple of ducks whose tiny pond is fed by a mountain spring. This marks the end of the climbing and from here on you can enjoy the winding woodland paths – which are fortunately well waymarked. There are views of the distant mountains – the Mézenc and Alambre – before the descent to the banks of the Loire itself. The way back follows just above the river and this is where the rock plants are at their very best – the path seems to be leading you through a giant rockery. And finally there are impressive views of the Château of Lavoûte-Polignac on its rocky perch across the river. Built as a fortress as long ago as the 10th century, its rather severe façade belies the interior elegance of this family home.

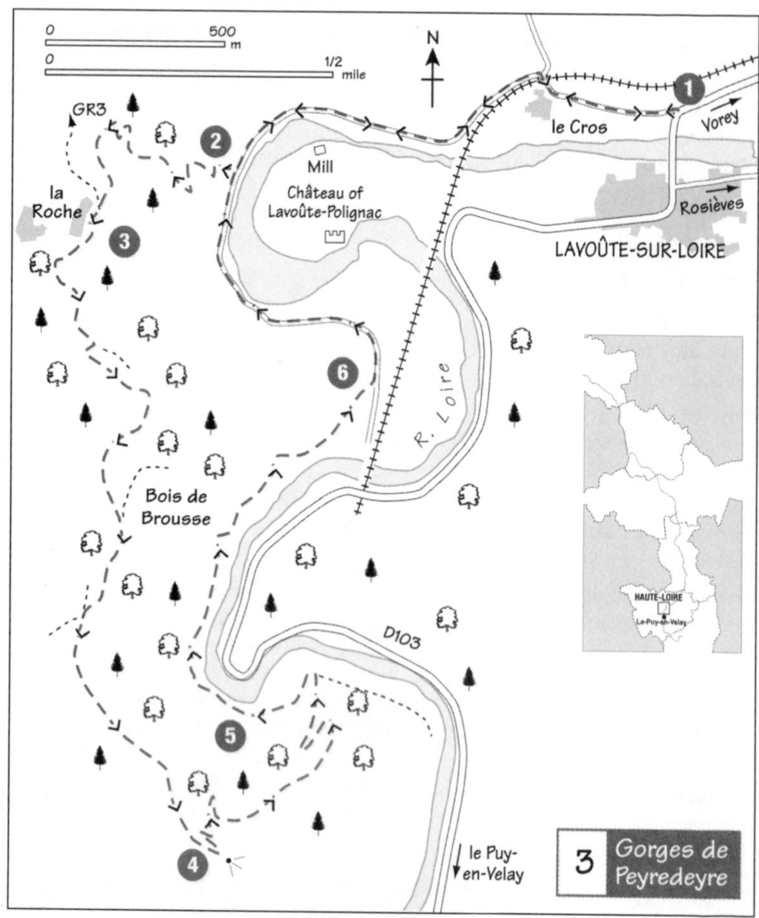


## *The Walk*

1. Leaving the car park, do not cross the river, but take the narrow road following the left bank of the river upstream – the route is signposted as the PR 227. In the hamlet of le Cros, pass under the railway and immediately take the road on the left. This comes down to the riverside beside the remains of a medieval bridge. Continue alongside the river with views of the mill ahead

2. At a little rise in the road, a path leaves on the right, climbing uphill into the wood – you are on the route of the GR3, with white on red waymarks. The path zig-zags up the slope until, after about half an hour, you emerge from the woods beside a couple of stone farmhouses – the hamlet of la Roche.

3. Turn left in front of the *fontaine* and follow the narrow track along the hillside. You have now left the Grande Randonnée and are following yellow waymarks. About 50 metres after passing a little waterfall, take a track doubling back uphill to the right. This swings left again and continues as a slightly broader track along the hillside. As you climb a little again, there are some excellent views of the curving valley and beyond to the distant mountains. On reaching a little stone building,

keep ahead where the track becomes quite wide. Continuing, there is a sudden sharp rise to reach a track cross-roads. Turn left here and carry on through the woods. Eventually you reach an open field on the right from where there are views ahead to the mountains, the highest of which is the Mézenc.

4. At another track junction, turn left and begin to descend steeply. The path winds down the hillside until you come to a major junction with a steep slope to the river ahead. Here leave the main track and turn left. The path soon comes down to the river bank.

5. After walking along the bank for about 30 metres you can go no farther and the not-too-obvious path now climbs on the left. The path bears right and, becoming wider, follows downstream above the river. There are good views of the river and the wild flowers are outstanding. At length you reach an open field dotted with broom, and can see ahead the Château of Lavoûte-Polignac.

6. Leave the field by a stile over the fence at the bottom to reach a tarmacked road. Turn left on the road, from which there are soon some superb views of the rather austere but very photogenic château. Continuing along the road, you again reach Point 2 and can retrace your steps beside the river and under the railway bridge to the town.

*The château of Lavoûte-Polignac*

## More Walks in the Area

This is all fine walking country, and the best routes are to be found in a Topoguide entitled *Le Pays de l'Emblavez à pied* (Ref. P433). The area referred to as l'Emblavez is the plain between the Loire and the volcanic mountains, a particularly rich and fertile territory (emblaver = to sow crops). So here, along with wild country, you get the fields of cereal and the vineyards. An excellent walk combining it all is the route from St Vincent (just to the north of Lavoûte-sur-Loire) encircling a peak known as the Suc de Ceneuil. From the vineyards around its slopes there are wide views to the distant mountains. For the best panorama of all you can climb to the summit – the path up from the village of Ceneuil is a *Sentier de Découverte*. The route is described in the Topoguide above, which you should be able to find in any local Office de Tourisme. Continuing down the valley of the Loire there are plenty more walking routes. Try those starting from Vorey (which likes to think of itself as *Petit Nice de la Haute-Loire*) or from Chamalières (see below). From the hamlet of Varenne south of Chamalières you can climb the Suc de Barthou (984m) – the route is again a *Sentier de Découverte* and you should be able to find the booklet describing both route and features (including the peaks to be seen from the summit) in the Office de Tourisme in Chamalières or Vorey.

Farther downstream the gorges continue and there are so many good walks that three folders relating to *Les Gorges de la Loire* have been published in the *Itinéraires Pédestres en Haute-Loire* series. Wherever you are there seems to be a good walk, and most of them have views of the river deep in its ravine and the distant peaks of the Velay. If you want to escape the Loire for a while, go along to the old town of Monistrol (which although dubbed '-sur-Loire' is at least 3km off). The Office de Tourisme is housed in the Bishop's Palace, and the square below (Place Néron) is the departure point of no fewer than seven marked itineraries. There is an excellent map with each, but the French text is lengthy and rather daunting – don't worry, these routes are well-waymarked and can easily be followed from map alone.

## Places of Interest Nearby

The Polignac family have been important landowners in these parts since the early Middle Ages. Today the Château of Lavoûte-Polignac is the residence of the Dukes of Polignac and you can take a tour around it any day from Easter to the 1st of November. Fine furniture and a prized art collection are on view. Outside is a Renaissance garden.

The first château was built on this site to guard the entrance to the river valley, but the Polignacs had another far superior fortress, which is well worth a visit. At Polignac itself (about 5km north-west of le Puy-en-Velay, off the N102), the Château de Polignac stands on a strange platform of volcanic basalt, raising it some 100 metres from the plains below. This curious place has an even-more-curious history. In Roman times it was the site of a Temple of Apollo – but his priests were rather worldly-wise! Those wishing to 'consult the oracle' would come to the rock and present their requests, along with an offering, in a room at its base. A hidden tunnel through the rock carried the spoken words to the priests in the temple on top, where stood a huge stone mask of Apollo. By the time the visitor had made it up the hill to the temple, the priests were ready with a reply – which, with the aid of a megaphone, appeared to come from the mouth of the god himself.

Around a thousand years ago, it was to this hill that the Polignac family came and they built an impenetrable fortress where Apollo's temple once stood. Over the years the family prospered and several members rose to positions of national fame and importance. The château was altered and added to over time and today you can see buildings from various epochs – along with some more ancient relics, including the mask of Apollo. And from the top of the keep, there is again a splendid view encompassing the distant range of the Velay and much more.

# 4. Views of the Lac de Grangent

The deep winding Lac de Grangent was formed when the Loire was dammed to provide hydro-electric power back in the fifties. On the plateau above, a medieval tower, a Gallic hill fort, a superb landscape of pines and broom and a ruined château overlooking an island in the lake all contribute to this excellent short walk.

**Grade:** Easy

**Distance:** 5km (3 miles)

**Time:** 2 hours (including time to look round the château).

**Map:** IGN Série Bleue 2833 E

**Start and finish:** The car park in the village of Chambles.

**How to get there:** The Lac de Grangent lies just to the west of St Etienne. Follow the D108 above the west bank of the lake, turning where signed to Chambles (approx. 9km south of St Just – St Rambert). There is car parking on the left just before entering the village.

**Refreshment:** There are two bar/restaurants in the village. A little bar that also serves snacks is conveniently situated beside the Château d'Essalois.

**Notes:** Trainers are quite suitable footwear for this easy short walk. Drink (and food) can be obtained from the bar beside the château, so you could perhaps give your rucksack the day off. Although the walk is short, most of it is exposed, so take appropriate precautions on a hot day. And finally, consider taking binoculars – there are excellent views all the way.

**Waymarking:** Four routes start from Chambles and there seem to be waymarks everywhere. It's probably best to ignore them and just follow the directions.

---

## Introduction

The countryside known as the Forez is in two parts – way over to the west are the impressive Montagnes de Forez, while centrally there is a wide plain through which the Loire wends its way north in leisurely fashion. On this walk you are in the south of the Forez, on the last of the high ground before that plain and the countryside here has a beauty of its own. Still deep in a gorge, the Loire now forms the Lac de Grangent, a most attractive expanse of water, very popular with the inhabitants of nearby St Etienne for their recreation. All around the lake, the steeply sloping banks are clothed with pines and heather, gorse and broom.

High on the left bank, the attractive little village of Chambles has an enviable position with fine views across the water. Even better views can be achieved by climbing the 11th-century tower, but the darkness inside and the rickety wooden staircase are not too encouraging. From Chambles, the path across the plateau leads you between yellow banks of gorse and broom to the 16th-century Château d'Essalois. Recent restoration has made this look quite smart, and the debate now is whether to upgrade yet more and install a roof. The château is open for exploration – look through the first floor window over the lake for an excellent view of the Île de Grangent, the only island in the lake. The island has its own ruined château and below it, a red-roofed chapel – although this is better seen from the opposite shore. The hill on which the Château d'Essalois is situated was once the site of a Gallic oppidum (Iron Age settlement) and you can see some of its outlines as you return.

## The Walk

1. From the parking area, walk up into the village square with its inviting restaurants. Leave the square at the top right-hand corner and continue ahead passing the steps to the tower on your left – climb it now or later if you dare. At the T-junction behind the tower, turn right and then immediately left. You will already have seen an amazing number of circuit waymarks. Don't take too much notice of them – the road you are now on should be above and approximately parallel to the shores of the Lac de Grangent. The road bends to the left (ignore the track on your right) and then to the left again. At this point take the road on your right. This road becomes a sandy track and heads over the brow of the hill. There are already views of the Château d'Essalois ahead (St Just-St Rambert is the town behind). Disregard the tracks going off on the right towards the lake. Soon you arrive at a major cross-tracks.

2. Here continue straight ahead towards the château. At a fork in the track, keep right on the main track. Alongside a pine wood on your right, turn sharp left on a less distinct path across a field into the valley. Cross the stream on a wooden bridge and take one of the tracks that climb steeply (but briefly!) up the slope on the far side. On reaching the broad sandy track turn right and follow it to the château. There are some excellent views across the water to the port of St Victor with its sailing club. Finally bear left on the track across the field to reach the château.

3. Take time to explore the château – there are views of the Grangent dam and the Île de Grangent from its windows. You could also enjoy a drink at the welcoming little bar opposite. When ready, continue down the broad track with the château on the right. There are views ahead across the Forez plain. Take the first track on the left (waymarked) and walk on around the side of the hill (the Suc du Pré) alongside an old wall. This hill was the site of the Gallic oppidum. Where the track forks, keep left (a VTT route goes downhill to the right). Soon you come down to a road with a car park opposite.

4. Turn right on the road and follow it to the top of the hill – you can walk on the grassy area beside it for part of the way. At the T-junction at the top of the hill, turn left into the village. Where the road swings right, continue ahead to another T-junction, passing some interesting old properties on the way. At the T-junction, go left, and, passing a *lavoir* (washing place) on the stream at the bottom of the hill, turn left again on a sandy track. A few minutes walking on this brings you back to the cross-tracks you passed earlier (Point 2). Turn right here and retrace your steps on the track uphill to Chambles. Reaching the village, do not turn left (the way you came) but continue ahead on the road and then take a narrow street ahead leading you back into the village square.

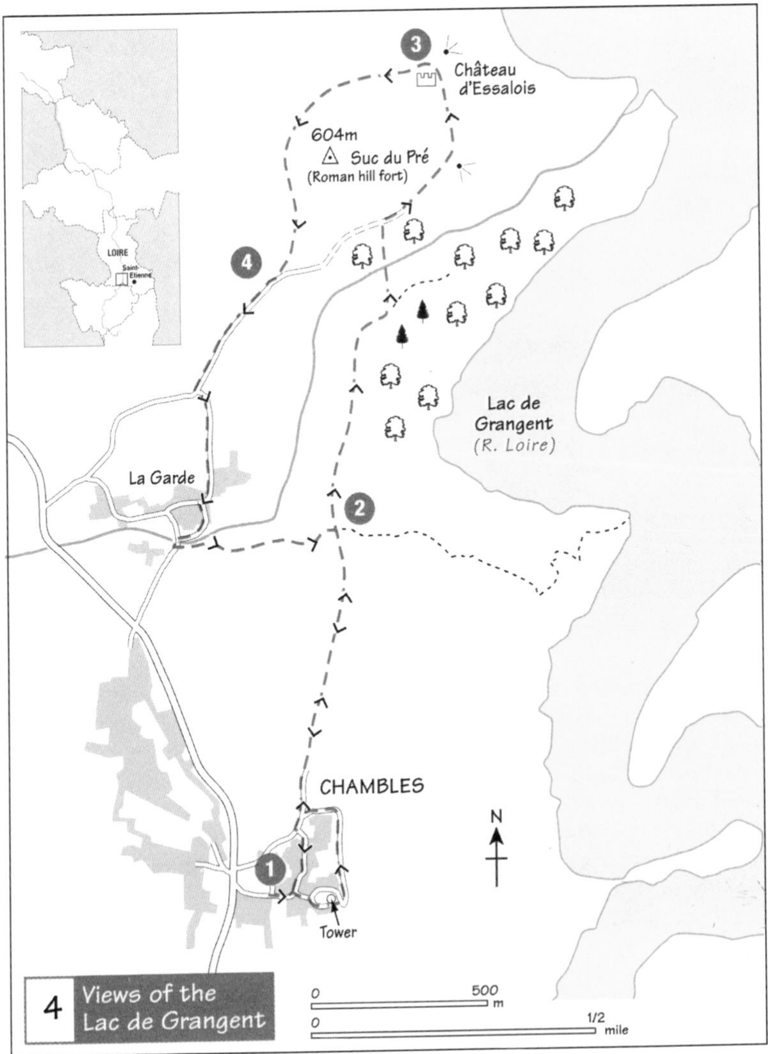


## More Walks in the Area

This is beautiful walking country, but strangely the GR3 is not here. It has left for its one diversion from the Loire Valley, a diversion west to follow the peaks of the *Monts du Forez*. This is an impressive range of high mountains (the highest is 1634m) whose lower slopes are clad in dark pine forest. The tops in contrast are bare wild moorland. In between are deep valleys with many tumbling rivers. The GR has chosen a worthwhile detour and you could opt to follow it – but it returns only beyond Digoin, thus bypassing the next two walks.

If you have time to linger in this area, the surrounding countryside has a huge variety of local circuits to offer. The best place to find details on these is the Office de Tourisme in St Just-St Rambert. The folder of walks for the immediate local area is entitled *Escapades en Forez Sud*, a most attractively presented collection of rambles with excellent maps. In this you will find that Chambles has in fact four circuits, not any one of them

*Île de Grangent viewed from the Château d'Essalois*

quite the same as the one described here. The waymarking of these circuits is, as you saw, first-class. The little town of Perigneux to the west has a choice of seven routes from 36km to 6.5km – see how energetic you feel.

If you would like a view of the island from the other side, you would need to cross the dam and follow the road around a huge hairpin bend. Just after the road bends to the left again, a track leads down to the lake shore. Farther south there are more excellent views from the many tracks leading to the lake from the village of Condamine. Get the IGN Serie Bleue map 2833 E and create your own route.

## Places of Interest Nearby

A drive of some 30km to the north west will take you to the edge of the Monts du Forez at the doubtful-sounding *Col de la Croix de l'Homme Mort*. It's a scenic drive all the way, but be prepared for a few bends. From there the mountain roads wind on through forest and high pasture and you are in the *Parc naturel régional Livradois-Forez..* The highest point, Pierre-sur-Haute, is not far away as the crow flies, but getting there and back will be a whole day's trip. The final ascent can be made either on foot or by cable-car and the view from the top is spectacular.

Heading in the opposite direction, south-east past St Etienne, you are in the *Parc naturel régional du Pilat* with more splendid scenery. Only a few kilometres from St Etienne is another spot with an evil-sounding name, the *Gouffre d'Enfer* (Chasm of Hell). Here the Furan River has been dammed to provide hydro-electric power and you can climb steps up the face of the dam, deep in the gorge. A path leads to 'hell' from the village of Rochetaillée on the D8. If you then feel like a stroll by the river, a waymarked path runs beside it and in another couple of kilometres you reach a second dam, the Pas du Riot.

St Etienne itself is big and busy and you may not feel like entering therein. If you do, most of interest is to be found in the old town sector, although there are several museums outside it. One museum you can visit without going near the town centre is the *Musée d'Art Moderne*. This vast exhibition of post-1900 art is housed in a not-too-attractive building in St Priest-en-Jarez, 5km north of St Etienne, and is well worth a visit if you have the time. It is open every day excepting Tuesdays and public holidays

## From the Source to the Sea

North from St Just-St Rambert the river widens as it flows through the plains of the Forez. This is not the most scenic part of its journey and you can quickly cover ground on the N82. There are distant views – to the west the peaks of the Forez line the horizon, to the east the Montagnes du Matin (so called by the early inhabitants of the plains because each morning they saw them silhouetted against the rising sun). The lively town of Feurs dates from Roman times and many artefacts are to be found in the town's *Musée d'Assier*. Just beyond Balbigny the terrain is again undulating, and here you should leave the N82 to follow beside the river. After St Jodard, turn downhill to cross the bridge to St Paul-de-Vézelin – but you might wish to continue on the right bank for a further 4km for a view of the photogenic Château de la Roche on its causeway out in the water. Returning to the bridge, cross it and continue to the village for the fourth walk in the series.

# 5. The Gorges Roannaises

Less deep and more verdant than those upstream, the Gorges of Roanne form what is possibly the most attractive part of the Loire Valley. Explore the area around St Paul-de-Vézelin, where this ramble takes you to a riverside beach in a picturesque setting and offers a choice of scenic routes for the return.

**Grade:** Moderate – with short strenuous climb on longer route.

**Distance:** 10.5km (6½ miles) or 9km (5½ miles) with an optional extra diversion for a view of the Château de la Roche.

**Time:** 3¼ hours or 2½ hours

**Map:** The route covers two IGN Série Bleue maps (2830 O and 2831 O). A much less expensive option would be to acquire the booklet *Découverte en Vals d'Aix et d'Isable* – the route can be found on the maps with Walk 4 and Walk 7.

**Start and finish:** Place de l'Église at St Paul-de-Vézelin.

**How to get there:** From Balbigny, take the D56 to St Jodard. After the village, turn left on the D26 to cross the river and climb to St Paul-de-Vézelin. Alternatively, turn where signed from the D8 (west of the river). The church is at the centre of the village and there is parking alongside.

**Refreshment:** St Paul-de-Vézelin boasts a bar/restaurant and a café – and there is a well-placed picnic site after the climb on the longer route.

**Notes:** This walk combines narrow tarmac roads and fairly rough woodland tracks. On dry ground you could probably get away with trainers, but to be honest, you would fare better with stouter footwear. St Paul-de-Vézelin is on a plateau 160 metres above the river, so on both routes some climbing is necessary – the longer route is the harder. Take plenty of fluids with you, particularly if the weather is warm – there are no possibilities for refreshment en route. In high season, the attractive sandy riverside beach is ideal for a swim – although it is not supervised.

**Waymarking:** The route is waymarked in white on yellow throughout apart from a central section on the long walk where there are flashes of green on white.

---

## Introduction

South of Roanne, the damming of the river at Villerest has created a wider, deeper stretch some 30km in length through most attractive gorges. At the southern end of this section and high above the Loire is the little old village of St Paul-de-Vézelin. There's not much activity about it now, but centuries ago it was a busy place where many people gathered on their way to catch the only ferry across the river – and so to the markets of Roanne. The building of the bridge changed all that, and St Paul-de-Vézelin has retired into its shell – but you can still find a bar/restaurant to resuscitate you after this walk.

The route here takes you from St Paul-de-Vézelin down thickly wooded slopes to the riverside. On the way a short diversion affords a distant view of the elegant Château de la Roche, sitting in the middle of the lake-like river below. Coming out from the trees, a narrow winding road brings you down to Arpheuilles, the old crossing place on the river. The promontory is now occupied by a small campsite with such an idyllic setting (friendly owners, too) that if you are travelling with your own accommodation it could prove difficult to move on down-river from this point. Farther on around the creek the grassy banks slope to a fringe of sand at the water's edge, making this a popular bathing place. If you are not swimming, just sit on the bank and take in the view – and choose your route home from here. Both options offer fine views of the winding river, but, in the usual way of things, the steeper climb gives the greater rewards. If you feel able to tackle it, the sharp ascent through the woods will take you to a site known as the *Pêt d'Âne*. This is a splendid viewing area with picnic tables overlooking a wide meander of the river around a flat-topped promontory of land far below. When you are ready to go on, the path over the hill offers a different prospect across the plains to the Monts du Forez. For those taking the lesser climb, there are still superb views of the river to be enjoyed. And if your visual appetite isn't satisfied after all that, you can stop off on the way home at another hilltop with a 360° panorama.

*The view from Pêt d'Âne*

## The Walk

1. Starting at the Place de l'Église, walk away from the church for a few metres to reach the war memorial. Here turn right, and very shortly, turn left in the direction of Marcilleux. Continue to a crossroads beside a farm and turn left. Following this track to its end, turn left on a road and immediately right on the 'main' road to the village of Clivier.
2. Where the road bends left, continue ahead on a narrow road signed to Pierre-Plate. After 500 metres or so you arrive at a junction where a road descends on the right. If you would like a view of the lovely but fairly distant Château de la Roche, walk down this road for about 5 minutes or so. The view improves a little (but not greatly) if you go all the way down to the hamlet. Don't forget it's a steep climb back. The full diversion will take about half an hour.

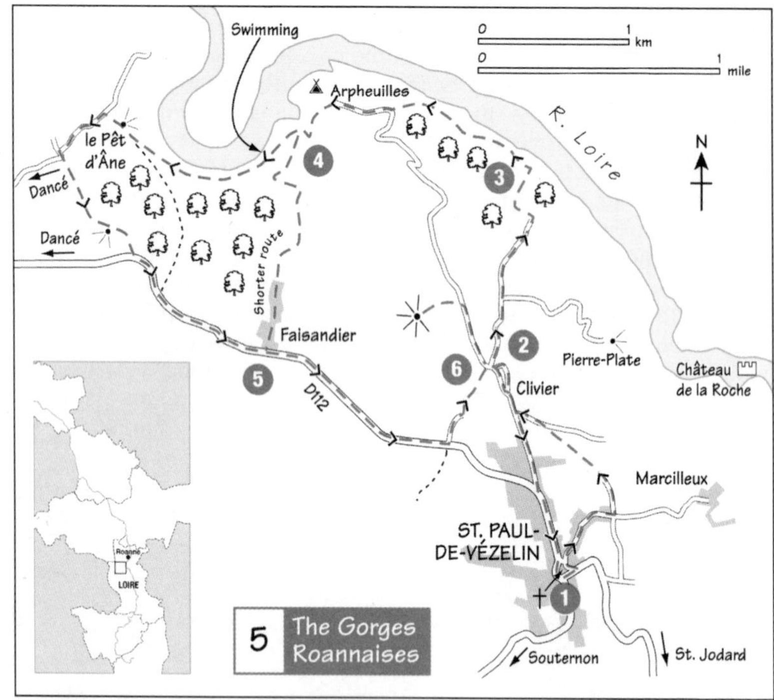


When you again reach the junction, maintain your previous direction along the road. After passing a farm, the way becomes rougher and begins to descend quite steeply through the woods. At a fork of tracks, you continue downhill. At length the path approaches the river itself.

3. A track leads off into a field on the left – ignore it. Arriving at the second field, there appears to be no track (only a possibly rather overgrown affair going down to the river). Notwithstanding, walk into the field and along its top edge. A tiny track soon appears and reaching some trees there are waymarks. You are now walking along parallel to the riverbank and the track gathers strength as it goes. There are views of the river through the trees. After some time, the path turns away from the river and climbs to meet the road. Turn right and descend to the attractive campsite. Turn left in front of the campsite gates and continue downhill to the tip of the creek.

4 If you are taking the shorter route, the track you now need climbs uphill on the left – but you will probably first want to walk a little further to the riverside beach where you can sit at a picnic table and take in the peaceful scene. On a hot day, a dip in the river may be very welcome.

**For the shorter route:** Return to the grassy track you saw earlier (just around the head of the creek) and climb uphill. Reaching the woods the track forks – turn left following the clear waymarks. Now you simply follow the obvious track all the way back to the hamlet of Faisandier at the top of the hill – but keep turning round as you go, there are splendid views down the winding river valley. Eventually you arrive at the road at Point 5.

**For the longer route:** From the beach, continue ahead beside the river. At the end the path enters the woodland and begins to climb – the waymarks here are green on white. A T-junction is reached and you take the track to the right. A steep climb follows until eventually you emerge from the trees at the *Pêt d'Âne* viewpoint with its picnic tables and play equipment. This is one of the highest points in the area and you can see across the river to the mountains of Beaujolais in Burgundy. Leaving the viewpoint, turn left (uphill) on the road. Where the road swings right, keep straight ahead on a sandy track beside the trees (yellow waymarks now). This opens out for more wide views – you are now looking in the opposite direction to the Monts du Forez. Reaching the road, turn left. Continue along this to the hamlet of Faisandier (there is no name, just some houses on a track on the left)

5. Continue ahead along the road. After about 15 minutes, as the road descends, take a narrow road going uphill on the left (not waymarked – in fact, the yellow waymarks turn off to the right at this point). This narrow road returns you to the 'main' road in the village of Clivier.

6. Turning right on to this road will take you directly back to St Paul-de-Vézelin. But for yet another fine view before you return, turn instead to the left and, almost opposite a farm in about 300 metres, take a track on the left leading to the very top of the hill.

## More Walks in the Area

The very well-stocked and most helpful Office du Tourisme in Roanne (follow the signs – it's near the station and there's parking behind) can find you all the information you need. If you are looking for another walk in the immediate area of this one, ask for the booklet *Découverte en Vals d'Aix et d'Isable*. You may well like to visit the nearby medieval village of Pommiers (see Places of Interest nearby) and take the short 2.5km walk while you are there. Realistically, you don't need the book for this one. From the car park in the centre of the village, take the little track (Chemin du For) down to the River Aix. There is a fine view from the old Roman bridge (Pont de la Valla) to the priory. Now turn right and keep strictly to the riverside path for about a kilometre – there are yellow waymarks. Turn right again and follow a field edge and lane to reach the road beside the priory and village.

Continuing downstream – and again mentioned in the Places of Interest section – are the combined villages of St Jean-St Maurice. Three routes of varying length start from these villages and the waymarking here is second to none. The routes are all described in a publication entitled *Rando Guide – À travers l'Ouest Roannais*. One of the routes here has a wealth of wayside crosses bearing witness to the passage of pilgrims on their way to le Puy-en-Velay and the Via Podiensis (see Walk 2). If you don't have time for this 12km circuit, you could at least take the 3km *Circuit du Patrimoine*. It is carefully marked out with a castle logo, and takes you on an excellent scenic tour of these beautiful old twin villages overlooking the river.

The most popular area for walking in these parts is to the north-west of Roanne – the Côte Roannaise. Even if you haven't time to walk you will probably want to take a detour – this is the last range of mountains you will see on this trip down river. The Côte Roannaise is part of the Monts de la

Madeleine, their highest point rising to 1164m. The lower slopes are covered in vineyards – higher up there are forests and then bare peaks. An excellent but rather expensive publication entitled *La Côte Roannaise* gives you a choice of 28 walking routes and a five-day ramble (with many variations), the 'grand tour' of the area. There are also excellent identification photos of flowers, birds, trees and insects. Unfortunately it's in French only, but the quality of maps and waymarking means you should have no difficulty following the routes. To help your choice of location, see the Places of Interest section.

## Places of Interest Nearby

7km to the south is the beautifully restored medieval village of Pommiers. The site is that of a Benedictine priory dating from around the 10th century, accompanied by a priory church of similar age. Towered fortifications from the Middle Ages enclose the whole, including some beautiful old houses that are still inhabited. A visit to Pommiers can be combined with a short walk (see above), and there is no doubt that the most impressive view of the priory is from the ancient Pont de la Valla beside the river. The priory is open for visits both morning and afternoon in July and August, and some afternoons only outside this time.

A few kilometres downstream on the left bank are the dual villages of St Jean-St Maurice. St Maurice is really the one that shouldn't be missed – a flower-decked village of beautifully maintained old buildings clinging to the cliff high above the swollen river. A couple of bars and a hotel have splendid views across the water, but the tower of the ruined château has pride of place. If you have time to spare, follow the *Circuit Du Patrimoine* (see above) or visit the *Maison de la Randonnée* in an old house that was once a girls' school on the road leading up from the château.

Farther downstream again is the medieval town of Villerest, accompanied by its *barrage*. If you cross the river here, there is a fine viewpoint at Commelle-Vernay, signposted from the D56.

Finally, there is plenty to see on the Côte Roannaise. On the lower slopes are the vineyards and *caves* open for tasting of the local AOC wines. Progressing higher, the roads are narrow and tortuous with many hairpin bends. This is obvious walking country – wooden fingerposts alongside the roads give the direction and time to various destinations. There is a rather bleak feel to it all, compounded by the decline of many villages and the destruction of forest by *la tempête* (the storm that ravaged France in the last days of the last century). Above Arcon (on the D51) there is a once-splendid arboretum, les Grands Murcins. At the time of writing in spring 2001, it had just reopened after coming to terms with the devastation. Nevertheless, it is well worth making the journey here if only for the view – in front of the gate of the arboretum is a *table d'orientation* from which you can just pick out the silvery Loire making its way through Roanne in the valley below. Don't forget the binoculars!

If you have enjoyed that view, you can continue on the D51 around its many bends to its highest point, the Rocher de Rochefort, with yet another orientation table. Despite all the signs on the way up, you could easily miss the site itself. At the top of the hill there is a rocky outcrop on the right-hand side with parking for just a couple of cars beside it. The orientation table itself is crumbling a little, but nothing could detract from that view – as a challenge, try to find the river bridge in Roanne.

Another spectacular site in these hills is the Barrage de la Tache. If you are up at the Rocher de Rochefort, follow the winding road down through the valley of the Rouchain (again with its dam) or, otherwise, take the D47 from Renaison. For a good view of both dams and reservoirs (for those with surplus energy) follow the fingerpost to les Noës from the car park below the dam. The path zig-zags steeply up the slope to a hamlet with the curious name of Le Py se Lance – the giant Gargantua was said to have thrown a rock here, thus carving out both valleys. This excellent walk now continues up the valley to La Croix du Sud – but you'll need another 5 hours or so.

## From Source to the sea

At Roanne the Loire finally leaves its gorges and flows north across wide plains. To the west it is accompanied by the Canal Roanne à Digoin, a canal once busy with the transport of wood, charcoal and wine, but now given over to leisure boating. If you have the time, the minor road (D210) that follows the canal – and crosses it several times – makes an interesting alternative to the busy D482/982. There are several locks along the way and plenty of action in summertime. Arriving in Digoin, head for the vast riverside car park, the starting place of the fifth walk in this series.

# 6. The canals of Digoin

The old town of Digoin is the meeting place of three canals – and one of them is carried over the Loire on a stylish 19th-century aqueduct. Riverside, aqueduct and canal junction all feature on this short ramble through the local countryside.

**Grade:** Easy

**Distance:** 8km (5 miles)

**Time:** 2 hours

**Map:** IGN Série Bleue 2827 O

**Start and finish:** Riverside car park at Digoin.

**How to get there:** The riverside car park is on the west side of Digoin, close to where the N79 crosses the river.

**Refreshment:** There are plenty of restaurants and cafés in Digoin, but none on the route.

**Notes:** This is a very easy walk and normally requires no more than trainers for footwear. The only possible difficulty is the grassy section of the towpath alongside the canal Roanne à Digoin. In summer this is cut short, but earlier in the year the long grass can be something of an impediment – particularly if it is wet. In this case, resort to the road alongside or wear boots and waterproof trousers.

Waymarking: Lots – but don't take any notice of it!

---

## Introduction

The attractive old town of Digoin is a watery place by anyone's standards. The wide Loire flows calmly through the heart of the town – and four rivers, the Arroux, the Bourbince, the Vouzance and the Arconce, join it here. Once the flat-bottomed old river boats set off down the Loire from Digoin and mariners thronged the quays where you have probably parked your car. But if you have heard of Digoin at all, it is likely to be not the rivers but the canals that have brought it to your notice. Digoin is placed at the junction of three of them and on a wider scale, is in watery contact with both the North Sea and the Mediterranean. The old canal port, once busy with the loading of coal, wood and wine, is now a basin crammed with pleasure craft of all kinds. Being able to offer a choice of cruising routes, Digoin is also a popular boat hire base.

From Digoin, the Canal Latéral à Loire runs to the west, the Canal Roanne à Digoin to the south and the Canal du Centre to the east. The latter is carried across the Loire on an aqueduct – an elegant eleven-arched bridge built back in the 1830s. Although an outstanding piece of architecture and engineering, its fame was eclipsed by Eiffel's much later *Pont-Aqueduct* at Briare. An interesting addition to the scene is the modern building of the *ObservaLoire* at the town end of the bridge. Due to open in June 2001, it should tell you everything you ever need to know about the river – a must if you are on the Source to the Sea trail!

This short and very easy walk from Digoin sets out across the splendid aqueduct. There is a lock at the far side which is very busy in summertime, so be prepared to spend a little time watching the action. After a wander through the country lanes, you arrive at the Canal Roanne à Digoin and

*Boats on the canal at Digoin*

another lock. From here the walk is simply a stroll along the towpaths beside the peaceful canals. After the triple junction, the tree-lined Canal du Centre is particularly pleasant – and having crossed the aqueduct again, you could choose to continue through the town to check out the scene at the lively Port de Plaisance.

## The Walk

1. Leaving the car park, walk beside the river away from the road bridge and in the direction of the aqueduct. On reaching the canal, cross the bridge and turn right on the towpath on the opposite side (canal on your right) to cross the aqueduct. Passing the lock, you meet the first of the waymarks. Just for the moment follow yellow – but not for long.

2. Take a small road dipping down to the left and leaving the canalside. Cross an iron bridge over the stream and then turn left on an earthen track under the trees. The track bends around and eventually reaches a T-junction. Here turn right on a wide unsurfaced track towards the village of Vivant. At the first house, a track leads off to the left – ignore it (although it may display yellow waymarks). Continue ahead on the now tarmacked road. At the first intersection, bear left. 150 metres or so further on you reach a T-junction.

3. Turn left here and follow the road under the new bypass and on for a farther 15 minutes or so to reach a T-junction. Turn right here and immediately come to a fork. Bear right, and in a further 5 minutes you arrive at the road beside the canal.

4. Cross over to the grassy towpath, turn right and follow beside the canal all the way to the canal junction. On the way you will pass a lock with the lock-keeper's house beside it. If by any chance you found the towpath overgrown and had to walk on the road, you can cross over

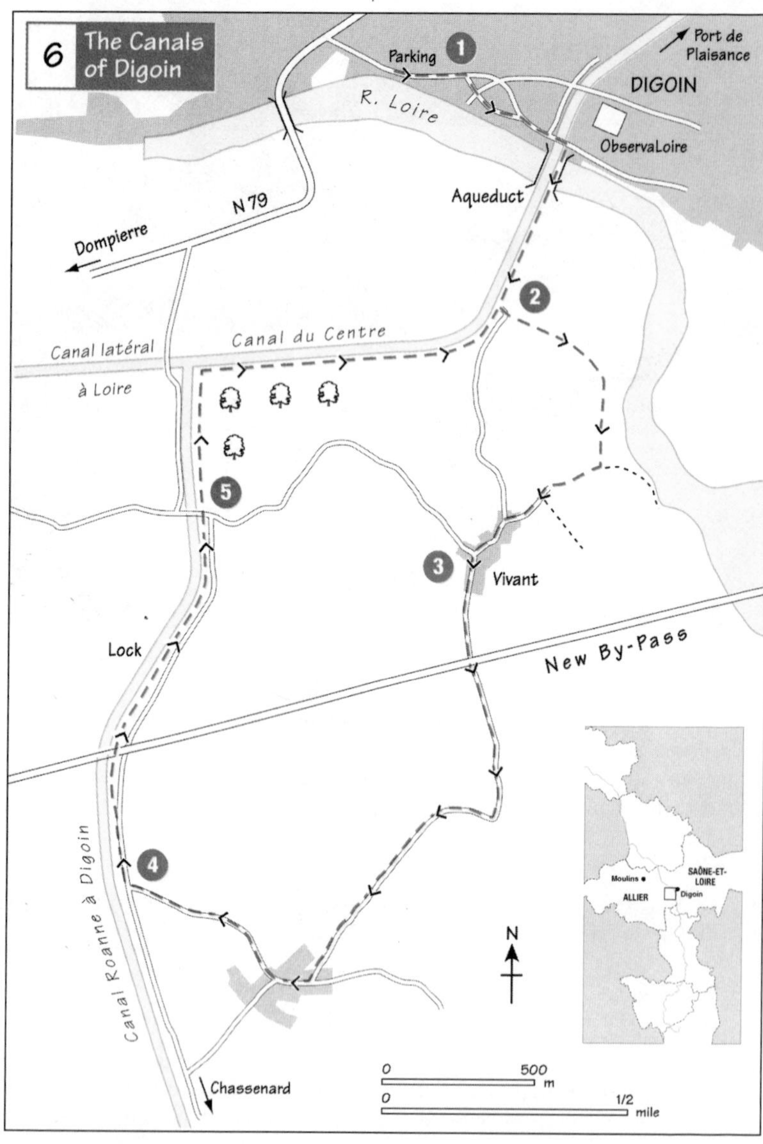


the lock gates here to reach a much quieter tarmacked track on the opposite side of the canal. Whatever you do, you will arrive eventually at a road bridge over the canal.

5. Yellow and green waymarks invite you to continue from this point on the road to the west of the canal – the idea seems to be that you will in the end cross the aqueduct on the towpath on the other side of the canal. The pleasanter route from this bridge is to continue on the track under the trees with the canal on your left. Soon you reach the junction with the Canal Latéral à Loire going off on the left. The towpath here swings right and follows the Canal du Centre all the way back to the aqueduct and town. And if you want to visit the port – just keep ahead beside the canal.

## *More Walks in the Area*

Although, in the guide books, Digoin claims to have numerous walking circuits, the Office de Tourisme can find only about half a dozen leaflets. The route described here – give or take a bit – is taken from two of them. The maps are photocopies of the IGN series and each leaflet carries two or three circuits – hence the mapping is not particularly clear. But in all fairness, the waymarking of these routes is far better than might be expected – the countryside is dotted with little coloured wooden arrows. (On a personal note, we did have a problem – our yellow-flashed path disappeared into an embankment where the new by-pass was being built. But this shouldn't occur on other circuits.) If you want another ramble in these parts, possibly the best choice would be the 7.5km orange circuit starting from Chassenard, 5km south of Digoin. Starting from the Château de la Croix (housing the *mairie*), you first dip down to the river before returning home on an interesting section of canal towpath.

It is probably worth mentioning a very short circuit popular with the inhabitants of Digoin. If you are staying in the town (there is plenty of hotel accommodation and a campsite on the riverside) it would make a pleasant evening stroll. First cross the aqueduct by the towpath on the right-hand side, and then turn right following the path beside the Loire. (More personal notes – there was a stork's nest here in Spring 2001. The locals were as surprised at this as we were). The path eventually turns away from the river and joins the main road. Follow this to the left for about 200 metres and turn left where signposted to Luneau. This road soon brings you to the canal bridge – where you can turn left and return along the towpath and over the aqueduct.

The town of Décize, on the way downstream to Nevers, makes an attractive place to pause on the journey. If you leave the by-pass and cross the bridge into town (the river here is the *Vieille Loire* – the old course of the river) you will reach a riverside car park and a kiosk housing the Office de Tourisme. Here you can find a most inviting-looking free booklet describing walks in the area. Unfortunately it's not quite as useful as it looks – most of the routes are not waymarked and the maps though colourful are stylised. A sense of adventure is needed! But if you have just a few minutes to spare in Décize, there is one local walk that is well worth taking. From the Office de Tourisme, walk out past the campsite on the tree-lined 985m. Promenade des Halles. The plane and lime trees were planted over 200 years ago and are classified as a historic monument. Arriving at the *Pointe* with its view of the barrage, turn left and follow the banks of the Loire as far as the main road. You can then return on the road or continue ahead beside the river, coming back on the Chemin du Gué du Loup with fine views of the ramparts. The whole route takes about an hour.

## *Places of Interest Nearby*

The ObservaLoire had not yet opened at the time of writing. Nevertheless, it promises to be a worthwhile visit for anyone wanting closer acquaintance with the river. The aim is to show everything from the flora and fauna – and fish – of the Loire to its one-time use as a commercial river and particularly to its capriciousness in flood and in drought. There should also be a range of displays and literature on the canals.

On account of the clays in its soil and its advantageous position on river and canals, Digoin has remained a centre for pottery-making since Roman times. Alongside the Office de Tourisme (from the aqueduct, take the first left into the town), the *Musée de la Céramique* spreads itself through 14 rooms. Starting with a 3rd-century Roman oven and working through to the elaborately decorated pottery of today it should make an interesting visit on a day too wet for walking.

## From the Source to the Sea

Leaving Digoin, head north-west on the road that parallels the right bank of the river. The countryside is typically Burgundian, gently undulating and pleasant in a gentle sort of way. At various times you pass signs directing you to river beaches away to the left. The pleasant town of Décize is, if anything, more watery than Digoin. Décize is on an island in the Loire – in fact, it sits between the 'old river' and the new. Joining the old river are the River Aron and the Canal du Nivernais, the canal passing through the heart of Burgundy. The Canal Latéral à Loire passes by to the south – but the two canals are connected via the Loire itself. The Barrage de St Léger-des-Vignes keeps the many pleasure boats from straying off down the river. If you have the time to explore Décize, take also a look at the Promenade des Halles (see More Walks) and the old ramparts, towers and other fortifications dating from the 12th century. From Decize, Nevers is merely half an hour downstream. There is ample hotel accommodation and a little campsite at the south end of the bridge over the Loire. The next walk, the sixth in the series, starts at the opposite end of this bridge.

# 7. Walking with a legend at Nevers

Nevers' most famous one-time resident appears to have been a parrot with a life-story as colourful as his feathers. Here his logo leads you on a riverside discovery trail, which you can extend to view the confluence of the Loire and the Allier.

**Grade:** Easy

**Distance:** 8km (5 miles) with optional extension to view the confluence (the Bec d'Allier)

**Time:** 2 hours. Taking the extension will add a further hour or so.

**Map:** IGN Série Bleue 2524 E – but it's not necessary as the route is quite clear. If you can get to the Office de Tourisme (in the middle of town), ask for the leaflet Sentier du Ver-Vert.

**Start and finish**: The car park at the start of the trail.

**How to get there:** From the north end of the river bridge at Nevers, take the road downstream (D504) for approximately 1km Walking this would make a pleasant addition to the route.

**Refreshment:** All manner of refreshment is available in Nevers – but there is none en route.

**Notes:** This is the very easiest of walks – a short ramble on a good path beside the river. On the return there is a short climb to a hillside viewpoint. The extension to the Bec d'Allier viewpoint is on quiet roads, and again there is a not-too- strenuous climb. Most of this walk is exposed, so take appropriate precautions on a hot day and carry fluid with you. And take your binoculars for the viewpoints.

**Waymarking:** None. You simply don't need it.

---

## Introduction

Everybody in Nevers knows about Ver-Vert the parrot. His fame has even carried downstream and, for example, you can find his effigy in the navigation museum in Briare. The story goes like this – and it is said to be true. Once upon a time the nuns of the Visitandine convent in Nevers owned a particularly intelligent and voluble parrot. Ver-Vert had a most extensive vocabulary and he was truly their pride and joy. The nuns of the sister-convent in Nantes heard of this remarkable bird and asked if they might borrow him for a short time. Back in Nevers his owners agreed rather reluctantly, and Ver-Vert was put on a barge to travel down river. Unfortunately the vocabulary of the bargees was not quite the same as that of the nuns, and by the time he arrived in Nantes, Ver-Vert had learned some new phrases. The nuns of Nantes were appalled and swiftly dispatched the parrot to his former home, where he was put into solitary confinement. As the days passed poor Ver-Vert gradually forgot his new repertoire. At length it was deemed fit to let him loose. The nuns were so delighted to have him back that they overfed him with tit-bits – and the unfortunate Ver-Vert died from over-eating.

And now you may be wondering what on earth all that has to do with going for a walk. Nevers has developed three *Sentiers de Découverte* – discovery trails – and the one here along the riverside has been named the *Sentier de Ver-Vert*. Along the way are many information panels, each with a speech from Ver-Vert telling you about the various features of the

Loire: flora and fauna [look for prints of the wild boar (*sanglier*) or beaver (*castor*)], erosion, floods, traditional river boats and more. Unfortunately the text is in French only, but you should still be able to glean something from it and from the diagrams and pictures. Some are quite obvious, like the one that shows the flood levels in various years – the highest is way above your head. Even if you disregard all the *panneaux*, this is a most pleasant riverside walk. At its end you can simply return the same way, including a detour to the hill beside for a wider view of the river. Alternatively, you can continue along quiet roads to a viewpoint over the Bec d'Allier – the mouth of the Loire's largest tributary, the Allier.

It's an attractive view, with the Allier arriving quietly at a confluence strewn with sandy reefs. It is said that the Allier here loses only its name-the Loire now takes on its character and henceforth becomes a slow and shallow river, its course dotted with many tree-topped islands and banks of white sand.

## The Walk

1. If walking from the Loire bridge in Nevers, just follow the riverside path alongside the D504. In about 1km you reach the car park at the start of the trail.

   Before you begin, just one word of caution – the route is usually very quiet, but Sunday mornings are an exception. Then it can seem that all the families of Nevers are out, on foot, on bikes and even on horseback and accompanied by dogs of all shapes and sizes. Between and among them the jogging fraternity chug by at regular intervals – this is also a *Parcours du Coeur*. By midday it's all over and everyone's on their way home to a well-earned family lunch. So avoid the time if you like – otherwise go along and enjoy the scene.

   From the car park the path is obvious and there are frequent information panels, which are quite interesting if you can work them out. The path itself is pleasant, winding in and out of woodland and keeping close to the river bank almost all the way.

2. A second car park is reached. The path after this sticks closely to the riverside. One of the information panels shows the flat-bottomed boats that once carried cargo on the Loire. The simplest were made of pine and were used to travel downstream only – they were broken up on reaching their destination. The ones with sails were made of more durable woods like oak and could navigate back upstream again. The trail soon reaches another parking area.

3. From here the path begins to swing away from the river and into the woods. Here the ground is soft and boggy and one of the most interesting panels shows you footprints you can recognise in the mud. Eventually you arrive at the road beside the fourth car park.

4. Here you can choose to continue to the viewpoint over the Bec d'Allier or to turn around and retrace your steps.

### For extension

Turn left on the road and walk along the grassy verge for about 20 minutes, passing a first road on the right signed to Marzy-Bourg and the Bec d'Allier viewpoint. Ignore this, but take the next road on the right and in about

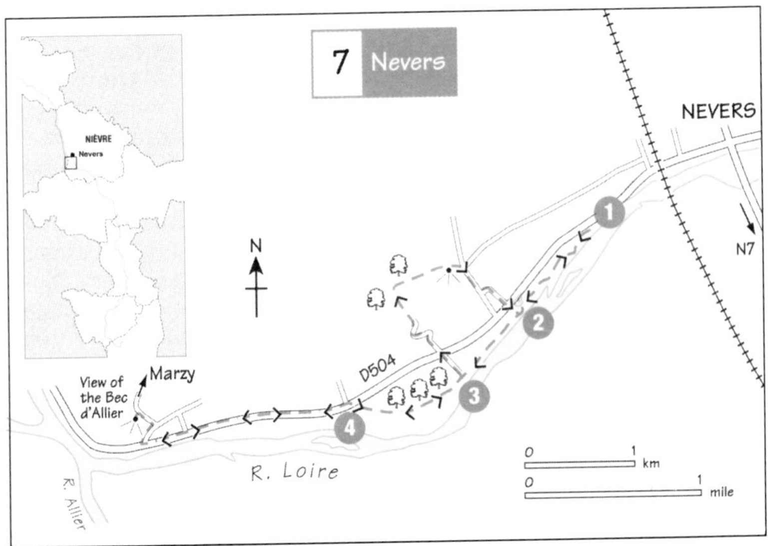


200 metres, turn left. The viewpoint is signed off on the left, a further 200 metres or so up the hill.

### To return

Retrace your steps as far as car park 3. Walk through the car park and keep ahead to the main road. Cross straight over and climb uphill on the road opposite. The road becomes a track and continues to climb. At the top of the hill it bears to the right and levels out. At the time of writing, this part of the *Sentier de Découverte* was still being developed and the track was being resurfaced. An information panel shown on the leaflet had not yet been installed. Nevertheless, an obvious track took you across the flank of the hill and there were some good views down the valley of the Loire to the distant mountains. Eventually, the path dips quite steeply to meet the road, the Rue Barreau.

Cross the road and walk downhill on the footpath. Take the first road on the left, which brings you down to the main road again. Crossing this you arrive car park 2, and can retrace your steps to the start.

## More Walks in the Area

Nevers has two more *Sentiers de Découverte*. The first is a short walk through a nature reserve to the north of the city – the *Sentier de Beue*. You can get a leaflet for this at the Office du Tourisme. The third of the discovery trails is the *Sentier du Bec d'Allier* – an excellent ramble along the banks of the Allier to its confluence with the Loire. The logo this time is the *Passeur* – the ferryman who once took people across the river here. The path is 3km in length and starts from the village of Gimouille about 7km west of Nevers. Along the way you pass 10 attractively presented rotating boards giving information and asking questions – in English as well as French. Finally you reach a large open hide looking out over the mingling waters. On its walls is a wealth of information for identifying the birds here – so take your binoculars. The leaflet for this walk can again be found at the Office de Tourisme in Nevers (and possibly at the *Mairie* at Gimouille if it is open), but it doesn't carry a lot of information. The display board in the car park at Gimouille has a clear map of the route, which is well waymarked.

The Office de Tourisme in Nevers is housed in the Palais Ducal – right in the heart of the city and not too easy to get at. In any case, much more walking information is carried by an organisation called *Randonièvre* (5, Rue de la Parcheminerie- a little road not far from the north end of the river bridge). If it's longer walks you are looking for, this is the place to go. There are various waymarked circuits starting from nearby villages and a wealth of information on other routes throughout the region. Two Grande Randonnées pass through Nevers. One is the GR3, the trail that follows the course of the Loire (here it has returned from its diversion to the Monts du Forez) – the other is the GR654, the ancient pilgrim route from Vézelay to Santiago de Compostela in Spain. This latter now has a whole Topoguide devoted to it – worthwhile only if you are spending some time in this area.

For an interesting circuit incorporating the GR3, the Loire and the Canal Lateral à Loire, take the 12km *Balade du Pont des Américains* from an excellent and cleverly-mapped series entitled *Balades entre Loire et Allier*. The route starts from Sermoise-sur-Loire, just south of Nevers. The series offers 25 routes in all – lots to choose from.

## Places of Interest Nearby

Most of Nevers' interest lies in the old town sector.. If you can negotiate the one-way systems and find a place to park your car near the Palais Ducal, the Office de Tourisme can offer two walking tours of the city. All you have to do is collect a brochure and follow the blue line on the pavement. Guided tours are also available.

Nevers is on the *Via Lemovicensis*, one of the four Chemins de Saint-Jacques pilgrim routes. Latter-day pilgrims can visit the Convent of Saint-Gildard where Saint-Bernadette spent thirteen years of her life and where her embalmed body remains in its chapel shrine. There is also a small museum relating to her life and work.

Coming up to the present day, motor racing enthusiasts will enjoy a visit to the circuit of Nevers-Magny-Cours. Here there is a museum devoted to Formula 1 racing and the Ligier team in particular. It is also possible to try go-karting, get a one-day driving lesson in a Formula 3 car (on the Grand Prix circuit) or take a 4 x 4 Toyota on an all-terrain track.

## From the Source to the Sea

The next place of any size downstream is la-Charité-sur-Loire, so named because of the generosity of the monks of the Middle Ages here. A little of the priory church is still standing, and it is one of the finest examples of Romanesque architecture in Burgundy.

Just a few kilometres farther on, you reach the little town of Pouilly-sur-Loire said to be the mid-point of the river, half-way between the source and the sea. It must be worth a celebration, and this is the start of the wine-producing country. A bottle of the local Pouilly should go down well! There are actually two sorts – Pouilly fumé from the Sauvignon grape and Pouilly-sur-Loire from the Chasselas. After Pouilly, the limestone slopes produce two more fine wines from the Sauvignon grape, both said to have a 'gunflint' flavour- Sancerre and Giennois. You could cross the river to visit Sancerre itself, a delightful hilltop town of narrow streets.

*Traditional river boats on the Loire at Nevers*

Continuing down river you will soon reach Briare and its remarkable *Pont Aqueduct*. But before you do so, stop in the village of Châtillon-sur-Loire and turn right, following signs to the Site de Mantelot beside the river. This peaceful watery corner with its fascinating history is the scene of the next walk in the series.

# Orléanais and Blésois

*The church at Thoré-la-Rochette*

# 8. The story of the Site de Mantelot

The green and peaceful canal basin at Mantelot was once the place where barges waited their turn to make the dreaded crossing of the Loire. Stand by the old lock gates and read all about it – then take this short walk through a nature reserve beside the river and look out for beavers.

**Grade:** Easy

**Distance:** 6km (3¾ miles) (see the More Walks section for an exciting extension)

**Time:** 2 hours

**Map:** IGN Série Bleue 2421 E

**Start and finish:** Site de Mantelot at Châtillon-sur-Loire.

**How to get there:** Châtillon-sur-Loire is 17km south-east of Gien on the D951. Turn where signed for the Site de Mantelot, cross the canal (but not the river), and follow signs to the right and then to the left. There is space to park cars at the Site de Mantelot.

**Refreshment:** None on the walk – although there is an interesting pizzeria/crêperie in a moored barge beside the road to Châtillon. Châtillon itself has several bars and restaurants. There are also picnic tables for D-I-Y lunches along the riverside near the Site de Mantelot

**Notes:** This is an easy walk on good tracks. The path through the reserve could be muddy after wet weather (or even flooded) and the field path has some long grass in summertime. The latter can be avoided by returning along the canal towpath – you may prefer to do this in any case. And although the nature reserve is wooded, the rest of the route is quite open so you should consider protection from the sun in hot weather.

**Waymarking:** The route is waymarked in yellow throughout.

---

## Introduction

The tree-lined lake and grey stone locks at Mantelot look as if they might have a story to tell – and indeed they do. Until the end of the 19th century, it was at this point that canal barges, travelling between Burgundy and the Seine, made the crossing of the Loire – and the only way was through the river itself. The Canal Lateral à Loire ended at Mantelot and one kilometre downstream, on the opposite side, was the lock at Combles, the start of the Briare Canal. That short distance was the most dangerous part of any bargee's journey, and it was especially so when the river was in flood or very low. A long submerged jetty (the *levée de l'Escargot*) was built out from the lock at Mantelot – you can see it today extending as far as the bridge downstream. When the river was low, boats could cling to that jetty to get them two-thirds of the way over. Then they were on their own. The passage upstream was most hazardous in times of flood when the *levée* was under water – two anchors were needed. On average, ten boats a year were wrecked on this crossing. From 1880, a tug and winch system was used and the loss of craft and life happened less frequently. Even so it was the perils of this stretch that prompted the building in 1896 of Eiffel's famous aqueduct just downstream at Briare. A new section of canal was needed to reach this – and on this walk you will see the two canals, new and old, side by side.

Behind the locks, the rectangular canal basin at Mantelot was once the place where boats waited for the river conditions to improve, or simply queued up to take their turn at the crossing. Today it's a beautifully kept heritage site, a splendid beginning to this short ramble. From here you walk out on a long path under the trees beside the Loire. At its end, you cross a stream to reach a wooded area known as the Île d'Ousson, a protected natural site. A little path winds down to the river edge where there are said to be beavers. There's not much doubt about it – if you can't see the animals themselves, you can certainly see the work of their teeth. Leaving the reserve, you cross both canals – old first and then new – and there is another lock where you may be able to watch pleasure craft. You can choose to return to Mantelot beside either canal, or make your way via a hillside path with distant views across the river.

## The Walk

1. From the Site de Mantelot, cross over the lock and turn right along the riverside. (A board on the left beside the lock shows you how the river crossings were achieved – don't miss it). The path keeps close to the river bank at first and then bends away. Reaching a track junction, a sign opposite announces the *Sentier de Gaston*. Turn left, and after about 30 metres, walk through the gate on the left and into the protected site.

2. Now follow the narrow grassy track that winds through the trees and is clearly signposted. An arrow invites you to turn left to the water's edge for a view across to the village of Ousson-sur-Loire. Returning, again follow the obvious track, which crosses a clearing before reaching another junction. Here again you can turn left and take a longer detour to the banks of the Loire where information panels tell you about the bird life. On these wilder tracks near the river, look for logs gnawed by beavers. Returning to the main track once more, keep straight on until you can see open fields ahead. Here the arrows direct you to the right and later to the right again. Soon you emerge from the wood and cross the stream on a little bridge. Continuing ahead, you reach bridges over the two canals.

3. Now you have a choice. If you simply follow the towpath beside either canal it will lead you straight back to the Site de Mantelot. The other option is to return over the hill. For this, keep ahead here on the road climbing uphill towards the village of Le Petit Chanoy. As the slope begins to level out a little, turn right on the Impasse de la Folie. At the fork in about 40 metres, bear right on the stony and grassy track again heading uphill. Continue on this track with some good views across the Loire. At length it meets another stony track and you maintain the same direction.

4. Immediately after a house on the right, turn downhill on a steep hollowed-out track (take no notice of the yellow cross on the tree). This track takes you down to a road above the canals, where you turn left. Soon the road crosses the new canal and carries on between the two. Arriving at a road junction, the long rectangular canal basin is ahead of you. Follow the track along either side of it to return to the Site de Mantelot.

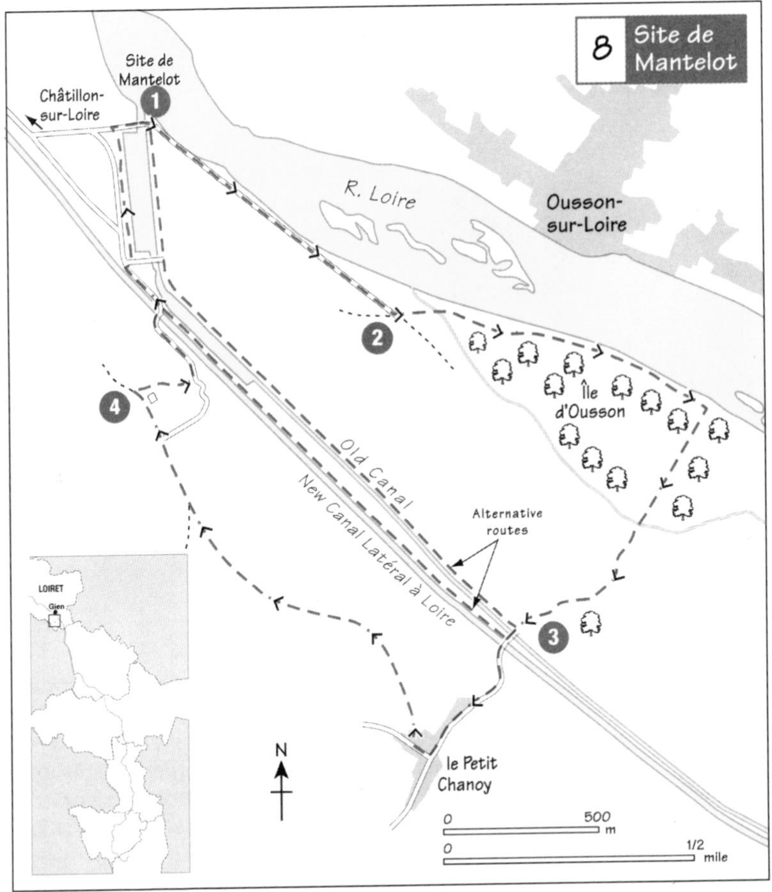


## More Walks in the Area

An exciting second walk – or a possible longish extension to this walk – is available only when the river is low. At such times, you can walk out along the jetty into the river and then climb up to the road bridge at the next-to-last pillar and cross to the other side. Continue then on the towpath of the old canal, cross the Loire again on the Pont Aqueduct and return along the towpath of the new canal – a distance of about 12km This circuit, and several others, are described in the free leaflet *Briare-le-Canal Promenades*: *14 Ponts, 7 Ecluses*, which you should be able to find in the Office de Tourisme in Briare. Sadly it's only in French, but the maps are clear and easy to follow.

Many other walks are described in the series *Randonnées en Loiret* covering virtually the whole of the *département*. The walks are grouped into folders of areas – there are around 20 walks in the Briare-le-Canal area and a further 20 around Gien. This comprehensive collection is presented with good readable maps, accompanied by much dense French text. If you have little knowledge of the language you could still follow them (the waymarking is good), but you would probably miss out a bit on the points of interest. For a route with obvious interest, take the 12km circuit *De la Loire et du Canal* from the Briare-le-Canal folder. It does what it says – follows the old canal south from Briare and returns along the river-

*Flat-bottomed Loire boats at the Site de Mantelot*

side. En route it passes the lock and basin at Combles, the downstream counterpart of Mantelot.

And here, with the aid of an excellent IGN map entitled *Loiret Randonnée (no. 6)*, you could easily follow that great footpath of the Loire Valley, the GR3. The route closely follows the right bank of the river from Bonny-sur-Loire through Briare to Gien – a total distance of around 18km, and bus connections are available. Just ask for times at an Office de Tourisme.

## Places of Interest Nearby

If you have enjoyed this walk you will certainly want to cross the river to Briare. Its seven locks and fourteen bridges make it a fascinating place – you can wander around the *Port de Plaisance*, along the various canals and over that famous aqueduct. If your feet are in need of a rest, take the little *Train Touristique* instead. Of course, boat trips are on offer, with or without sustenance as you go. Moored beside the aqueduct, La Péniche offers information and canal literature along with the souvenirs (of which the best is undoubtedly the Giennois wine). For yet more watery interest, the enthusiastic staff at the *Maison à Deux Marines* will offer you a conducted tour in English – among its many exhibits are the old flat-bottomed river boats and a working model of canal barges making that fearful crossing of the river. If you then want to see the site at Combles, which has not been preserved, follow the riverside road out of the town for a few kilometres. The remains of lock and basin are near the end of the road bridge, opposite the campsite.

## From the Source to the Sea

From Mantelot, cross the river bridge and turn left to Briare where you could easily spend a day looking around. Continuing on the north bank the road runs along the riverside and past the bridge at Gien (château, pottery museum). Further on, at Ouzouer, continue on the D119 for a superb view of the Château de Sully across the river. You may want to cross the river here to explore further. If you want to avoid Orléans entirely and stick to more rural pastures, continue west on the D951, which will bring you to Cléry-St André and eventually, Beaugency. It might be worth a detour to Olivet on the way. Olivet is on the Loiret, the river that gives its name to this *département*, yet is only 13km long. Walk through the lovely park to the riverside and look across to the houses opposite, each with its boathouse. There's a slight hint of the 'Grand Canal' about it all.

For those who can face the traffic, Orléans awaits on the north bank. The cathedral can be seen for miles around, a magnificent edifice dating from the 13th century. Orléans will always revere Joan of Arc, who in her finest hour, relieved the siege of 1429. At the centre of the town, in the Place du Martroi, is a statue of her on horseback. On the south side of the river is another statue, close to the site of the fort les Tourelles and the bridge she once captured. Across the bridge, the Quai du Chatelet offers a peaceful walk. Other attractions are the Maison de Jeanne d'Arc in the Place de Gaule and the splendid floral gardens at la Source. It would be impossible to describe the sights of Orléans in a few words – go to the Tourist Office and equip yourself with a map. And when you are ready to continue, the ancient town of Meung-sur-Loire is just down the river, followed by Beaugency, the scene of the eighth walk in the series.

# 9. In the Forest of Orléans

The Forêt Dominiale d'Orléans is fine mixed woodland with a colourful undergrowth of gorse, broom and wild flowers. Here is a walk that combines forest tracks with a ramble along the green and peaceful banks of the disused Canal d'Orléans, now under restoration.

**Grade:** Easy

**Distance:** 16km (10 miles). The short cut will reduce the overall distance by about 3km, or you could choose to start at Grignon (Point 4) and simply follow the eastern loop of the circuit (approximately 8km).

**Time:** 4½ hours for the whole circuit

**Map:** IGN Série Bleue 2319 E

**Start and finish:** The church at Châtenoy.

**How to get there:** Châtenoy is north of the Loire to the east of Orléans. From Châteauneuf-sur-Loire, turn north on the N60 for 11km At a cross-roads, turn right (SP Châtenoy). There is parking beside the church.

**Refreshment:** There is a bar/restaurant opposite the church in Châtenoy. En route, the *Auberge des Trois Écluses* has an appealing location beside the canal in Grignon – and the village has another very pleasant bar/restaurant just up the road.

**Notes:** This gentle ramble is on easy tracks all the way and trainers are quite suitable footwear unless the ground is very wet. Although it is almost entirely in forest, there is not perhaps as much shade as you might expect. The towpath and some forest tracks are fairly wide and not overhung by vegetation – take appropriate precautions on a sunny day. Take fluids with you – although you should be able to get both food and drink in Grignon.

**Waymarking:** The first part of the route is waymarked in yellow. After Grignon, you return on the Grande Randonnée, waymarked in white on red.

---

## Introduction

The Forêt Dominiale d'Orléans is said to be the most extensive tract of woodland in France. Stands of oak and pine, banks of gorse and broom and a changing carpet of wild flowers make it a splendid place for a walk in any season. The forest is criss-crossed by many paths and trails, and even the GR3 takes a detour from the banks of the Loire to enjoy the canopy of trees by way of a contrast. Also crossing the forest is the Canal d'Orléans. Although now being restored, it is not at present open to water traffic. Silent and tranquil, the canal seems like a ribbon lake, with patches of bright yellow water lilies stretching from bank to bank and plentiful dragonflies in the heat of summer.

The Canal d'Orléans runs from Orléans to Montargis, and so connects the basin of the Loire with that of the Seine. The walk here is along the summit section, the stretch that crosses the watershed between the two. Walking beside the canal you will pass the wide tree-fringed Étang de Noue Mazone, a lake created to supply the summit with water. Further on you reach the Écluse du Point-de-Partage (Lock of the Watershed) and then two more locks in the pretty village of Grignon. Beside these stands

*Auberge des Trois Écluses*

an old auberge with tables and brollies on the lockside – guaranteed to be irresistible on a hot day! From here the way home is through the forest, following the route of the GR3. The Grande Randonnée winds through the trees on the opposite side of the lake and passes through a variety of forest landscapes before you are returned to your starting point in the village of Châtenoy. Just before arriving at the church, check out the scene at the splendid village pond where the men fish while the womenfolk chat comfortably in a shelter that appears to have been provided for just that purpose.

## The Walk

1. From the church, walk away from the main road (following signs for walking routes A6 and A8), and where the road bends to the right, continue ahead on the Route du Port. Soon the A6 route is signed off on the left. Continue ahead (following A8) and just around the corner you reach the canal. Now turn to the right and follow the towpath. A little further along the towpath joins a tarmacked road, which again follows the bank of the canal.

2. Reaching a bridge (the Pont de Verrerie), cross the canal and join the towpath on the opposite side. The canal curves gently, its banks shaded by tall trees. After 20 minutes or so walking, the trees on the opposite side part giving open views of the Étang de Noue Mazone. Continuing on the towpath, you soon reach the old lock, the Écluse du Point-de-Partage.

3. Take the road on the left here, and after about 20 metres, take a track on the right beside a pine wood. Follow the track around the bend, keeping the wood on your left and then continue ahead on a track crossing a field. Reaching the road in the village of Grignon, turn to

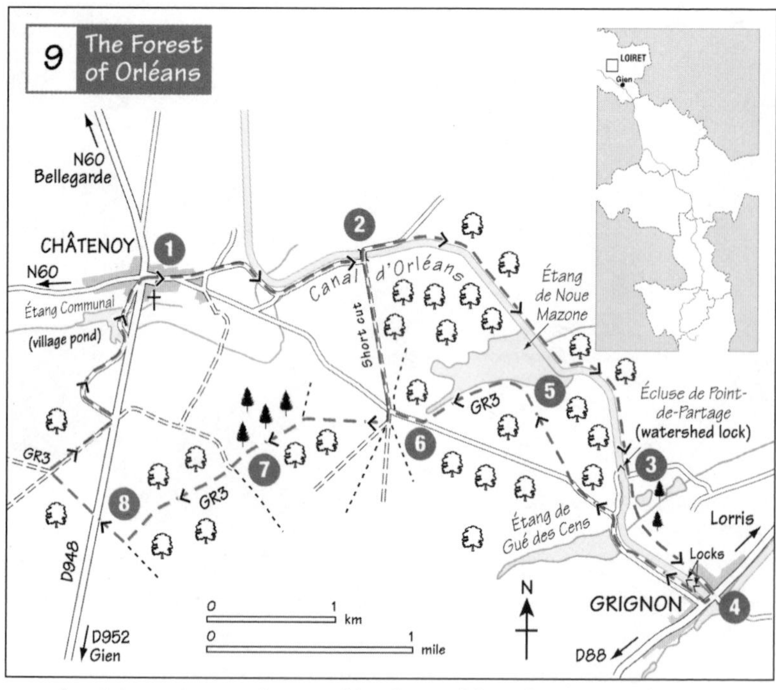


the right and cross the canal bridge – although you may first want to pause at the Auberge des Trois Écluses.

4. Immediately after the bridge, turn right down some steps and continue beside the canal on the opposite bank. You are now on the GR3 with white on red waymarks. The track soon leads up to join a road beside another lake, the Étang du Gué des Cens. Now follow the road, which soon bends left to enter the forest. Almost immediately after crossing a broad stream, take a waymarked track on the right, just before forest block 398. This straight track, flanked by forest on the right and new plantation on the left, brings you to the shores of the wide Étang de Noue Mazone.

5. Following the white on red waymarks, turn left on a narrow track winding its way through the oaks along the edge of the lake. Eventually the path turns away, and emerges on a road running through the forest. Follow this to the right for about 300 metres to a multiple junction.

6. If you are tired at this point, you can take a short cut home. Follow the forest road immediately to the right of the main road (at an angle of about 45º). This will take you to the Pont de Verrerie again and you can retrace your steps to the start.

   To continue with the main walk, turn left at the multiple junction on to a gravelled road. After about 50 metres, turn right on a broad track (Route Feuillue) and in a further 150 metres or so, turn right again on an attractive woodland path waymarked in both white on red and in yellow. At a T-junction at its end, turn to the left on a track skirting a pine wood. This brings you to a track crossing beside some forestry buildings.

7. Continue ahead at this cross-tracks, passing a smart residence dwarfed by the line of pylons. The track continues to a T-junction, where you turn right to meet the road.

8. Cross the road directly to a forest track on the opposite side. Continuing on this, you soon reach a junction with a broad chalky track. Turn right on this (leaving the GR, which goes straight ahead) and keep ahead to the road. Immediately turn left on the Chemin du Breuillard, now following yellow waymarks. In about 200 metres, the road bends to the right and becomes a gravelled track, which again curves around to the main road. Again bear to the left, and now you are taken past the attractive village pond to return to the cross-roads and church at Châtenoy.

## More Walks in the Area

There are many paths through the forest of Orléans. If you have taken this walk, you will probably have noticed the display board outside the church at Châtenoy with its map of all the footpaths in the region. The Office de Tourisme in Châteauneuf-sur-Loire can find you a folder of these walks (*Randonnées en Loiret – Châteauneuf-sur-Loire*) – the French text may look a little daunting, but the maps and the waymarking on the ground are very reliable. One very simple (and different) walk to take from this collection would be that following both banks of the Loire between Jargeau and Châteauneuf, a longish circuit of 19km.

Another suggestion for forest walks would be to head for the Carrefour de la Résistance, a beautiful and tranquil spot in the forest north of Ouzouer-sur-Loire (see *Places of Interest Nearby*). Here a couple of routes are marked on a huge sign board – or you could simply choose to ramble at will.

Further downstream from Châteauneuf, towards Orléans, an interesting circuit of 15km starts from the village of Mardié. Known as the *Circuit du Passage aux Cerfs*, it includes the stretch of the river bank where the deer (*cerfs*) cross the river in their mass migrations to the Sologne. You would be lucky to witness this awe-inspiring event – but nevertheless this riverside section is most attractive. For just a short there-and-back amble along the banks, head south-east from Mardié to the Château de Latigny and then take the narrow road to the riverside where there is a small parking area. Otherwise you could find the whole route at the Tourist Office in Orléans (and possibly Châteauneuf). An alternative suggestion would be to follow the Grande Randonnée du Pays (yellow on red waymarks) all the way between Châteauneuf and Mardié, a distance of about 16km.. There are bus connections for the return (or outward) journey

## Places of Interest Nearby

At the heart of the forest, 7km north of Ouzouer-sur-Loire, is a major intersection of tracks known as the Carrefour de la Résistance. In this remote and silent place stands a huge memorial to the heroic members of the *Maquis* of nearby Lorris, who had a secret camp in this forest. Lorris itself, 7km to the north, is the home of a Resistance museum. Opposite the memorial, a Forest Centre offers information and there is also a pleasant area of picnic tables.

Not far away, and sign-posted from the Carrefour de la Résistance, an *observatoire* (a hide) has been built looking out over a lake deep in the forest. This is the Étang du Ravoir and in the trees on the far side, the osprey (*balbuzard pêcheur*) makes its nest – the Forest of Orléans is the only such site in France. On summer weekends between May and September, a specialist guide will loan you binoculars and tell you what is happening. After 15 years of nesting in this place, this year (2001) the nest was sadly abandoned – hopefully things will return to normal next year.

The Arboretum des Barres (20km north of Briare and signed off the N7) is well worth a visit – devote at least an afternoon to wandering through the three separate collections from all over the world. There are some amazing trees here – a thuja with 80 trunks, a caramel tree, huge giant sequoias – but the bonus is finding the ground carpeted with tiny delicate cyclamen. And for those who remember their youth when trees meant climbing, there are opportunities to indulge again. In high season, groups are escorted through the branches – under the strictest supervision!

# 10. Woods and lakes of the Sologne

The well-marked forest trails of the Sologne offer some of the finest walking in the Loire Valley. Oaks, pines, broom and heather, dark brooding lakes, remote brick farmhouses and a wealth of wildlife all feature on this typical ramble

**Grade:** Easy

**Distance:** 12km (7½ miles) or 6km (3¾ miles)

**Time:** 3 hours

**Map:** This is one of those routes that manages to cross the corner of several maps (2220 and 2221 of the IGN Série Bleue series). The route appears on one of the *Randonnées en Loiret* series of leaflets – if you need a further map, you could get this leaflet from the Office de Tourisme in La Ferté-St Aubin.

**Start and finish:** The church at Ménestreau-en-Villette.

**How to get there:** Ménestreau-en-Villette is 7km east of la Ferté-St Aubin on the D17. There is parking in the square beside the church.

**Refreshment:** The little village of Ménestreau-en-Villette surprisingly supports a bar/café, an auberge and a hotel/restaurant – plenty of choice.

**Notes:** This lovely flat walking country is suitable for everyone. A pair of trainers is quite adequate footwear in summer, but note that, after rain and out of season, the forest tracks can be muddy. There is plenty of shade here on a hot day, but nevertheless, it would be as well to take sun cream. And don't forget the fluids – there is no refreshment available en route.

**Waymarking:** You start off on a Grande Randonnée (white on red), after which the route is waymarked in yellow. This route has been entitled *La Dernière Harde* (The Last Herd) after a book describing the life of the deer by local resident Maurice Genevoix. Its name appears on some of the wooden signposts.

---

## Introduction

Around Orléans the Loire seems to change its mind, forsaking its northerly course and heading instead for the Atlantic. Cradled in its bend is a marshy wooded area known as the Sologne. Not too many of the Loire Valley's tourists find their way to this corner – although it certainly has great appeal to walkers. The Sologne is atmospheric countryside. The thin sandy soil of the region gives rise to an unusual forest of various species of oak interspersed with Scots and Corsican pines and huge Douglas firs. In spring the undergrowth is bright with yellow broom, while later in the year the forest floor has a carpet of purple heather. Lakes of dark brackish water are scattered across the region. The houses and farms are unusually almost all of brick – there is no stone for building beneath the sand. Many of them display characteristic patterns of different colours. Here in the Sologne deer, both red and roe, are more numerous than anywhere in France and there are foxes, squirrels and the elusive wild boar. If you don't spot some wild creatures on this walk you will be very unlucky – or simply making too much noise.

The Sologne did not always look as it does today. Not too long ago, it was a vast marshland, an unhealthy place to live where unexplained illness and fever were common. Its transformation was largely brought about by Napoleon III, whose grandfather came from the Sologne. Pine trees were planted to soak up the water and, across the marshes, dykes and roads were built, retaining many lakes. On each lake you will see a sort of cross of heavy wood. This is the *bonde* – a huge plug. Simply remove it and the lake will drain – a procedure often carried out over the winter with much excitement among the local population. When the lake is almost empty the fish can be caught in nets – not to be eaten for supper, but mostly to be transferred to re-stock other lakes. Fishing – and hunting of all kinds – are popular pursuits in the Sologne.

This fascinating country has its own network of paths and tracks, and the forest junctions sport handsome wooden signposts pointing the way. Many short circuits are possible – the one chosen here starts from the little brick village of Ménestreau-en-Villette and has all the typical ingredients. Hopefully it should give you a real feel for the region. And if you become hooked, just up the road is the Domaine du Ciran, a sort of reserve devoted to all things *Solognot* – see below for more details.

## The Walk

1. From the square beside the church, pass the *Mairie* on your left and continue ahead (away from the village) into the Rue du Moynard. At the end of the village, opposite a brick farm on a bend, leave the road and keep straight ahead on a track (*Chemin Communal*) into the woods – it bears the white on red flashes of the Grande Randonnée. You are immediately in fine forest with a variety of oaks and many other species. Soon you reach a cross-tracks with a wooden signpost.

2. Turn right here, still following the Grande Randonnée. This most attractive path soon comes out at a narrow road, where you continue again on the path opposite (leaving the GR to go off to the left). Soon the path passes a reedy lake behind a fence on the right, and coming up to a wider track, you bear round to the left. The chateau of le Briou is now on your left before you reach the very beautiful Étang du Donjon with its water-lilies, and opposite it, the Étang du Briou. The well-signposted path turns left between lakes and heads again into the forest. Keep straight ahead on this track, passing the brick farm of le Cheret and ignoring all side tracks, for about 20 minutes. The main farm track you are now on bears right, but you continue straight ahead to meet the main road.

3. Turn left here, and walk along the grassy bank beside the road for about 10 minutes. Cross the road to a wide gravelled track (again a *Chemin Communal*) signposted to Bois Brûlé. Almost immediately, at a fork, your track bends to the right, after which you keep straight ahead at all junctions. The path becomes narrower and less well-surfaced as it again becomes engulfed by woodland, but there are yellow flashes and a signpost referring to *La Dernière Harde*. After three quarters of an hour of walking through superb woodland you reach a gravelled track.

4. Turn right here, now following the GRP du Sologne with its yellow on red waymarks. At an obvious fork, take the left-hand sandy track. The

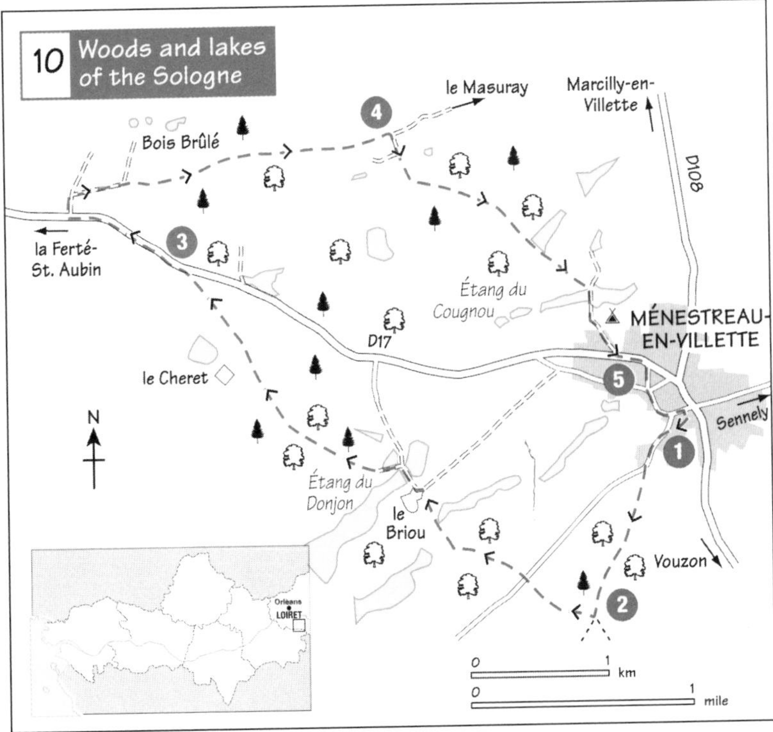


track continues through the woods and then passes another lake on the left before descending beside the dammed *étang communal*, evidently well-stocked with fish! Turn right before the campsite beside the vast Étang de Cougnou and climb to meet the road.

5. Turn left and follow the road for about 300 metres. Now turn right on the Chemin du Moulin Lagarde. At its end, turn left on the Chemin du Moulin Mitaine to return to the church.

## More Walks in the Area

If this walk has made you want to see more of the Sologne, you might do well to invest in a Topoguide entitled *La Sologne à pied*, which can be found in any Office de Tourisme (try the one at La Ferté-St Aubin) and even in some bookshops. It offers a selection of 19 walks scattered across the area. This Topoguide is produced only in French, but the maps are reproductions of the IGN series (and therefore first-class) and the waymarking on the ground is generally very good. One of the most interesting circuits starts at the Pont du Coudray near Brinon-sur Sauldre. It initially follows the now disused but still attractive Canal de la Sauldre through one of the most remote parts of the Sologne.

For more local walks, each Office de Tourisme in the Sologne should be able to offer its own regional selection – at la Ferté-St.Aubin, the office stocks the leaflets of the *Randonnées en Loiret* series. But if the sight of those wooden signposts has tempted you to try a linear walk, the IGN produces a map covering the whole of the Sologne in its *Plein-Air* series (scale 1:100,000). All the main walking routes are shown on this map – but, since the last edition was 1992, there is one important omission. This is

*Lake in the Sologne*

the newly-created GRP of the Sologne, a short section of which you used on this walk.

## Places of Interest Nearby

About 4km north of Ménestreau, on the road to Marcilly, is the excellent Domaine du Ciran. Sited in the extensive grounds of a château, it describes itself as 'neither a nature reserve nor a zoo, but rather a conservation site'. Regard it as an extra walk! A trail of around 6km in length invites you to divert to various hides to observe both birds and mammals. The route is punctuated by display boards that will test your French, but nevertheless are packed with visual information. This is the place to sort out all those oaks and pines that you met on the walk, get a glimpse of the deer that you possibly didn't meet, and enjoy once more the colourful and diverse vegetation of the Sologne. The Domaine du Ciran is open throughout the year, except for Tuesdays between October and March – but remember the long French lunch break and time your arrival accordingly. A restaurant is open in high season and at weekends.

Those interested in learning more of the Sologne, should ask Tourist Information for a pack of leaflets entitled *Rencontres en Sologne* describing (in English and German as well as French) the various museums of the region. You can choose among establishments devoted to deer-life, poaching, rural crafts, ponds, hunting and more. All seem to be combined in the Musée de Sologne, housed on an attractive site of three water-mills at Romorantin-Lanthenay.

And if you need a château to complete the day, try the rather different brick edifice at La Ferté-St Auban. You can wander through the usual rooms furnished in 17th-century style, but the added attractions are an island of Lilliputian houses for the children and a 'living kitchen', where the cook in mob-cap seemingly devotes her life to baking little honey cakes in a traditional oven for the delight of the visitors.

# 11. Orchards by the Loire at Beaugency

From the medieval streets of Beaugency, follow this path through the apple orchards to the pretty village of Baulette and return along the banks of the royal river.

**Grade:** Easy

**Distance:** 12km (7½ miles). A short cut could halve it, and another reduce it by a couple of kilometres.

**Time:** 3 hours

**Map:** IGN Série Bleue 2120 E

**Start and finish:** The end of the bridge at Beaugency.

**How to get there:** Beaugency is on the Loire 20km south-west of Orléans. There is parking on the quayside.

**Refreshment:** Beaugency has a wealth of eating places. Continuing ahead past the church at Baule (Point 4) will bring you to the main road, where again there are bars and restaurants.

**Notes:** This walk could not be easier, and there are lots of opportunities for shortening it as you go. Trainers would be suitable footwear – except perhaps when the grassy tracks are wet after rain. The first part of the walk is totally without shade, so you would need protection on a hot day. The latter part beside the river offers more cover. Carry fluids, although there is refreshment en route at Baule. You might like to take binoculars for the wildlife on the river.

**Waymarking:** The route is waymarked in yellow to Baulette, after which you join the Grande Randonnée. There is no waymarking along the riverside – but the path is obvious.

## Introduction

Beaugency is a medieval gem. In the space of a few ancient streets are a château, an abbey church, a huge 11th-century keep and a clock tower dating from the same period. Add to that 15th-century fortifications, the Tower of St Firmin, the Renaissance façade of the Hotel de Ville, the Rue du Ruisseau with its mills and pretty bridges and it's obviously a scene worth exploring at the end of your walk. And although it may be busy in summer, if you come out of season you could well think you were the first to discover it. Below the town, the low bridge that spans the wide river here has no fewer than 23 arches. The original was apparently built by the devil in one night (although goodness knows why, as it subsequently carried thousands of pilgrims across the river on their route to Santiago de Compostela). Whatever its origins, the first bridge crossed the Loire at Beaugency over a thousand years ago. The version you now see is mostly 16th century, although the south end has been reconstructed after it was blown up by the allies in 1940. Beside the bridge are the pleasant tree-shaded old quays – and it is from here that this walk sets out.

The land beside the river is rich in alluvial silt, a medium obviously conducive to the growing of fruit trees. Apples and pears line the route, a delightful sight with the blossom of springtime, while in autumn you wonder at the abundance and variety of the fruit. The outward path leads through the orchards to the pretty floral village of Baule, after which you join the Grande Randonnée to follow the River Mauve on its way to join

*Cabane de vigneron*

the Loire. The way back follows the banks of the Loire all the way. Offshore are the sandy wooded islands for which the river is famous, islands giving shelter to many species of birds and also to beavers. Before reaching the quays there is a pleasant picnic spot beside the river, an alternative to the many restaurants of Beaugency. And from here the path back to town is everybody's favourite Sunday morning stroll – you could time your walk to join in the scene.

## The Walk

1. Leave the quays walking upstream, and from the end of the car park, continue ahead on the Rue des Îles (this is not the riverside road, which bears the waymarks of a Grande Randonnée, but rather the parallel road inland). You are soon walking on a path between walls with good views across the fields to the Loire. At the barrier, turn left and head uphill on the gravelled road. At the T-junction, turn right on the Rue Entre-Deux-aux-Vallées.

2. At the end of the road, keep ahead on a track between hedges. This opens up to give wider views over the valley of the Loire to your right. You pass the first of the orchards, mainly of pears, and a circular stone *cabane de vigneron* (winegrower's hut). After about ¾ hour or so walking (ignoring all side tracks) the path descends to a road beside a *station d'épuration*.

3. If you would now like a short cut, turning to the right here and keeping to the right will bring you down to the banks of the Loire, which you can follow back to Beaugency – around an hour's journey.

   To continue with the main route, bear left on the road and leave it almost immediately (at the corner) to follow a track along the right-hand edge of a field. This climbs gently to the village of la Baule – you first pass behind the gardens of some newly built houses, and then come out on a gravelled road.

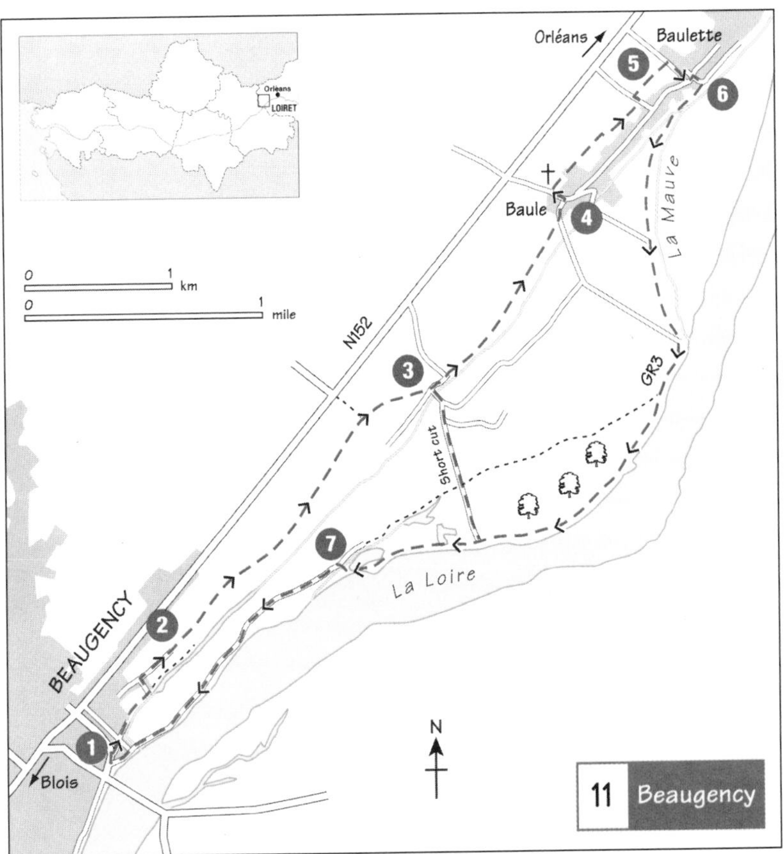


**4** Another road joins from the right (you could also short cut back to the river that way) but you keep ahead to the junction in front of the cemetery wall. Turn left here, and then turn right on the little road in front of the church. The road becomes a broad gravel track and continues alongside fields. Reaching a tarmacked road, turn left for a few metres and then right on a grassy track between fields.

**5** Rising to another tarmacked road, turn right into Baulette (signed as *Baule*) – a hamlet delightfully decked with flowers in summertime. At the road junction, turn left and then bear right at the roadside cross to join the Rue de l'Abbé-Pasty. Soon you arrive at the riverside (a pleasant site with picnic tables is just to your left)

**6** Turn right here, and join the raised bank (*levée*) beside the River Mauve. The Grande Randonnée has joined you from the bridge on your left. There are open views to enjoy as you follow the river to its confluence with the Loire (the short cut from Point 4 meets you here). Continue now along the bank of the Loire – there are views upstream to the bridge at Meung-sur-Loire and alongside you the river soon skirts a maze of sandy wooded islands, which are a paradise for birds. Apple and pear orchards line the path on the right. If you are here in the late summer the abundance and quality of these crops will surprise you. The path is largely through light woodland offering welcome shade on a hot day. At a hard-surfaced area you are joined by the short cut from Point 3. At length you reach a parking and picnic area alongside some lakes

7 Coming out to a tarmacked road, simply turn left and follow it all the way back to Beaugency. The road soon regains the riverside and you can count the arches of the splendid bridge as you approach the town.

## More Walks in the Area

Two villages in the vicinity of Beaugency offer walks leaflets which have also been translated into English. Just west of Beaugency, Tavers is an ancient Roman site. There are also prehistoric remains – the *Circuit de la Pierre Tournant* (7.3km.) takes you past an ancient dolmen and again along the riverside. The other village, Lailly-en-Val, is across the river from Beaugency and on the edge of the Sologne. Two waymarked circuits head out into the surrounding woodland. The Office de Tourisme in Beaugency can give you all the details.

Following the river 6km upstream from Beaugency will bring you to the attractive little town of Meung-sur-Loire (see below). Meung is built on *les Mauves*, arms of water that intertwine and thread their way through the streets and support many water-mills. At le Mail (the quayside) there is plenty of parking, and alongside the area an information board displays the very many waymarked circuits of the area. The Office de Tourisme has details of all these – it is in the centre of the town, just a few minutes walk from the quayside (past the covered market). To enjoy the best of les Mauves, follow the yellow-flashed circuit as far as la Nivelle, then choose any of the well-waymarked options.

The GR3 sticks quite closely to the river bank all the way from Beaugency to Orléans, and of course is well-waymarked. Meung is 6km away, and Orléans a further 14km – a good day's walk, and there are bus and train services to return you to your starting point (check the times with the Office de Tourisme before you go). The best walking map covering this area and giving the route of the GR is the IGN *Loiret Randonnée (no.1)* A similar distance following the GR downstream (but not across the river at Muides) would take you to Suèvres, a town worth visiting in itself – see Walk 13.

## Places of Interest Nearby

The attractive village of Meung-sur-Loire (mentioned in the More Walks section) was apparently a favourite retreat of Georges Simenon's detective hero Maigret.. The floral streets and water-mills on the Mauves are delightful, and the riverside is a very pleasant place for a stroll if you haven't time for a long walk. All is overlooked by the collegiate church and, of course, a château. This one is built in many styles spanning around 600 years, but the eerie feudal dungeons are perhaps the most impressive.

Cross the river from Meung and you will see a church of impressive proportions dominating the flat landscape. This is the 15$^{th}$-century basilica of Notre Dame at Cléry-St André. Although there was a church here from the 13$^{th}$ century, this one was largely built by courtesy of Louis XI – during the Siege of Dieppe he vowed a donation of his weight in silver for victory. His tomb is in the church – where you can also see the elaborate carvings in the Chapelle St Jacques, bearing witness to its importance on the pilgrim route to Santiago de Compostela.

## From the Source to the Sea

From Beaugency, continue on the north side of the river at least as far as Suèvres, where you could escape the traffic for a few minutes to look at some of the mills and *lavoirs* just behind the main street – see Walk 13. This is the very heart of château country and you may now want to cross the river (by the bridge at Mer) to visit Chambord and Cheverny. Carrying on downriver you arrive at Blois, whose château is as rich in history as it is in architectural style – but you will have to contend with the traffic and one-way systems on the north side of the river to visit it. The best views of Blois are from the south bank (the road closely follows the river) from where you can see the château, the Cathedral of St Louis and the triple-towered Église St Nicolas.

Below Blois, roads hug both banks of the river, the north side being the busier, but possibly with the better views. Just downstream the elegant Château of Chaumont perches on rock high on the south side of the lovely sandy-banked river. For many years now the château has been the home of an international garden festival running throughout the summer months. At Amboise, too, the town and château are south of the river, with classic views from the opposite bank. But here you must surely halt and find your way to Clos Lucé, the home of Leonardo da Vinci for the last three years of his life. The cellar is packed with models of his inspired futuristic inventions. And for more château there is Amboise itself, and a few kilometres away, Chenonceau on the Cher. But now continue on the north side of the river and head on beside the vineyards of Vouvray towards Tours. The next walk in this series is at the hillside village of Rochecorbon – where it is time to meet the first troglodyte dwellings.

# 12. Through the parkland of Chambord

Every tourist in the Loire Valley must visit ornate, flamboyant Chambord – or at least, so it seems. Here you do it in style, following the Grande Randonnée through the woods to arrive at the back door of the château itself.

**Grade:** Easy

**Distance:** 13km (8 miles)

**Time:** 3½ hours walking – but allow time to look round the château.

**Map:** IGN Série Bleue 2121 O

**Start and finish:** Car park at the centre of the village of Maslives (opposite the *Mairie*).

**How to get there:** Maslives is on the D 84 north-west of Chambord

**Refreshment:** There is an auberge in Maslives adjacent to the car park. In *The Village* at Chambord you can get everything from a take-away snack to a very substantial meal.

**Notes:** This is an undemanding walk with virtually no change of contour. Trainers would be suitable in a dry summer, but, as always, wet weather means mud in the forest. The latter part of the homeward route is without shade – protect yourselves from the sun on a hot day. Allow at least an extra hour if you want to visit the château, and more time to wander around outside, perhaps for photographs - it's so big you have to get a long way back.

**Waymarking:** Two-thirds of this walk are on the Grande Randonnée, waymarked in white on red. The latter section bears the occasional yellow waymark.

---

## Introduction

Chambord, the 'truly royal' château, was the dream and creation of just one man – François I. In his youth he bought himself a small hunting lodge in the forest, had it razed to the ground, and in its place began the building something just a little more grand. Involved in its design was his friend, Leonardo da Vinci, who at the time (1519) was living at the Clos Lucé in Amboise. Chambord was to have 440 rooms and 365 fireplaces – and at its heart was the now famous double spiral staircase. Outside, the jumble of turrets, lanterns and chimneys that grace the roof terrace has in latter days been likened to an overcrowded chessboard. At one time François' grandiose ambitions even included diverting the Loire to fill his moat – but he was persuaded to settle for the lesser River Cosson instead. François I emptied the royal coffers, raided the funds of his churches and melted down the silver of his subjects for Chambord – and lived long enough to see his vision almost to completion.

The great château stands at the heart of its vast forest parkland, an area enclosed by a wall that, at 32km, is said to be the longest in France. The park is a *reserve cynégétique* (a game reserve), where deer, wild boar and *mouflon*, the wild Corsican sheep, are free to roam. Roads run across the park and a section of it is open to the public. There are nature trails, circular walks and hides for observing the game, while the GR3 considers Chambord worthy of a diversion from its usual Loire-side course. The walk described here starts from Maslives, a quiet village just outside the

*The Château de Chambord*

château grounds and well away from the throngs of tourists. Picking up the GR3 outside the village, you follow it through the park gates and into the woods. Suddenly it emerges at the wide road leading to the back of the château, a stunning sight. Once over the bridge on the Cosson you are among all the visitors – and there are plenty! A row of shops known as *le village* caters for all needs. You can buy tickets to enter the château here – and at the very least find a bite for lunch. The return home is on a long wooded track through the parkland, followed by a path between the maize and sunflowers, across flat fertile farmland with views as far as the Loire itself. This country has little to do with the mighty château on its doorstep, and you can enjoy a tourist-free meal at the village auberge when you return to Maslives.

## The Walk

1. Leaving the car park, turn right on the road running through Maslives. Take the first road on the right, the Rue du Puits Casseau, which is not waymarked. Follow this straight road to the farm at its end (les Grands Champs) and then continue on the gravelled track. This soon bends to the right, and, immediately after, you are joined by the Grande Randonnée with its characteristic waymarking. Continuing into the woods, the path bends to the left and then to the right, but is clearly waymarked. This most attractive path emerges at the road junction in front of one of the entrances to Chambord (Pavillon de St Dyé).

2. Cross the road to enter the park gates and then take the second track on the left - the long, straight Route de la Reine. Soon you will need to pass through a pedestrian gateway in the fence. After 5 or 6 minutes walking you reach a second gateway, and through it immediately turn right on a track alongside the fence. After about 400 metres (opposite another gate) turn left on a waymarked track which is part of the *Sentier les Parquets Assegonds* – a nature trail. Now take the second

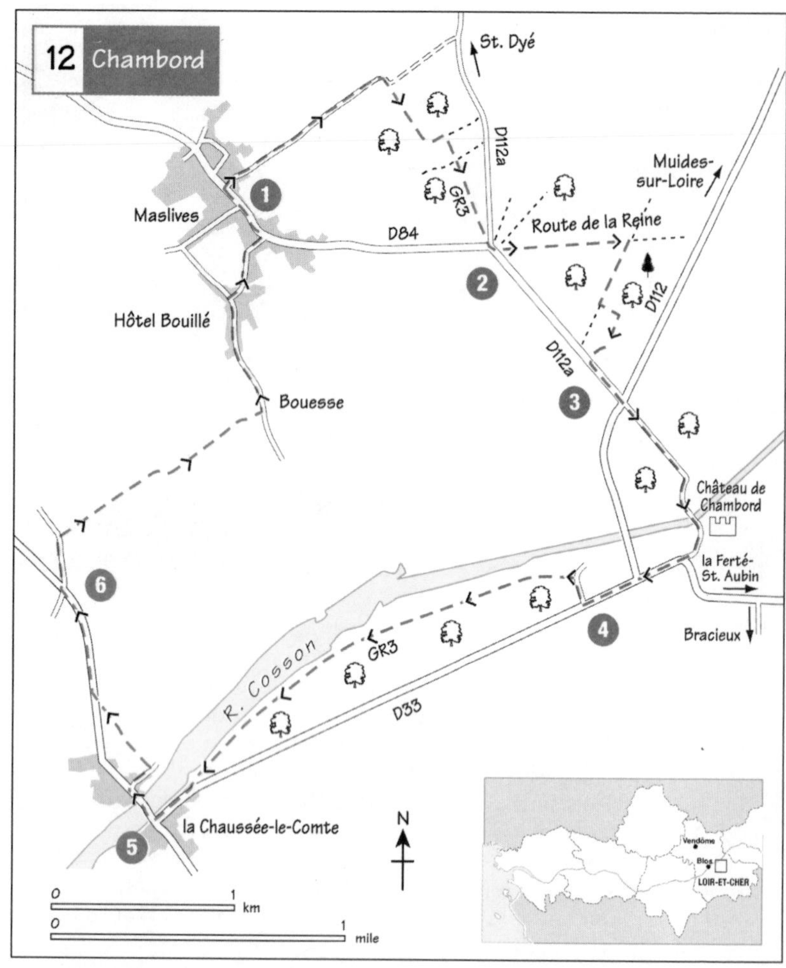


path on the right, still marked as a Grande Randonnée, which winds through the woodland to reach a parking area. Here the waymarks lead you left, through another parking area and down to the road.

3. Here you have the first dazzling view of Chambord. Turn left, cross the roundabout directly and walk down the broad pedestrian road towards château. Bearing right, you cross the bridge over the Cosson and mingle with those who arrived here on wheels. To the right is the commercial area of *le village*. When you are ready to leave, walk past it (not through it), and turn right on to the main road (there is a broad verge). Cross over the end of a road on the right and continue for 300m.

4. Now turn right down a road to a parking area. At its end turn left on a broad track under the trees. This long track in fact follows the south bank of the Cosson, but the river is always hidden behind the trees. After about 45 minutes walking, you reach a road, and turn right on it to arrive at another gate to the parkland (Pavillon de la Chaussée-le-Comte)

5. Through the gate you at last leave the Grande Randonnée and turn instead to the right (Rue de Saumery). After about 200m, turn up the first road on the right through the houses, and after the last house, take a grassy track leading between fields on the left. This again brings you to the road, which you then follow to the right for a distance of about 500m to a junction.

6. Here turn right in the direction of Maslives. The road soon bends left, but you take instead a broad earthen track on the right between the fields, heading for the distant village of Bouesse – there is one brief right-left kink in the path on the way. Arriving beside a farm in the village, turn left on the surfaced road. Continue through the village, and after 10 minutes or so you will reach another group of houses (the hamlet of Hôtel Bouillé). Here you turn right and soon reach the main road – where you turn to the left to regain the car park in Maslives.

## More Walks in the Area

Chambord sits between the Loire and the woods and lakes of the Sologne. For more woodland walking – rather more on the wild side than at Chambord – you could get hold of the Topoguide *La Sologne à pied* (available from most Offices de Tourisme in the area). Among the 19 routes offered are those at Crouy-sur-Cosson (6km.), La Ferté-St Cyr (15km.)and Villeny (16km.), all villages to the east of Chaumont. Any would make a good choice – and you can be sure that, although the Topoguide is in French only, the maps and waymarking are excellent.

For other circuits in the area, the Office de Tourisme in Blois (opposite the château) stocks individual leaflets in the extensive *Loir-et-Cher Promenades et Randonnées* series. The nearest town to Chambord to have an individual leaflet – and an Office de Tourisme – is Huisseau-sur-Cosson, 6km south-west. Two circuits are described, both passing small châteaux. If another walk including a major château appeals, there is a pleasant and interesting route in this series starting from Chaumont-sur-Loire – the Office de Tourisme at Chaumont (on the main road) is sure to have it in stock.

Returning to Blois, the superbly waymarked circuits in the vicinity of the town itself are well worth exploring – see Walk 13 at Suèvres for details.

## Places of Interest Nearby

The Château of Chambord is open to the public every day of the year except, Christmas Day, New Year's Day and the 1st of May. You may wander around the château at any time, but there are also conducted tours, some in English. Various other themed tours take place throughout the year. Chambord was the originator of the *Son et Lumière* (in 1952) and still offers a *spectacle nocturne* on summer evenings.

The grounds of Chambord are always open for walking and simply observing the game. It is also possible to take a 'game drive' in a 4 x 4, accompanied by a forest ranger, or to do the same more cheaply in a coach. Daybreak and night-time excursions into the forest are arranged – and in the rutting season (September), occasional evening trips to hear the haunting 'belling' of the deer. For information on all this and lots more, visit the Tourist Information in the village of Chambord – or phone 02.54.20.34.86 (English spoken)

For another of the great châteaux, head just a few kilometres south to Cheverny. This one is quite different –a more simple classical white tufa building with grey slate roof, purely an elegant residence with nothing of the fortress about it. Cheverny may have more appeal to children than most chateaux – it was the model for the Marlinspike Hall of the Tintin cartoons, and now houses a permanent exhibition of Tintin's adventures. It is also home to a large pack of hounds, which you can watch being fed at 5pm every day.

# 13. The Water-Mills of Suèvres

No fewer than fifteen water-mills are passed on this walk through the countryside around the pretty floral town of Suèvres. And a few châteaux, *lavoirs*, *fontaines* and ancient buildings are included for good measure.

**Grade:** Easy

**Distance:** 12km (7½ miles). Two loops of around 6 and 8km are possible and there are other short cuts – see map.

**Time:** The walk itself should take around 3 hours, but add time for just looking – and for photography.

**Map:** IGN Série Bleue 2121 O

**Start and finish:** The Office de Tourisme in Suèvres. There is car parking in the square opposite (beside the main road).

**How to get there:** Suèvres is on the N152 north-east of Blois.

**Refreshment:** There is a pleasant bar/restaurant in the square at Suèvres.

**Notes:** This very easy walk is largely on minor roads, although south of the River Tronne you follow a long field track for about 3km This is a walk that should be taken at leisure – allow time to look into all the nooks and crannies of Suèvres. There is little shade, so remember the sun cream on a hot day – and if you are taking the whole route, carry fluid as there is no refreshment along the way. Some of the mills and *lavoirs* are quite photogenic, so take your camera.

**Waymarking:** The route is waymarked in yellow throughout

---

## Introduction

As you hurry along the N152 between Blois and Beaugency, you could almost not notice the little town of Suèvres. It doesn't get much of a mention in the guidebooks either – only a passing reference to its St Christophe Church (you can see that beside the main road) and a suggestion that the Rue des Moulins with its water-mills is worth a quick look. This hardly does justice to this fascinating little town – as you will find on this walk.

Suèvres is on the edge of the Beauce, the plateau of rich fertile cereal-producing land north of the Loire – if you arrived in these parts by *autoroute*, you must already have been impressed by its extent. There would certainly have been plenty of work for water-mills. The town is built on a former Roman site above the river, an area crossed by tiny streams of crystal-clear water fed by springs. Along the watercourses are the many mills, no longer working but still picturesque in their restored state. *Lavoirs*, the old covered wash-houses, are dotted all over the place – not now needed for the weekly laundry, many have instead been decked with flowers. A handful of châteaux in various architectural styles are likewise scattered about the town.

The route here wanders through the back streets of Suèvres and out into the surrounding countryside, taking in as many of the mills and *lavoirs* as possible. It would be easy to divide the circuit into two loops or to shorten it in other ways. Whatever you do, don't miss the picturesque Rue des Moulins where banks of flowers overhang the sparkling water and take a look at the old town gate and 15th-century houses before you leave.

## The Walk

1. Leave the main street on the Rue des Desjoyeaux, which runs alongside the Office de Tourisme (S.P. La Chapelle-Martin). Turn right on the Chemin des Sablonnards, at the end of which is the first mill, the grey stone *Moulin des Crotteaux*. Continue on the broad track to the left of the mill, which winds around fields and passes a couple of houses before again reaching a tarmacked road.

2. Turn right, passing the *Moulin de Bonne Eau* on the right and a red brick château on the left. Turn left around the wall of the château on the Rue des Choiseaux. The *Moulin Neuf* is soon across paddocks on the left, and then on the right, the pretty *Moulin de Choiseaux* with its little restored wheel. Now turn left on the Rue des Yvonnières, where water bubbles from a spring and you pass the fine *Moulin de Dizier* with its *lavoir*. A little further on is another château, this time in white stone. At the fork in the road bear right along its wall.

3. Reaching the wider road, turn left and immediately right on the Rue de la Folie. This bears left and heads towards the church, but you soon turn away to the right keeping to the tarmacked road across the fields. At the wider road just before the village (Laloin), turn left, then immediately right.

4. Now take the first earth track on the left (before the village) – it looks as if it goes straight to a farm. In fact, it emerges between the buildings to a tarmacked road, where you turn right. In front of you are a flower-decked *lavoir* and yet another fine château. Turn left around the château and then left again, following the broad track beside its wall to reach the main road

5. Turning left here will take you straight back to the centre of town. But to continue with the walk, cross the road. This is now the Rue du Grand Port, and at its end is a cross-roads. For another short cut (saving 2km approx.), keep ahead on the track to reach Point 7. Otherwise, turn right on the Rue du Petit Port. As you go you can see the turret of the *Manoir de la Motte* (it also has a mill) ahead and across the fields on the right. After about 500m you reach the Moulin de Rechevet, and shortly afterwards, a road goes off on the left. This you are going to take in a minute – but first, walk another 200m or so to two more mills, the Moulin de Gâtines and the Moulin de la Nuzée. A sparkling stream runs alongside the road.

6. Returning to the road junction, turn now and follow the road across the River Tronne. After about 400 metres, just after a track on the right, a grassy track on the left leads across the fields to the riverside (well before the road climbs the bank). Following this track, turn right before the woods and keep ahead.

7. Here you are joined by a track on the left – the short cut suggested in Point 5. Keep ahead on the track, which eventually reaches a tarmacked road. Turn left on this, and then right on to another track, just before the bridge. Continue for another 15 minutes or so, following the river, to reach another road

8. Turn left and cross the Tronne – the Moulin de Ruabourg is on your

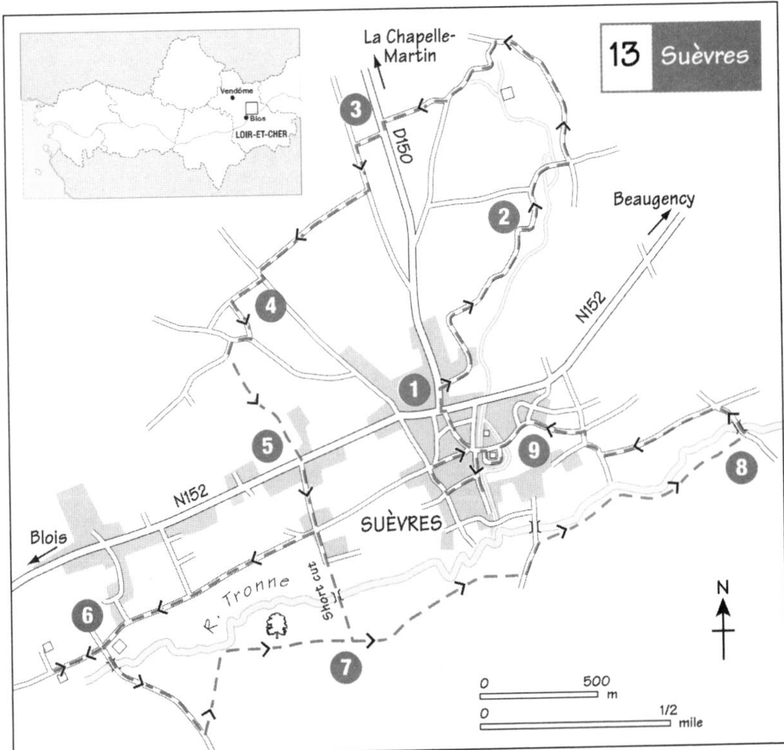


right. Immediately turn left on the Rue des Châteliers – the château of that name is behind the wall on your right. The road bears to the right. Coming to a junction before a grey stone wall, bear right and in a further 100m turn left. Arriving at a T-junction, the Église St Lubin and the Château des Forges are opposite.

**9.** Turn left and find ahead a *lavoir* and the vestiges of the old medieval gateway. Beyond, take on the left the Rue St Martin, which loops to take you past the *Moulin de Gastines*. Arriving back on the road, turn left and cross the Pont aux Choux – the *Moulin de Rochechouard* is on your right. Now turn left on the picturesque Rue des Moulins to see the *Moulin Fort* and the *Grands Moulins* (once a textile mill) beside the lovely clear stream. Returning up the Rue des Moulins, do not go as far as the road bridge, but rather turn left on an alley between gardens. Across on the right you can see the ancient fortifications of the town. At the end of the alley turn right, and then right again on the Rue des Juifs. Arriving at the Rue P. Pouteau, turn left to return to the square – but on the way, cast your eye on no. 27 and no. 11, both residences that have survived from the 15th century.

## More Walks in the Area

Just down the road is Blois, which has devised its own set of local routes and waymarked them charmingly with little walking hedgehog signs. These are presented in a folder entitled *Sentiers de Blois* – there are nine routes in the immediate vicinity of Blois, and two more in the neighbouring village of Villersfins. Several circuits are included on each map, but nevertheless, the routes are quite clear – and the hedgehog waymarks are

The Moulin de Rochechouard

excellent. A little French text is offered for each walk, interesting but not essential. This folder of walks is free and can be obtained from the Office de Tourisme in Blois (opposite the château).

Having obtained the folder, you may then feel you want to retreat from the traffic – there is less of it on the south side of the river. On this bank, about 300m east of the stone bridge, is a pleasant riverside parking area known as les Croisilles, from which there are undoubtedly the best views of Blois. The routes south of the Loire start from here, and there is a display board describing them all. The 6km *Boucle des Levées* is probably nearer 8km (there is no scale on the maps), but is interesting. These curious *levées* were apparently built to protect the town from floods (but how? – they seem to be on the wrong side) – nevertheless they give splendid elevated views as you return. The way out is similarly scenic along the riverside, followed by a flat but pleasant section through the countryside and a park beside the River Cosson. Other circuits stay north of the Loire – one of them, the 10km *Boucle entre Loire et Forêt*, offers a longer riverside stretch, returning along the edge of the woods.

If you prefer to stay out of Blois altogether, any Office de Tourisme should stock leaflets in the first-class *Loir-et-Cher – Promenades et Randonnées* series. These are sold both individually and in packs – see under the More Walks section of Walk 12 for those nearby

## Places of Interest Nearby

Two of the mills passed on this route (Moulin des Crotteaux, Moulin de Rochechouard) are open to visitors in summertime – the Office de Tourisme in Suèvres can give you details.

Nearby Blois has lots to offer. A leaflet in English entitled *Walking Tours of Blois* describes four circuits taking you past all the historic buildings. You could also visit the National Stud or enjoy a *Son et Lumière* at the château. Just a little north of Blois is a dammed, wider area of the river known as the Lac de Loire. From here you can take a 2-hour trip on a traditional Loire sailing boat to see the flora and fauna of the riverside. Book at the Office de Tourisme in Blois. For more information about Loire navigation, the Observatoire Loire (in the Rue Vauvert, near the quay) offers a permanent exhibition.

Suèvres is on the doorstep of château country – Chambord, Cheverny, Chaumont, Blois, Talcy, Villesavin, Fougères-sur-Bièvres and many lesser ones are only a short drive away. And to be a little more green, you could cycle. The Office de Tourisme is well-stocked with cycle routes and almost every small town has an establishment hiring bikes. Other attractions of the region include visits to vineyards and winetasting, farm visits to watch sheepdogs or see cheese being made – and a tour of the local nuclear power station at Saint-Laurent-des-Eaux. 75 % of France's energy is produced this way and the French are ever-mindful of the need to improve public relations.

# 14. A Train Ride through the Vineyards at Thoré-la-Rochette

Farms, woods, fields, villages and the vineyards of the Vendômais region are the ingredients of this walk on the slopes above le Loir. And you could complete the day with a ride on the *train touristique* of the Loir valley.

**Grade:** Easy

**Distance:** 12km (7½ miles)

**Time:** 3½ hours

**Map:** IGN Série Bleue 1920 E

**Start and finish:** The station for the *Train Touristique*, just out of Thoré-la-Rochette.

**How to get there:** Thoré-la-Rochette is just off the D917, 8km west of Vendôme. The station is signed from the village and is about a kilometre to the south on the D62.

**Refreshment:** The route passes a good restaurant in Thoré-la-Rochette, but there is no other possibility for refreshment en route.

**Notes:** This ramble is almost entirely on easy tracks across the countryside – between open fields, through woods and through vineyards. Walking boots would be preferable but you could get away with trainers in a dry spell in summer. Thoré-la-Rochette, where there is refreshment, is a good three-quarters way round the circuit, so you should carry plenty of fluid with you. And on a sunny day, take the appropriate precautions. The attractive *train touristique* runs at weekends in summer, and there is a wine museum and shop selling regional products at the station – see the Places of interest section for details.

**Waymarking:** The first and last parts of the route are on the Grande Randonnée (marked in flashes of white on red). Elsewhere there is yellow waymarking.

---

## Introduction

North of the Loire itself, the valley of 'le Loir' also has its wealth of châteaux, vineyards and cliffs with troglodyte dwellings. To the west of Vendôme there is a particularly scenic stretch where the beautiful village of Lavardin with its hilltop feudal ruin is followed by the historic market town of Montoire-sur-le-Loir, again with a château. A few bends more and the Loir is beneath the cliffs of Trôo, a hillside village famous for its cave-dwellings and viewpoint on the motte of a one-time fortress.

Trôo is the destination of the *Train Touristique* of the Loir valley, a cheerful little train that begins it journey where this walk also begins, just south of the wine-growing village of Thoré-la-Rochette. The train is brought out of its shed only on weekends in summer – but the infrequent service is no indication of a lack of popularity. Crowds arrive for the event, which begins when the station is opened up to reveal an interior teeming with local produce, and in particular wines. And across in another track-side building the Musée de la Vigne with its collection of old wine-growing equipment has its home.

*The train touristique*

Wine is really the theme of this walk. The fine AOC wines of this region bear the title Coteau du Vendômois – both red and white are rather light, dry and sharp in taste. Above the river valley the slopes are clothed with vineyards and here the tracks cut across them, giving you the chance to view the progress of the crop at first hand. A feature of this region are the *cabanes des vignerons* – the little winegrowers' huts, often complete with window and chimney. But the walk is by no means only vineyards – there are open fields and paths through the woods above the Loir, a crumbling ancient dolmen under a wayside tree and the village of Thoré-la-Rochette where you climb to the 12th-century church up a path worn in the rock by the feet of pilgrims long-gone.

## The Walk

1. Cross the tracks behind the station building and walk up the steps to the broad path beneath the rock face (it's used as a climbing wall by youth groups). Turn right and walk down to join the road. Turn left on the road and almost immediately (just after the electricity transformer), take a track on the right. This still follows the railway, and soon arrives at the hamlet of la Saulnerie.

2. Turn left on the narrow road and climb through the village. Where the road bends left, leave it and continue straight ahead on the track into the woods (do not bear right on the broad track). The track you are on now climbs beneath a road and eventually comes up to join it just before a road junction

3. At this junction, cross straight over to a wide gravely track opposite. After about 150m the track forks – bear left towards the farm on the horizon. Continue straight ahead past the farm and little group of houses to meet another tarmacked road, which you cross directly to the track opposite. Now you come to the vineyards and there are wide views to the east across the valley of the Loir as you descend the hill. The track bends right and left to meet another cross-track. Turn

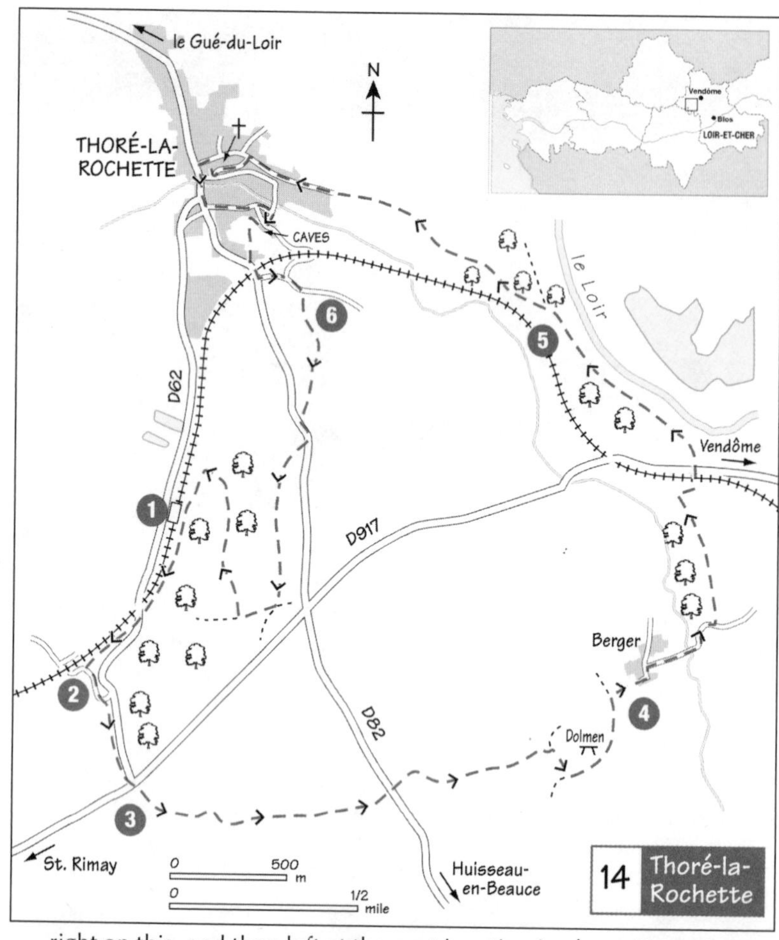


right on this, and then left at the next junction in about 200m. Soon, on the left, you pass the Dolmen of Vaugouffard. Continue on the track, which descends and bears right to reach the farm at Berger.

4. Bear left around the buildings, and then turn right on a road that crosses a stream and then climbs. Coming to the top of the hill, a grassy track on the left runs along the edge of the wood. Following it, you eventually bear right to cross the railway, and beyond it, arrive at the road (D917). Now take the broad track directly opposite, heading across a field and into some beech woods. Through the trees there are glimpses of the Loir way below. After a few minutes walking you arrive at a fork in the track.

5. Take the left-hand option, a very pleasant track leading you out of the woods and across fields to Thoré-la-Rochette. With the steeple ahead of you, continue downhill on the road and then climb again. Just before a road junction, turn sharp left down the narrow Rue des Fondées. At the bottom, turn right on the Sentier de l'Église and after about 50m, look for some rough steps in the rock on the right. These are the Pas des Fidèles (Steps of the Faithful), which lead you up to the church with its panorama. With the church on your right, cross the gardens and take a road opposite the point at which you arrived – the

Rue du Tertre des Boulangers. Turn left on this to descend to the main road where you again turn to the left and cross over the stream. At the junction continue in the direction of Vendôme, and then turn left on the Rue de la Basnerie. At its end turn right on the Rue de l'Orangerie. Just after the bend, pass the *Caves de la Rangerie* and immediately take a path doubling back and heading uphill on the right – you are now following the white on red flashes of the Grande Randonnée. This path brings you to a main road, on which you turn left, cross the railway bridge and then take the road on the left.

6. After about 200m, take an uphill track on the right, which turns right at the top of the hill. Here again you are in the vineyards. The path eventually reaches the main road. Turn left on this road, and, after about 50m take a track on the right through the vines. Continue on this for about 600m, passing the little hut on your left. At a cross-tracks turn right, still following the waymarks of the Grande Randonnée. The track bears to the right and descends through the wood. At the bottom of the hill you again reach the track of the *train touristique*. Turn left and continue on the path beneath the rock face to return to the steps and the station.

## More Walks in the Area

Nearby Montoire-sur-le-Loir is an interesting place for many reasons – see below. From here, a 16km circuit (*Chemin des Châteaux*) takes you past both the Château of Montoire and that of Lavardin. Crossing the river on Lavardin's picturesque bridge, it heads for the cliffs of les Roches-l'Évêque with their cave dwellings and goes on to pass the *Parc botanique de la Fosse*. You could take a detour to visit the Château of Fargot or the historic station at Montoire and pop in to the church at Lavardin to see the remarkable wall-paintings – all in all, a full day's excursion. The route of this walk – and two others – is described on the leaflet *Montoire-sur-le-Loir* from the *Loir-et-Cher – Promenades et Randonnées* collection. Visit the very helpful and well-stocked Office de Tourisme in Montoire (alongside the market place) to find this leaflet and many more in the same series. Again the text is only in French, but the maps are excellent and the waymarking on the ground generally good (the route is almost entirely on a GR or a GR du Pays)

Another leaflet in the same series describes walks starting from Lavardin itself. It's worth a visit (see below) and you could at least consider the 2.5km *Sentier Panoramique* – although two longer routes are described on the same leaflet. All these route leave Lavardin in the same direction – and if you follow the French text you have a fair chance of getting lost! From the centre of the town, simply turn up the hill to the château drawbridge and entrance. Just afterwards you can pick up the waymarks of the GR335 (white on red) leading you up a track on the left – and from there on you will have no problem following the map.

Other walk leaflets worth getting are those of Couture-sur-Loir and Trôo. At Couture there are three routes, one leading you past the Manoir de la Possonnière, the birthplace of the poet Ronsard. Trôo is one of those places not-to-be-missed – see below. If you get the leaflet, you will have a 4km tour taking you past every feature of interest.

## *Places of Interest Nearby*

The Train Touristique of the Loir valley comes out of its shed at Thoré-la-Rochette on summer weekends between June and September. July and August see the heaviest schedule with three excursions every Sunday. Otherwise there's just one trip in the afternoon on Saturdays, Sundays and other fête days. The little train goes as far as Trôo, stopping at Montoire for you to view the station, but first trundles down to Varennes, ironically crossing the TGV line at the place at which the world rail speed record was broken (515.3 kph). If you want time to explore Trôo, you will have to take the morning train on a Sunday and return by one later in the day. The Office de Tourisme in Montoire-sur-le-Loir will give you a timetable, and one is posted outside the station at Thoré-la-Rochette. The station building here opens about half an hour before the train leaves and sells tickets – although you would do well to reserve a place in high season (apply to the Office de Tourisme in Vendôme or Montoire, or the *Mairie* in Thoré-la-Rochette). The station remains open every Saturday and Sunday afternoon for the sale of local wines and regional produce – ideal for presents to take home. Look particularly for the Coteaux du Vendômois *gris* wine with its strange pinkish-grey colour.

If you would like to investigate the Coteaux du Vendômois wines more thoroughly, there are several *caves* open to the public in both Thoré-la-Rochette and Montoire. Apply to the Office de Tourisme (or the *Mairie* in Thoré-la-Rochette) for details.

At Montoire-sur-le-Loir you could visit the Chapelle St Gilles to admire the wall paintings, walk down to the bridge from where there are some very pretty views of the Loir, or explore Musikenfête, a museum of folk music and the home of an annual festival. The château dominating the town is dangerously crumbling and therefore not open to the public. Montoire has another claim to fame. In October 1940 the station was the meeting place of Hitler and Maréchal Pétain, a fateful rendezvous at which they agreed the establishment of the Vichy government and the occupation of northern France. Fortunately Pétain could not be persuaded to declare war on England. Hitler arrived on an armoured train, positioned to withdraw into the St Rimay tunnel should the RAF happen by. The station at Montoire has an exhibition of photographs and documents relating to this event. Admission is by arrangement with the Office de Tourisme at Montoire.

A few kilometres up river from Montoire is Lavardin, a village that has gained the designation of *plus Français des villages de France*. From the riverside there is a fine view of the ruined château on its hill above the town. The château is open all year round. In the town, the priory church of St Genest has some fine murals.

Trôo, the *Cité Troglodyte* is just a short distance to the west. Here the hillside is riddled with caves, many used as hideouts in time of war. Along the narrow paths winding up the hillside are many troglodyte homes, their terraced gardens cut from the rock and brimming over with flowers. A cave show-house can be visited, and there is even a cave-hotel. At the top of a hill is a mound where once a castle stood – a fine viewpoint. Behind is an old priory church and farther back, near the old gateway, the *puits qui parle* – the well that speaks. 45m deep, it has a splendid echo. At the bottom of the hill is *la grotte pétrifiante* – a cave with stalactites.

# Touraine (the *département* of Indre-et-Loire)

*Pagode de Chanteloup, Amboise*

# 15. Under the Arches of Chenonceau

Everyone knows Chenonceau, the most romantic of Renaissance châteaux, its long gallery supported on arches spanning the tranquil River Cher. Crowds flock to visit it, but you can be almost alone on this walk along the opposite bank, with undoubtedly the best views of all.

**Grade:** Easy

**Distance:** 8.5km (5¼ miles)

**Time:** 2¼ hours

**Map:** IGN Série Bleue 1923 E and 2023 O

**Start and finish:** The main car park in Chenonceaux.

**How to get there:** Chenonceaux is about 30km east of Tours on the north bank of the Cher. Heading east you will first pass the château entrance on the right. The Office de Tourisme comes almost immediately afterwards, followed by a well-concealed but largish car park amid abundant vegetation. Should this be full (just possible in high season), there is another car park in the village of Chenonceaux – follow the signs.

**Refreshment:** Plenty in the village of Chenonceaux.

**Notes:** This easy walk is largely along riverside tracks, with a sort section through the village of Chenonceaux. Trainers would be quite suitable in dry weather, although stouter footwear may be appreciated out of season or after heavy rain. There is no refreshment en route, so carry water. On a hot day, take the sun-cream – and whatever the weather, don't forget your camera.

**Waymarking:** About three-quarters of this walk is on Grande Randonnée with white on red waymarks. A short riverside section is not waymarked – but you can't get lost.

---

## Introduction

Chenonceau has the epithet *Château des Dames* – its destiny over the years has been shaped by a succession of women. The first of these was Catherine Briçonnet, the wife of one Thomas Bohier, a Tax Collector under François I. He bought here a manor with a mill – and as he was abroad for long periods, it was his wife who was responsible for the design of the four-turreted château they had built in its place. Chenonceau bankrupted Thomas Bohier, and after his death, the estate was seized by the crown. When in turn it was passed on to Henri II, he gave it to his mistress, the beautiful Diane de Poitiers. She added a formal garden and, most famously, a bridge over the Cher. Diane loved Chenonceau – so when Henri died tragically in an accident, his widow Catherine de Medici was at last able to take her revenge. Diane was expelled from the château and sent to Chaumont. Catherine herself lived in Chenonceau, added more parkland and garden, and topped the bridge with its two-storey gallery. A further contributor to the history of Chenonceau is Madame Dupin whose popularity in the local community saved the château from destruction by the Republican revolutionaries – she is buried in the park. And finally there is Madame Pélouze who bought the château in 1864, and put all her life's energy into restoring it to its former glory.

Chenonceau is stunningly beautiful, and naturally is one of the most

*The hamlet of la Roche (Walk 3)*

*Flowers and fungi found along the Loire, clockwise from top left: mountain pansies (viola lutea, sub-species sudetica); cowslips (primula veris), fly agarie (amanita muscaria), shaggy ink caps (coprinus comatus)*

*In the vineyards*

*Walk 14: market day*

Bridge and cathedral at Blois (Walk 13 – 'More Walks')

The Loire at Gien

Château de Mont Poupon (Walk 16)

Château de la Roche (Walk 5)

Château d'Essalois (Walk 4)

Château de Saumur (Walk 25)

*Formal gardens at Villandry (Walk 21)*

*Pont aqueduct at Briare-le-Canal (Walk 8)*

*Church at Rochecorbon (Walk 18)*

*Ruined château of Arlempdes (Walk 2)*

*Château du Lude (Walk 24)*

*Château de Chenonceau*

popular of the Loire châteaux. The walk here starts from the village of Chenonceaux (unlike the château, spelt with an x). Passing the château gate you will no doubt see the throngs of tourists, but there is no view of the building itself. You have a little while to wait for that as the route first takes you away downriver – although at one point the path does just touch a corner of the moat and parkland. Walking through woods and fields, you arrive at the north bank of the Cher and then the lock at Civray where you cross the Cher. The path on the south side of the river is at first an open track with views. Farther on you reach the woods at the edge of the park and then, as you round a bend, there is suddenly this glorious vision of Chenonceau itself, its gallery and arches reflected in the calm waters of the Cher. The riverside path goes right under the arches and there are splendid views on each side. Unfortunately it is not possible to enter the château from this bank of the river – although visitors from the inside may get a pass to visit the parkland here and return. But your path continues under the trees by the river bank, and soon crosses the bridge to return to the village of Chenonceaux. If at the end of the walk you are keen to see the interior and gardens at closer quarters, it is easy to return to the main entrance.

## The Walk

1. Leaving the car park, turn to the left. Continue alongside the road, passing the Office de Tourisme, the main entrance of the château and then the château vineyards. Continue along the road for a further 300m or so, and (coming up to the *Civray de Touraine* sign) turn left on a hard-surfaced track, waymarked with the white on red of a Grande Randonnée. This track crosses the railway and immediately turns left alongside the lines. Follow the track (there are no other options) as it turns right and heads downhill towards the poplars. Reaching the woods, you find you are beside the stagnant waters of Chenonceau's moat, with its wooded parkland on the far side – but you still can't see the château.

2. After a couple of minutes beside the moat the main path swings to the right. This pleasant path follows the edge of the wood and eventually crosses open land to reach a broad gravelled track in front of more woodland. Turn left on this and continue to the river bank. Now turn right and keep to the riverside path, soon passing the lock with its classic lock-keeper's house (look for the surprising flood levels marked on its façade). Continue past the campsite to the bridge.

3. Pass under the bridge and immediately turn right and double back to cross it. Now turn left (leaving the GR, which turns right) and continue on the path along the south bank, enjoying views of the lock from the opposite side. The path becomes rougher for a while but improves as you approach the woodland of the château. Huge sign boards warn boats they are nearing Chenonceau – and asking them not to bump into its pillars. Farther along the Grande Randonnée joins from the right and you meet again the familiar white on red waymarks. The first sight of the château is stunning – and the view improves as you go on. The path runs right under the arches and it is possible to divert into the parkland on your right (follow signs for Madame Dupin's grave). Visitors to the château are allowed access to this but must show a card to re-enter – sadly, there is no way in for you here (but go up and ask – you at least get a glimpse of the long gallery). Your path continues under the trees beside the river as far as the next bridge.

4. Climb the steps and turn left to cross the bridge. On the far side, take a road on the left, immediately before the railway. Still following the waymarks, pass a picnic area, some tennis courts and the municipal campsite, before turning right to pass underneath the railway. This little road now climbs to join the main road. Turn left at the junction and continue through the village of Chenonceaux, with its tempting variety of cafés and restaurants. Your car park is on the left-hand side, just after the bend.

## More Walks in the Area

The route of this walk was largely on the GR 41, the Grande Randonnée of the Cher valley – it takes a big loop to go under the arches of the château. Continuing east on the GR41, in just 19km from Chenonceaux (a day's walk) you will arrive at Montrichard with its château, boat trips and riverside beach – and there's a bus to return you at the end of the day (or take you out in the morning). Heading in the opposite direction, 24km will

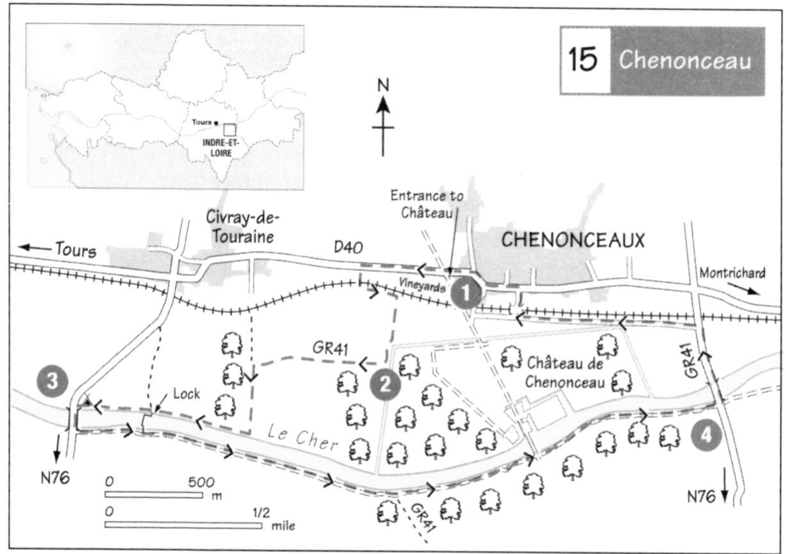


bring you to Veretz, similarly served by bus. Whereas the eastern route wanders through the countryside and villages, the western one mostly stays close to the riverside – and passes four châteaux en route. The route of the Grande Randonnée is marked on the appropriate IGN Série Bleue maps, but you would need more than one of them for each of these journeys. Better than these maps is an excellent booklet *Guide des Randonneurs – Sentier Historique de Touraine*. This describes a 170km circular route taking in the valleys of the Cher (GR41) and the Indre (GR46). The maps are excellent and if you have some knowledge of French you can get a lot of historical detail. You would be lucky to find the book in a local Office de Tourisme – write (or go) instead to the desk of the *Comité de Touraine de la Randonnée Pedestre* at the Office de Tourisme in Tours.

To the north of Chenonceaux is the Forest of Amboise, an excellent choice for a walk, especially in hot weather. The Office de Tourisme in Amboise can offer you a map of the western part of the forest showing all the main tracks, and suggesting a waymarked circuit of 35km (it can be shortened.). A separate leaflet entitled *Chemin de la Forêt* describes an 18km circuit (again with short cut) farther to the east. Amboise also boasts a 9.5km waymarked circuit of the town (*Sentier des Artistes*), taking you from riverside to the *Pagode de Chanteloup* in the forest and visiting everywhere of note on the way.

## Places of Interest Nearby

Heading north on the road to Amboise you will pas the fairly recently opened Parc Mini-Châteaux. Here you can see 'all the most beautiful châteaux of the Loire Valley at a glance' – at least 60 of them are beautifully and accurately laid out with miniature vegetation (bonsai trees) and tiny people in their courtyards and windows. Photographs taken here can be indistinguishable from the originals. Fountains play, hounds chase the deer, model trains trundle by (a TGV 'races' in and out of its station at Vendôme) and tiny boats ply the waterways. Parc Mini-Châteaux is open every day with illuminations on Saturday evenings in summer. Entry is not inexpensive, but strangely includes the nearby donkey park (where there are as many donkeys as châteaux)

To the west of the Parc Mini-Châteaux, on the D31, you come across the curious *Pagode de Chanteloup*. The building is the only surviving part of an 18th-century château belonging to the Duke of Choiseul. He fell foul of the hierarchy of the day in the form of the king's mistress and was exiled in his sumptuous château – the pagoda was built as a thank-you to those friends who did not desert him. The château is now demolished and the pagoda, set beside an ornamental lake, has something of the leaning tower of Pisa about it. But you can still climb the spiral staircase to the rather doubtful platform at the very top for a view of Amboise and the forest. In keeping with the gentile nature of the place, handsome lunch-baskets of local produce can be purchased to enjoy at the lakeside, and you can play traditional outdoor wooden games at tables under brollies in the garden.

Arriving in Amboise, there is plenty to see, but the must-be-visiteds are the château, and the Clos-Lucé, the last home of Leonardo da Vinci. Housed in the basement, the models of his brilliant inventions (recreated from his drawings by IBM) must be worth an hour or two of anybody's time. The Clos-Lucé is open every day throughout the year with the exception of Christmas Day and New Year's Day.

# 16. Céré-la-Ronde – a landscape of Touraine

This is a walk not to be missed, passing acres of sunflowers and fields of grazing Charollais cattle, then meandering through woods to a pretty valley where three rivers meet, overlooked by the impressive Château de Montpoupon.

**Grade:** Easy/Moderate

**Distance:** 13km (8 miles). A short cut can create two circuits of about 8 and 6km.

**Time:** 4 hours in total.

**Map:** IGN Série Bleue 2023 O

**Start and finish:** Car park at the church at Céré-la-Ronde. (If taking only the 6km circuit, start from the Château de Montpoupon, Point 5).

**How to get there:** Céré–la-Ronde is about 9km south of Montrichard on the Cher – take first the D764, followed by the D281.

**Refreshment:** There is a pleasant bar/café not far from the church at Céré-la-Ronde. Beside the stream at Montpoupon, the old Moulin du Bailly serves excellent light lunches – ideal for walkers.

**Notes:** This pleasantly undulating walk is mostly on field tracks and woodland paths – boots or stout shoes would be preferable footwear. There is a section of about 400m alongside the D764, a fairly busy road with narrowish grass verges – take care. Part of the route is in the open, so remember sun-cream, hat and water on a hot day. The route can be divided into two loops by a 'short cut track'. The north loop of about 8km is enjoyable but you would miss the Château de Montpoupon. An alternative is to start from Montpoupon and take the south loop, a total distance of around 6km.

**Waymarking:** This well-documented circuit has been waymarked in red throughout. The latter part is on the *Sentier Historique de Touraine*, so you will also find the yellow on red waymarks of a GRP

---

## *Introduction*

Touraine is one of the ancient provinces of the Loire Valley, a land rich in history – today the modern *département* of Indre-et-Loire broadly shares its boundaries. Touraine has many landscapes – the gentle sandy-banked riverside, cliffs of white tufa rock, endless slopes of vineyards, the marshlands and forests of the gâtine (between the Loire and the Loir), and here the fertile farmland of the Champeigne. Every village claims its own little parcel of the region's history. Flitting from great château to even greater is no way to appreciate Touraine – instead, try walking between fields of bright sunflowers and towering maize, past old manor houses and farms with their courtyards, under walnut trees, through oak forests and beside tiny streams and pausing to browse in every village. A newly created walking route, the *Sentier Historique de Touraine*, aims to do just that – but at 170km it's a bit on the long side. The walk described here follows just a short section of it.

Your starting point is the village of Céré-la-Ronde, where the hilltop church has a 12th-century octagonal tower and the nearby old school boasts oak trees more than 200 years old. At a 189m, this is the highest point in Touraine. Charollais cattle graze the high fields and there are many distant views before the descent into the woods, which are part of the hunting forest of Montpoupon. When you emerge, there is first the attractive old Moulin du Parc, and then, at the top of the hill, the elegant château itself (dating from the 13th century) with its splendid view of the green valley below. The way back is on the Sentier Historique – initially through the woods and later through a valley whose tufa flanks conceal extensive caves. Take time before you leave to look at the old houses of Céré-la-Ronde.

## The Walk

**1.** From the church walk away from the village (church on your right). On the left is the old École Saint-Vincent with its aged oaks. Turn left around it (note the *Sentier Historique* sign) and walk downhill to the road at the bottom. Turn left (leaving the *Sentier Historique* and now following red flashes) and continue to the road junction. Now turn right and cross the bridge over the Aigremont, heading in the direction of Montrichard.

**2..** After about 800m, almost at the top of the hill, turn left where signed to la Souderie. At the junction in about 150m turn left and then follow the narrow road as it bends around to the right. Charollais cattle enjoy the views all around you. Before reaching a low white farmhouse, take a grassy track on the left between fields. This soon passes a small coppice and then continues to a track cross-roads. Turn right here (water tower now behind you) and head for the wood. The largish pond on the right as you reach it rejoices in the name of *Mare de la Taille-Marteau*. As you emerge from the wood, a track joins from the left and you immediately arrive at a cross-tracks. An information panel on the right before the junction describes the features of a large sessile oak tree. Turn left at this cross-tracks and enjoy walking along the roof of the world (although not a very high one!), between fields of sunflowers to reach the road

**3** Turn left and continue on the road for about 150m Turn right on a track that soon passes the edge of the wood – if you reach the bend in the road you have overshot it. Again continue past those sunflowers (do they always face the east?) to reach the wood. After a few minutes under the trees you reach a field on the right and the track turns left and immediately bears right. A couple of minutes later, at a fork, bear right. There are several more junctions as the path descends through the forest, but at each of them you keep to the main track, which in any case is well-waymarked. The final descent is on a hollowed-out track that takes you down to a clearing and a plantation of poplars above the stream (again, the Aigremont)

**4.** Here it is possible to take the short cut (not waymarked). Walk ahead and cross the stream on stepping stones. Follow the track to the left and then bear right up the hill. A steady climb takes you to Point 7.

To continue with the main walk, turn right here and follow the broad waymarked track to the D764. Turn left on the road and walk beside it with care. You can immediately see the old building of the Moulin du

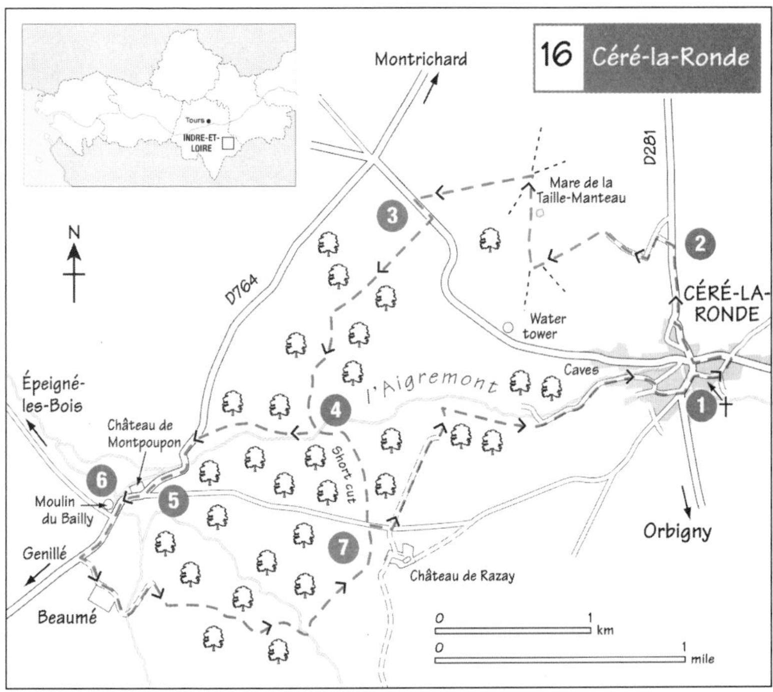


Parc, after which the road starts to climb. Before reaching the summit, take a non-waymarked track leading up through the woodland on the left to arrive at the car park for the Château de Montpoupon.

5. Cross the car park and the road to arrive in front of the Château de Montpoupon – there is a lovely view into the valley below where an old *lavoir* stands beside the Aigremont. Again you must walk down alongside the road to cross the stream – on the right is the old Moulin du Bailly with its restaurant tempting you for lunch.

6. Now continue uphill on the road and after about 500m take the first road on the left, signed to Beaumé. You have once more picked up the *Sentier Historique de Touraine* with its yellow on red waymarks. Passing the farm, the road becomes a stony track, which crosses a stream, turns and climbs into the woods. The track doubles back to the right, after which you arrive at a wayside cross. Bear left here, and in a few more metres, bear right leaving buildings on your left. Now just follow the excellent waymarking through the forest – bear left at a fork, ahead at a cross tracks and, reaching a younger plantation, bear left. The path now gradually descends to run alongside a stream, and then crosses it on stepping stones. On the far side a grove of poplars leads you on to a broad uphill track under beech trees, which eventually meets a tarmacked road beside the Château de Razay (now a *centre de vacances*). (From here, the short cut is the non-waymarked track opposite. It descends, and crosses the Aigremont to join the main route at Point 4).

7. The main route here turns right along the road. After a couple of minutes walking, turn left (SP La Guignardière). The multi-coloured waymarks show other circuits have now joined. The narrow road

*The Château de Montpoupon*

descends past a house, after which all the colours direct you on to a grassy track on the right. This long track eventually comes out on a gravelled road and then a tarmacked road. Here a board tells you that the bank on the left harbours the extensive Cave Charrault – apparently occupied by a deserter in 1870, but re-discovered rather more recently. You can see its now boarded-up entrance as you continue along the road. At the T-junction, turn right. At the next junction continue right on the Rue de Chesnaie and then left on the Rue de la Poste with its fine views of the village. Descending to the road beside the bar/restaurant, bear right up the hill to return to the church.

## More Walks in the Area

You may well be interested in following the *Sentier Historique* a little farther. To the north it joins the Cher at Montrichard, while heading south it eventually reaches the Indre at Chambourg-sur-Indre. Both rivers are then followed downstream and the loop is completed at Tours. While the sections along the river valleys are served by bus routes, unfortunately there is none between Montrichard and Chambourg. The booklet describing the circuit can be obtained from the *Comité de Touraine de la Randonnée Pédestre* – see under Walk 15 (Chenonceau) for details.

Other nearby villages have circular walks published in the *Sentiers Pédestres – Touraine* series. These leaflets have excellent mapping and usually a small amount of French text, which you can take or leave. The waymarking on the ground is generally well-maintained. To the south-west, the lovely old village of Genillé is set in attractive countryside and has a choice of circuits in this collection, which you can obtain from any Office de Tourisme (there is one in Genillé)

Nearby Épeigné-les-Bois has its own series of 3 photocopied leaflets – and amazingly, these have been translated into English. The routes are all different lengths, but you might enjoy the 9km circuit passing through woods, vineyards and open countryside. The leaflets can be found in the Office de Tourisme in Bléré (in the main square)

## Places of Interest Nearby

The Château de Montpoupon can be visited on the walk. Only the towers remain of the original 13th-century fortress – the main building dates from 200 years later. Several rooms are open for visiting, while the displays in the outbuildings convey a 19th-century 'everyday story of château-folk'. The multiple rooms of the Musée de Veneur tell you everything you want (or maybe don't want) to know about hunting. The Château de Montpoupon is open every day in April, June, July, August and September and at weekends in May and October. The long French lunch-break is taken out of high season.

South of Céré-la-Ronde is the village of Montrésor with a fine 15th-century fortress-like château above the River Indrois. Its décor is the work of a 19th-century Polish count – military souvenirs and hunting trophies – but there are also some fine paintings. More early paintings are to be found in the Gothic church along with other treasures. The château is open daily from 1st April to 1st November.

# 17. Azay-sur-Indre – a tale of two rivers

The pretty village of Azay-sur-Indre sits at the confluence of the Indre and its tributary the Indrois. Here you follow each green river valley in turn and enjoy some good views from the high ground between.

**Grade:** Easy

**Distance:** 12km (7½ miles)

**Time:** 3 hours

**Map:** IGN Série Bleue 1923 E

**Start and finish:** The *Mairie* at Azay-sur-Indre where there is a small car park.

**How to get there:** Azay-sur-Indre is about 25km south-east of Tours. From the N143, turn north to Reignac-sur-Indre and then south-east to Azay. Turn right at the cross-roads and immediately right again to find the *Mairie*.

**Refreshment:** L'Auberge des Deux Rivières stands by the bridge at Azay-sur-Indre – but there is nothing more than a picnic site en route.

**Notes:** Field and farm tracks and woodland paths are the ingredients of this walk. All can be muddy after wet weather, but should not require footwear other than trainers during dry spells. Carry fluid with you – there is no bar or café on the route – and wear appropriate protection from the sun on a hot day. Note that as you are following river valleys, no short cut is possible – there are no other crossings of the rivers.

**Waymarking:** The route is waymarked in blue throughout.

---

## Introduction

In the south of Touraine, the land forms a plateau where tracts of forest alternate with rather bare cereal-growing farmland. Cutting through this plateau are three almost parallel rivers, the Cher, the Indre and the Vienne, each on its way north-west to join the Loire. Their valleys, lush and green, offer a sharp contrast to the plains above – ancient villages, farms, mills and old manor houses are gathered amid poplars and willows along the river banks. Nearing the Loire, each river has its share of the great châteaux – on the Indre are the fairytale Ussé and the beautiful Azay-le-Rideau. Upstream the châteaux are less spectacular, but equally numerous. Azay-sur-Indre where this walk begins has a château on each bank of the river and you will catch glimpses of one or two more along the route.

Azay-sur-Indre is a pretty floral village at the confluence of the Indre and its tributary the Indrois. Beside its double bridge, a pleasant park with picnic tables overlooks the mingling waters. From here the route climbs to the Château-Manoir de la Follaine and then wanders through farmland and water-meadows beside the Indrois. A forest of oaks, pines and chestnuts leads up to the summit between the rivers before the path descends again to the village of l'Île Thimé with more picnic tables beside the Indre. Following the river, a green track between forests of poplars brings you back to Azay. Its impressive 16th-century château is well-hidden behind a long stone wall but you can just take a peep at it through the gate before you return.

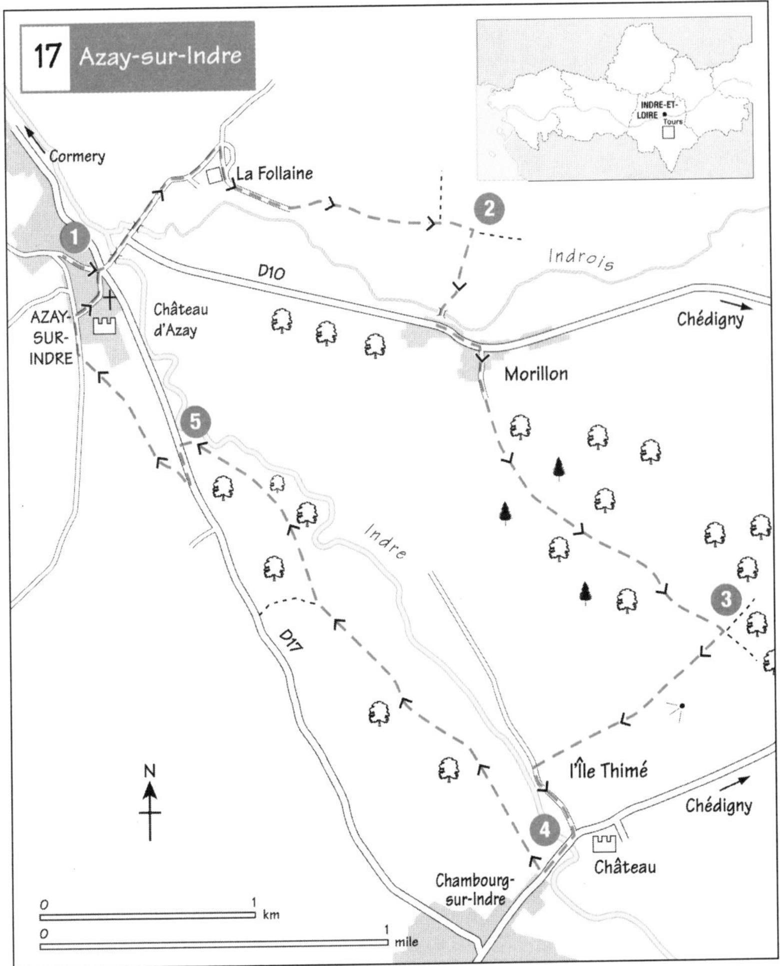


## The Walk

1. Leaving the *Mairie*, walk downhill towards the 12th-century church (look for the Madonna and Child above the door). Turn left and cross straight over the main road. The road now takes you over the bridges at the confluence of the Indre and Indrois and then climbs the hill on the far side. Ignore the road to the Moulin de la Follaine, but take the next right, just after the farm. This doubles back past the 15th-century Château-Manoir de La Follaine, a one-time hunting lodge with a fine view. The road then descends and after passing the water-garden centre on the right, becomes a grassy track. Continue on this pleasant track through fields alongside the river. After passing a grey hut on the right, a couple more minutes walking will bring you to a track junction.

2. Turn right here on a broad track that soon crosses a stream and heads towards a village. The track crosses the Indrois with its willows, reeds and water lilies and then climbs to the road. Turn left on the road to walk through the village of Morillon – on the left is an old water-mill.

*The confluence of the Indre and Indrois*

Just before the bus-shelter, take a road on the right climbing out of the village. After passing several properties, the road becomes a lovely sandy track heading into the woods. Leaving the trees behind, the track passes under a line of pylons just before arriving at a cross-tracks in front of another wood.

3. Turn right here and climb to the brow of the hill. From here you can see (ahead and to the left) the village of Chambourg-sur-Indre. To its right on the hillside is the Château des Helas. The track descends to meet a tarmacked road, where you turn left into the village of l'Île Thimé. Passing farms you arrive at the junction with the main road. On the opposite side yet another chateau hides in its grounds, but you turn to the right along the road. After crossing the first bridge there is a picnic site beside the Indre.

4. Before the second bridge, take a path dipping down on the right alongside the poplar trees. This now bends to the right and becomes a broad track running between fields of cattle and scattered woodland. After about 15 minutes walking you arrive at a major fork of tracks. The left-hand track is the wider, but you bear right around the edge of a field towards the river and more poplar trees in the distance. Walking through these lovely poplars, the River Indre briefly flows alongside you, and then the path bears left to meet the road.

5. Turn left and walk beside the road (with care) for about 200m On the opposite side is the wall of the Château d'Azay. At its end, take a path on the right, doubling back and climbing through woods alongside more wall around the château grounds. Soon the path is running beside fields before meeting a tarmacked road. Bearing right, you pass the gateway of the 16th-century château – it was once the residence of Lafayette, soldier and statesman at the time of the Revolu-

tion, and 'hero' of the American War of Independence. Continue alongside the grey stone wall, and then take the first road on the right. The walls are high on either side as you walk down under a bridge to return to the church and *Mairie*. Note the springs pouring from the ground as you pass the school on the corner.

## *More Walks in the Area*

The neighbouring villages of Reignac-sur-Indre and Chambourg-sur-Indre both have walks featured in the *Sentiers Pédestres –Touraine* series – the Office de Tourisme in Loches has them in stock. Reignac is a pretty floral village that has a lot in common with Azay – an attractive riverside overlooked by a château. This one, too, belonged to Lafayette. Chambourg is set just off the river and has no château. Here the 14km circuit *le Gué du Grain* leads you away from the river valley into the forest of Chanceaux where the deer are plentiful. The *Gué* (ford) referred to is a crossing of the Ruisseau de Châtres on stepping stones – so don't go after heavy rain.

At the heart of the forest of Chanceaux is the very pretty little hamlet of Chanceaux-près-Loches – a château overlooks the stream and there is also a priory church, an old hunting lodge and a mill. This is the start of the 20km long *Chemin de la Forêt,* again described on a *Sentiers Pédestres – Touraine* leaflet. Fortunately the map on the leaflet is excellent – the waymarking certainly isn't. But this lovely forest is worthy of a wander – and there is a short cut so you don't need to do the whole distance. Again beware after prolonged rain – there's lots of mud and at least one ford.

The very best way to explore this region is to follow the GR 46, the Grande Randonnée of the valley of the Indre. A bus service runs down the valley from Loches to Tours, so you can pick your stretch. Azay to Cormery is about 12km, and on the way you could explore Reignac and Courcay (look at the Sentier des Rochers behind the church). Cormery, with the ruins of its Benedictine abbey is one of those little-known gems – see below. To help you with the route you could get Série Bleue maps 1923 E and O – or try to get hold of the booklet *Guide des Randonneurs – Sentier Historique de Touraine* (see under Walk 15 – Chenonceau)

There are many walks in the nearby Forest of Loches. There is no waymarking, so you will need the accompanying booklet – see Walk 19, Sepmes)

## *Places of Interest Nearby*

Just outside Reignac is a leisure park by the name of Labyrinthus. The essence of this is a series of quite complex mazes, created each year by growing - maize! There are Labyrinthus parks all over France, and each is ploughed over and given a new design and a new theme each year. These mazes are quite difficult (although by the end of the season you may be able to pick out the most-used paths) and certainly not only for children. There is even a wooden maze where doors open only when questions are correctly answered – try out your French! Labyrinthus is open broadly during July and August only – confirm the dates at an Office de Tourisme.

And for more leisure activities, Chemillé (20km east on D10) boasts a large and most attractive *Plan d'Eau* with a swimming beach and boats and pedalos for hire – a good place to cool off on a hot summer's day.

For something in a different vein, travel a few kilometres downstream to Cormery. This pretty village with its mill beside the river is the site of an abbey founded in 791. A thousand years later it was all-but destroyed in the Revolution. The impressive 11th-century Tour St Paul still stands, and there is a chapel and other remains. And while in Cormery, eat macaroons – they were once the speciality of the monks.

Not far away is historic Loches – and in its forest, the Chartreuse du Liget. See under Walk 19, Sepmes for details – there is so much in this area it had to be spread out!

# 18. The Lantern of Rochecorbon

At Rochecorbon, the watchtower of a long-demolished château clings to rock-face above the town. Other constituents of this classic walk are narrow streets of troglodyte houses, wine cellars, vineyards, an ancient chapel and a long path beside the Loire.

**Grade:** Easy / Moderate

**Distance:** 12km (7½ miles). An easy short cut could reduce this to a circuit of 7km (4½ miles).

**Time:** 3 hours for whole route. The shorter circuit would take just over half this time.

**Map:** IGN Série Bleue 1822 E

**Start and finish:** The church at Rochecorbon.

**How to get there:** Rochecorbon is north of the Loire between Tours and Vouvray. From the N152, turn north where Rochecorbon is signed and continue past the lower part of the village to reach the church, where there is parking.

**Refreshment:** There are several bars and restaurants along the riverside at Rochecorbon, and one or two more near the *Mairie* at the start of the walk

**Notes:** The walk very easily divides into a lower and an upper circuit. The lower circuit is almost entirely on hard-surfaced paths and minor roads – there is just a short section through vineyards on earthen tracks. If you continue with the upper circuit you will meet more cross-field paths – choose your footwear accordingly. Take fluids and sun cream on a hot day, and perhaps binoculars for the views of the Loire.

**Waymarking:** The route is waymarked in red throughout

---

## Introduction

Approaching Tours, the Loire flows beneath high cliffs of yellow tufa. On its way to join the mighty river, the little River Bédoire carves out a deep valley through this rock, and almost pressed into its sides is the village of Rochecorbon. Many of its houses have back rooms in the rock, or at the very least, outhouses and garages. Some are complete troglodyte dwellings – cool in summer, warm in winter, and no worries about the roof. On the very edge of the cliff a thin grey finger points to the sky. This is the *lanterne,* all that is left of an 11th-century fortress that tumbled down the crumbling slopes centuries ago. The *lanterne* was probably a watch tower – but as well as having a wide view, it could also be seen from a distance. There are suggestions that it could have been used to signal to a garrison at Amboise, or as an aid to navigation for boats on the Loire. Enjoying not quite such a wide vista, a latter-day look-out known as the *Observaloire* has been built on the riverside beside the Office de Tourisme. Climbing its metal staircase gives you a view down the Loire (better when there are no leaves on the trees) and a different angle on the jumbled houses and cliffs of Rochecorbon.

The walk here starts from the light stone church beside the River Bédoire in the centre of the village. Passing through the vineyards (the wine produced here is AOC Vouvray), you are soon heading down the

*La Lanterne*

narrow twisting alleys to the riverside with its *Observaloire*. A long path beside the sandy-banked river leads to the village of St Georges where an ancient chapel stands beside a tree-shaded square. If you have time to get the key, there are interesting wall paintings inside. From here, paths through the vineyards soon return you to the church. But you can choose to go on, climbing past the Caves Rupestres (wine cellars in the rock) and a row of troglodyte houses to reach the plateau above. The way home takes a pretty path beside the Bédoire to arrive again at Rochecorbon.

## The Walk

1. From the church, climb up the main road to reach a cross-roads. The *Mairie* stands on your left here, and you take a path that skirts to the left of the building to arrive at the tennis courts. Walk around the tennis courts to emerge on the road. Now turn to the left to reach a road junction, where you continue ahead on the Rue Raphaël Lagarde-Pouan. At the T-junction at the top of this road, turn left.

2. After about 30 metres, the road swings right. Here you bear left on a track through the vineyards, and in about 50 m, take the right fork. Now the *lanterne* is directly ahead of you. The track descends to meet a narrow road, where you turn left. Heading steeply downhill on this road, take an alley leading off on the right (just before the junction) – there are good views across the river. After another steep descent you reach a narrow road. Turn left here, and after about 40m, look for an alley on the right leading out to the main road and the river. Cross the main road to reach the *Observaloire*, and continue to the riverside .

3. Turn right and follow the riverside path, first passing houses and gardens and eventually the Parc de Loisirs, a children's playground with mini-golf and roundabouts. On your left the river flows between its

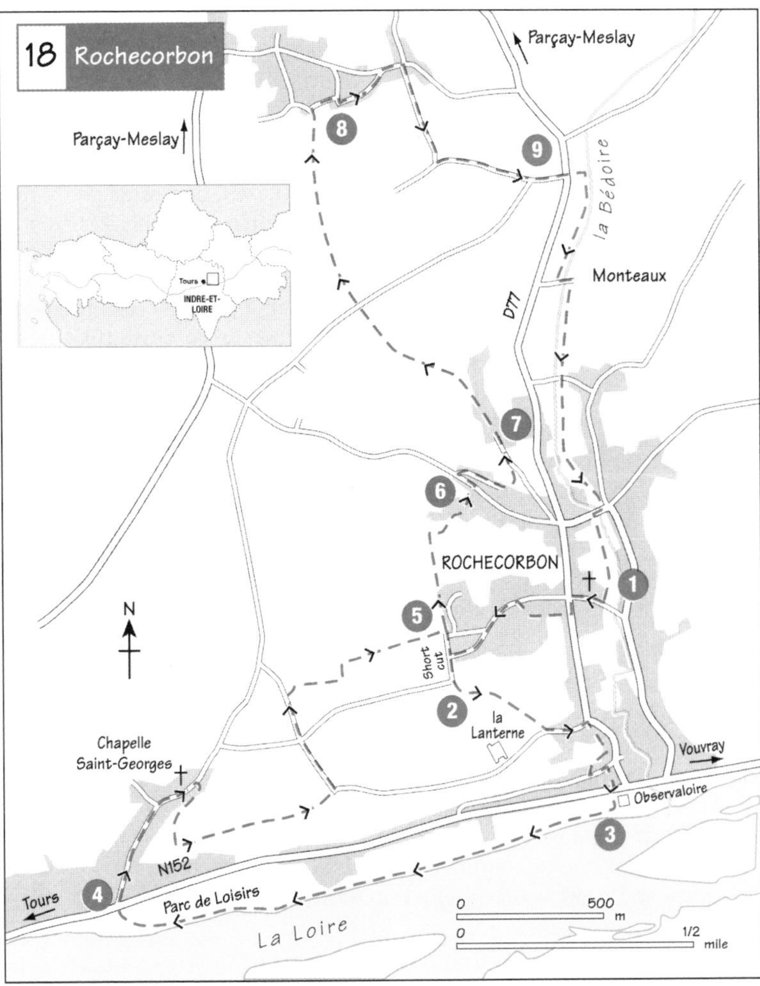


wooded sandy banks and islands, a haven for birdlife. After the Parc de Loisirs, a small car park is on your right and you walk across it to the main road

4. Cross straight over and continue up the road opposite, the Rue Saint-Georges. Soon you arrive at the Chapelle Saint-Georges beside the peaceful village square. Continuing up the road, in just about 20 m, look for a track doubling back on the right. The track climbs the bank to arrive at some vineyards. Bear right and keep to the track skirting the edge – you can see the Loire way below you. At length the track reaches a road at a corner. Turn left on the road, and at the cross-roads, keep straight ahead on the Promenade des Vignes. In about 100m the road swings left. Here you take a track on the right beside a house. At the corner of the vineyard keep straight ahead towards the water-tower with the vines on your left. The track bears left, after which you take the first track on the right to walk between the vines.

5. Arriving at the corner of the vineyard you are very close to your start-

ing point and have a choice. Walking out on to the road and turning right and then left will bring you back to the junction above the tennis courts and you can retrace your steps to the church.

To extend your walk, turn left here and continue along the edge of the vineyard. The path passes a little hut and you arrive at a cross-tracks. Turn right (a sign ahead says *Proprieté Privé*), and after about 30m take a broad and rather overgrown track on the left (if you reach the houses you have gone too far). This track soon runs along the edge of the vineyard with woods on the right (the waymarking here is very worn out). Look out for a track on the right descending steeply through the woods. It continues between the gardens of houses to come out on a road, the Rue de Vaufoynard. Turn left here and walk up to the corner and the *Caves Rupestres*.

**6.** Turn sharp right here, climbing the Rue Elisabeth-Genin with its troglodyte houses. At its end, take a narrow track on the left running uphill alongside the garage of the last house. The path now crosses a small field and then runs through a little spinney. At the far side of this, turn right on a grassy track, which soon swings left and comes out beside another vineyard. Turn right here to reach a track leading to a road junction a few yards along on the right.

**7.** At this junction, turn left on the road, which becomes a gravelled track. Now continue on this track for over a kilometre, at one point crossing a tarmacked road. Finally the track descends to a village and a junction with a huge lime tree on the corner.

**8.** Bear right here and follow the road around to climb to a road junction. Turn right, heading for a village with caves in the cliff. At a cross-roads turn right again and keep to the road through the valley. The road climbs, corners to the left and after about ½ kilometre, descends past the road junction to the main road.

**9.** Cross the main road, then cross the little bridge opposite and turn right. This path soon brings you to the right bank of the Bédoire. At the hamlet of Monteaux, cross over the river and now follow the attractive path along its opposite bank. Eventually you reach Rochecorbon and emerge at a roundabout. Turn right here and again cross the Bédoire. On its far side, take a track on the left, the Chemin des Petits Jardins, which leads you through some well-kept allotments to return to the church.

## More Walks in the Area

Walking along the riverside at Rochecorbon you will have noticed the white on red waymarks of a Grande Randonnée – in this case, the GR3, the long-distance trail that follows the Loire all the way from the Cévennes to the Bay of Biscay. There are one or two major diversions en route, but here the GR3 is sticking fairly closely to the riverside. Following it to the west will take you through the centre of Tours – not perhaps everyone's choice for a day's ramble, but the riverside path is definitely the most pleasant way of arriving in Tours. To the east of Rochecorbon is Vouvray, after which the GR3 crosses the river to Montlouis – both towns are renowned for their fine wines. Farther on the GR3 continues to Lussault and Amboise. Bus routes connect all these towns – you would have to check at an Office de Tourisme for times. A suitable stretch might be from Amboise to Montlouis (17km.) or Vouvray (22km.) Grandes Randonnées are always very well waymarked, but to help with route-finding you could get hold of the local IGN Série Bleue maps (1622 E, 1922 E.) There is also a booklet describing the route of the GR3 through the *département* of Indre-et-Loire (Touraine) – see the More Walks section of Walk 22 at Villandry for details.

If circular walks are more to your taste, the Office de Tourisme in Rochecarbon can offer you a wide selection of routes based on villages and towns in the area. The leaflets are in the *Sentiers Pédestres – Touraine* series and you can buy (or sometimes be given) them individually or get the whole local package to browse through. Nearby Vouvray has two waymarked circuits (6km, 14km.) – both give the opportunity to wander through the famous vineyards. And crossing to Montlouis there are more vineyard-based circuits of similar length, including some fine views over the Loire. The text on these leaflets is, as usual, only in French, but the maps and waymarking are so good that you will have no problem in following them.

## Places of Interest Nearby

Here you are in the heart of the AOC Vouvray region and Rochecorbon has devised a short circuit around the town visiting at least a dozen *caves* welcoming visitors for tasting. Ask for the leaflet *Promenade des Vignes* from the Office de Tourisme.

Continuing with the wine theme, the Caves Rupestres and the Grandes Caves Saint Roch (on the riverside) each have an entry fee, but also offer you something of the history of man and the vine along with a free glass of the magic liquid at the end of the tour. Both *caves* are open every day in high season – for other times, consult the Office de Tourisme.

The Manoir des Basses Rivières, also on the riverside, is a country residence dating from the 18th century. The caves in the hillside behind are rather older – back a thousand years or so, they belonged to the monks of the nearby Abbey de Marmoutier. You can explore the caves on three levels and descend on a staircase through the heart of the rock. The manor and caves are open every day except Tuesday in July and August and at weekends from April to September.

And for more exploration above ground, the trip boat St Martin-de-Tours is based on the quayside beside the Office de Tourisme. It offers short excursions on the Loire with 50 minutes commentary (in French) inviting you to *découvrez toute la richesse naturel du dernier fleuve sauvage d'Europe*.

## From the Source to the Sea

Passing through (or around) Tours you could leave on the D7 south of the Cher to visit the château and gardens at Villandry (see Walk 21). Just across the river on the north bank is Langeais with its splendid 16th-century furnishings, and if you return to the D7 you will pass the pepper-pot turreted Château of Ussé, the inspiration for Perrault's story of Sleeping Beauty. Farther on you will need to ignore the nuclear power station – just beyond it there is a fine view of the beautiful old town of Candes St Martin as you cross the bridge over the Vienne at its confluence with the Loire. You could consider a short diversion to Chinon, where the château tells the story of the meeting of Joan of Arc and the Dauphin. A couple of kilometres downstream from Candes, the gleaming white Château of Montsoreau stands beside the Loire, and now the road follows the sandy-banked river all the way to Saumur. Above the town, the Rue des Moulins provides that most famous view of the château looking down the wide river with its islands and bridges (see Walk 25).

From Saumur the D751 again renders many views of the Loire as you follow it downstream to the little town of Gennes. On the way you will pass the Musée du Champignon, caves producing just the right conditions for the cultivation of an amazing variety of edible fungi. You could pause here to sample the mushroom platter of the day in the little restaurant. From the bridge at Gennes, the scenic D152 will carry you the last 4km along the river to the picturesque site of Le Thoureil and the tenth walk in the series – an unusual excursion into prehistory in the woods above the river.

# 19. A woodland of wild flowers at Sepmes

North of Sepmes, all the woods are brightly carpeted with daffodils in early spring. But don't worry if your holiday is a little later – you can still enjoy an abundance of wild flowers on this gentle ramble in and out of the woods.

**Grade:** Easy

**Distance:** 7km (4½ miles)

**Time:** 2½ hours

**Map:** IGN Série Bleue 1824 E

**Start and finish:** The water tower at Sepmes.

**How to get there:** Head for St Maure-de-Touraine, 22km south of Tours on the N10. From there, take the D59 south-east for 6km to reach Sepmes. The water tower is an obvious landmark, and there is parking at the recreation ground opposite.

**Refreshment:** There are one or two bar/restaurants in the village of Sepmes, but none on the route.

**Notes:** This is an easy walk for anyone and could normally be undertaken in trainers. But note that, after heavy rain, some of the woodland tracks can be muddy and even grassy tracks can be very wet underfoot, making stouter footwear desirable. The woodland offers shade, but there are some exposed sections, so remember sun-cream on a hot day. The recreation ground at Sepmes is provided with picnic tables if you are thinking of an alfresco meal at the end of the walk.

**Waymarking:** The route has been waymarked in mauve throughout.

---

## Introduction

In the Loire Valley, spring comes early. From late February onwards, the woods between Sepmes and Ste. Maure-de-Touraine are ablaze with yellow daffodils. The magnificent sight attracts quite a few visitors, but you can probably escape them all on this short waymarked walk that will take you through the pretty valley of the River Manse. Even if you are too late for the daffodils, you can still enjoy cowslips, celandines, wood anemones, stitchwort, herb Robert, star of Bethlehem, early purple orchid, lungwort and plenty more besides. And if you should be here in autumn, take a bag for the blackberries.

This short walk starts at the park at Sepmes where there are picnic tables under the trees. From there the path dodges in and out of woodland, passing old stone farmhouses tucked out of sight. In clearings are vineyards and orchards. At one point you pass the attractive old château of la Roche-Ploquin deep in its wooded valley, and further on a little lake in a sunken hollow in the woods. If this brief ramble leaves you with an appetite for more, you could combine it with one of the suggestions in the More Walks section – or, in total contrast, take an urban stroll around the splendid nearby medieval town of Loches.

## The Walk

1. From the water tower, walk back a few metres towards the village, to

*Lake in the valley*

the fork in the roads. On your right at the junction is a newish house, and along the right-hand side of that house runs the broad track you are looking for. The track follows the woodland edge, with the back gardens of houses to your left. If you are here at the right time, you can already see the bright yellow carpet of daffodils. Turn right around the corner of the wood and then left at the next corner, to cross the field. The path then dips through another patch of woodland to reach a track junction, with a farm ahead.

**2.** Turn right here and walk downhill to the road. Turn left on the road and immediately bear right. Down on your right is now the River Manse and across it are the fields and buildings of the riding school. Behind them on the hill is the Château de la Roche-Ploquin. Having passed the château, turn right and cross the river on a road that now climbs past the gatehouse.

**3.** At the top of the hill, where the road bends right, turn left on a track. On the right is a field, and to the left a small vineyard and then a hedge laden with blackberries. At the top of the field bear right and keep to the track. Eventually it passes between hedges and comes out at a T-junction where you can go ahead no more.

**4.** Turn right and continue on the track which runs beside apple orchards and soon crosses a tarmacked road. Keeping ahead, you come to the farm of La Guilleraie, after which the track descends through the trees into a deep valley. Soon you can see below you a house and a lake with a picnic table in a pretty valley. At the fork in the track, bear left and walk between the house and the lake. The path then bears right to cross over the stream and climb on the far side. At first the track hugs the woodland edge, but soon continues into the open field.

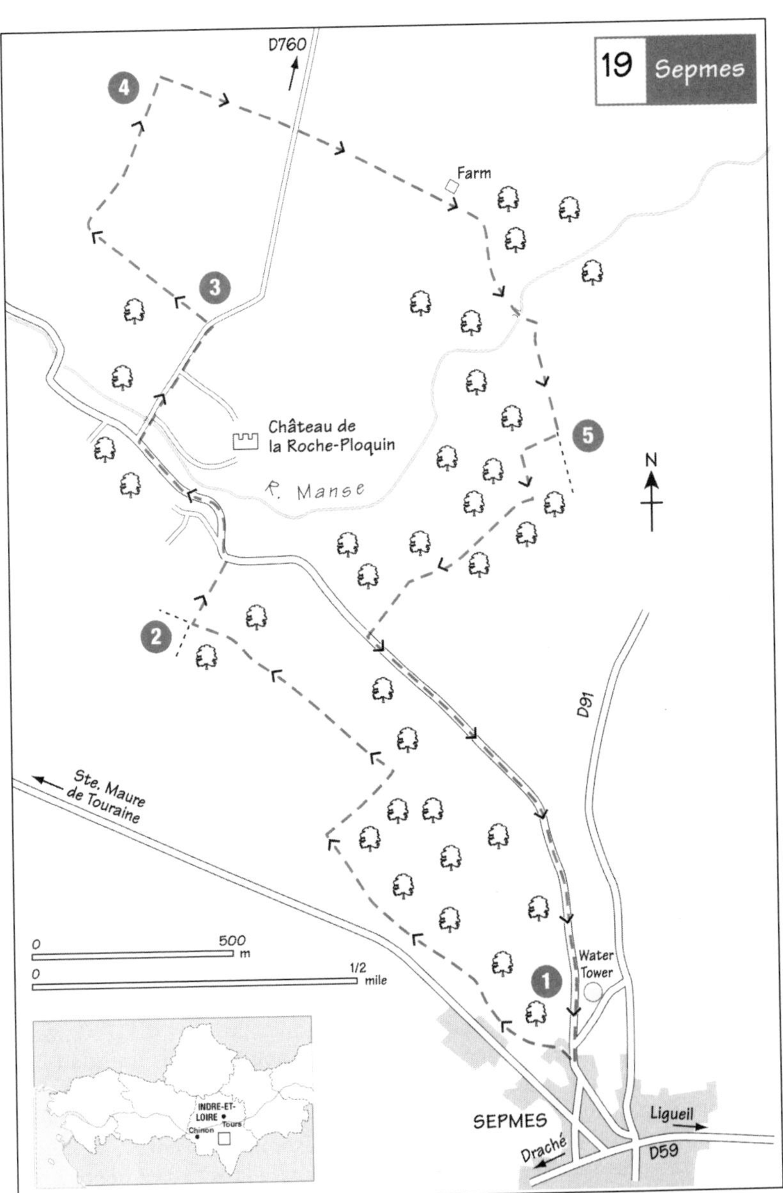


5. In mid-field you reach a track junction and turn right on a track heading into the wood again. Under the trees the track bears left and later right, always keeping alongside the fenced off sector of the wood. After a while you have a field on your left and shortly afterwards the track meets a tarmacked road. Turn left, and about 10 minutes walking will bring you back to the water tower.

## More Walks in the Area

The historic town of Loches is only about 16km away and well merits a visit. While there, it is possible to take a short circular walk. There is parking beside the Office de Tourisme (near the station) and they can supply you with a town map to help you round. From the Office de Tourisme, cross the Place de la Marne and take the road to the right of the ancient bell tower to reach the Place aux Legumes. Turn right on the Rue St Antoine. This will lead you up past the Hôtel de Ville and to an old archway, the Porte Royale. Beyond is the Logis Royale and donjon. When you come out of the Porte Royale again, turn left and continue around the walls. At the first road junction, turn left on a path that runs below the ramparts (a rock fall had closed this in Spring 2001, but it should open again). This path will bring you down to the riverside, which you can then follow to return to the Office de Tourisme.

For many more rural walks, go along to the Forêt de Loches, just east of Loches. You can pick up an interesting booklet, *Promenons-nous en Forêt de Loches*, from the Office de Tourisme before you go. The booklet details 9 walks from three separate starting points. The routes are not waymarked – instead, the booklet offers a sketch map of each forest junction. Just regard it as a challenge! Although there is not a lot of text relating to each walk, a little knowledge of the language would help you to identify the odd named landmark. But if all this sounds too much like hard work, you could simply drive along to one of the starting points, the Kiosk de Pas-aux-Ânes (From Loches, take the D760, and at the Pyramid de Chartreuse cross-roads, go straight over, then first right). Here there is a very pleasant waymarked trail of 2km, which leads you beside a lake deep in the woods to reach the Chartreuse du Liget, a ruined monastery with an ornate entrance gate – see below.

For other walks in the vicinity, both St Maure-de-Touraine and Loches have a stock of leaflets, describing routes from local villages. The maps in these leaflets are very good, as generally is the waymarking, so they can be followed quite easily. Some knowledge of French would add interest to the walks. The leaflets have the simple title *Sentiers Pédestres – Touraine*.

## Places of Interest Nearby

Both the medieval city of Loches and the ruins of the Chartreuse du Liget have been mentioned in the More Walks section. Loches is more than worth a visit – simply follow the walk directions to visit all its most notable features. You don't have to walk through the forest (pleasant though it is) to reach the Chartreuse du Liget – the ruins stands beside the D760 from Loches to Montrésor. This large Carthusian monastery was founded by Henry II (of England) in expiation for the murder of Thomas à Becket. To see more of it, drive a kilometre or so along the road towards Montrésor. The curious round Chapelle de St Jean houses some 12th-century frescoes – and farther east again there are yet more ruins to the left of the road.

In the opposite direction from Sepmes, through Draché and half a kilometre or so up the N10 (or via minor roads), you can find a strange menhir with a hole through it – the Pierre Percée. The countryside south of Loches is rich in megaliths of all kinds. If you want to know where to find them, ask for the leaflet *Préhistoire en Sud Touraine* at an Office de Tourisme.

And you might want to pop along to Ste. Maure-de-Touraine for a little goats' cheese – if not to tour the historic buildings. See under Walk 20 (Avon-les-Roches) for details.

# 20. In the valley of the Manse at Avon-les-Roches

The pretty valley of the Manse is famed for its ancient villages and troglodyte dwellings. In addition this walk passes the dramatic ruins of a 15th-century collegiate church high on a hillside and goes on climbing through the woods to a plateau of moorland with distant views

**Grade:** Easy / moderate

**Distance:** 10km (6¼ miles)

**Time:** 3 hours

**Map:** IGN Série Bleue 1823 O, 1824 O

**Start and finish:** The church at Avon-les-Roches.

**How to get there:** From L'Île Bouchard, take the D751 north. After 3km turn right on the D21 and very shortly turn left (SP Avon-les-Roches). The church is in the centre of the village beside the *Mairie*, where there is a car park.

**Refreshment:** The focus of local life is the Café de la Vallée (beside the *Mairie*)– drinks and light refreshments are served. There is no refreshment en route.

**Notes:** The walk is almost all on field and forest tracks, with just a couple of short sections on very minor roads. Although the tracks are very well defined, there is some long grass and the possibility of mud after rain – unless the weather is exceptionally dry, stout footwear is recommended. The route is a little 'up hill and down dale', but none of the climbs is particularly steep. Carry fluid with you (there is none on the way) and, as part of the route is exposed, take appropriate precautions on a hot day.

**Waymarking:** The route is well waymarked in yellow throughout

---

## Introduction

The Manse is not much of a river in itself, flowing a mere 30 or so kilometres to its confluence with the Vienne east of Chinon. But its short valley is one of the prettiest and most interesting in Touraine, and is well worthy of some exploration. The Manse begins with two tributaries, both called 'Manse', and both arising on the plateau beyond Ste. Maure-de-Touraine. The northernmost of the two has the more exciting course, and soon enters the steep wooded Valley of Courtineau – a valley whose tufa slopes are riddled with tunnels and caves, many of which are still-inhabited. There is even a troglodyte chapel. After the Manses join, the valley becomes wider and more sweeping, its hollow now filled with fields of cereal and maize and dotted with ancient farms of crumbling stone. At St Épain an old archway beside the church is part of the medieval fortifications and there are houses dating from the same era. The village of Crissay with its old houses, church and ruined castle is almost in its entirety a designated heritage site. A few kilometres downstream, Avon-les-Roches is not quite in that league, but it does have a fine medieval church with a beautiful colonnaded porch from the 12th century.

The walk from Avon-les-Roches sets out up the valley of a stream that is a tributary of the Manse. Here again are the ancient farms, and deep in the valley is an old *lavoir*, a one-time washing-place, shaded by a weeping

*Ruins of the collegiate church at Les Roches Tranchelion*

willow. The dignified ruins of a 16th-century collegiate church dominate the skyline above the hamlet of les Roches Tranchelion – it is worth climbing up to take a closer look at some of the delicate Renaissance carving before continuing on your way. Beyond the ruins, a row of troglodyte dwellings has been dug into the cliff. None of them is still in use although it cannot have been long since they were abandoned – you can look through the windows to see some of the furniture inside. The top of the hill is clothed in fine oak forest and leads to a descent through the hamlet of Sévaudières – by which point you may feel you have gone back a couple of centuries or so. A final climb takes you to the Landes de Ruchard, a wide moorland of gorse and heather. Unfortunately it is now a military training ground, but you can still enjoy the colourful distant views from these heights before returning to Avon-les-Roches.

## The Walk

1. Facing the church, take the road alongside it on the left, the Rue du 8 Mai, which climbs to reach the cemetery. Turn left along its stone wall (Rue de la Boulinnière) and then right along the top wall and keep ahead. At the junction in about 350 m, take a wide sandy and grassy track on the right, This leads along the side of the valley with some pleasant views. At a cross-tracks, keep straight ahead and go on into the woodland. Emerging from the trees, turn right on the broad track to descend to the road.

2. Turn left on the road and continue to the fork where a *lavoir* stands beside a weeping willow on the little stream (inside are the old washing implements – but don't get excited, they're cemented to the wall). On the hill above, the ruins of the church stand out against the sky. It's an attractive spot, and a picnic table has thoughtfully been provided. Continue by bearing right to pass the old farm, and then immediately turn left and bear right on the track that climbs below the ruins. A

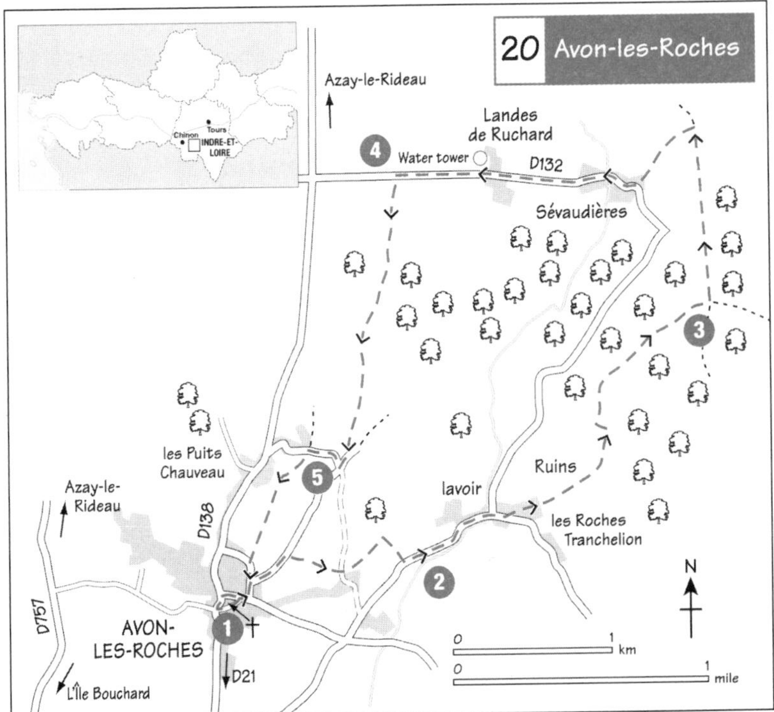


zig-zag track on your left will take you up to them – it's worth exploring. When you are ready, continue on the track that climbs along the side of the valley and soon passes a long row of troglodyte dwellings. After more steady climbing the track enters the woods and, at the top of the hill, turns sharply to the right – it's not a turn you could miss and is well-waymarked. Continue now on this obvious track for another 10 or 15 minutes – at one point the route turns right and immediately left again, but just follow the yellow flashes.

**3.** At a major cross-tracks, turn left on the broad sandy forest road. Keep to this for just over a kilometre, after which the forest has been left behind. As the track finally curves to the left, take a grassy track doubling back through fields on the left and heading downhill again. The track winds down to a road where you turn right to reach the tumbling old stone buildings of Sévaudières. Below the houses on the left is a *lavoir* on the stream – several paths lead to it, but the intended one is marked with a yellow arrow. Continuing, the road soon begins to climb and to take you back to the 21st century. At the top of the hill you reach the splendid expanse of the moorland of Ruchard – and the military enclosure. Passing the water-tower, keep ahead for a further 5 minutes or so

**4.** Now take a waymarked track on the left. At first the land is open, but soon the track enters woods again. Leaving the trees behind, keep to the track for about another 10 minutes to reach a tarmacked road at a junction. Turn right on the road and walk downhill.

**5.** About half way down the hill, a track crosses the road. Turn left here (there is lots of waymarking – a possible extension to this route lies ahead). Climb the grassy track from which there are good views of the hamlet of le Puits Chauveau below you. The track reaches a tarmacked road and descends again to the cemetery you met at the outset of the walk. Passing it, turn right to return to the church.

## More Walks in the Area

Several nearby villages have walks described in the *Sentiers Pédestres – Touraine* series – the Offices de Tourisme in St Maure de Touraine, Azay-le-Rideau and Chinon each stock the leaflets of their particular area. Unfortunately, not every route on every leaflet is well-waymarked. One that is – and also has lots of interest – is the yellow-marked circuit of 16km from Villaines-les-Rochers, about 10km north of Avon-les-Roches. Villaines-les-Rochers is a basket-making town in a valley again lined with some remarkable cave dwellings. In addition, the route passes several osier beds, a couple of chateaux, some pretty villages and a viewpoint across the valley of the Indre to the north.

Other circuits that might be of interest are those at Neuil, a few kilometres to the east. A display board beside the *Mairie* will tell you about them, and the *Mairie* itself may have a leaflet. Neuil has a *lavoir* and spring, some fine old buildings and more troglodyte dwellings. Three pleasant rural circuits are described, dipping in and out of the surrounding woodland.

If you are thinking of visiting Ste. Maure-de-Touraine – it's the home of an excellent goats' cheese – you might consider the 11km 'red route'. Rambling through the countryside to the village of les Coteaux, you can admire cave-dwellings, vineyards and, of course, herds of goats. A leaflet can be obtained from the Office de Tourisme in Ste. Maure – attractively situated with the old château, on the top of the hill.

## Places of Interest Nearby

Just a few kilometres north of Avon-les-Roches is Azay-le-Rideau with its exquisite château beside the Indre, a sight not to be missed. Still on the Indre (but just a little less trumpeted) is another château, that of Saché. Balzac was a frequent visitor here in the 1830s and wrote at least part of his novel Le Père Goriot (Old Goriot) in a room that has not been changed to this day. There are many other mementoes of Balzac's life and work on view. The château is open throughout the year with the exception of December and January.

The town of Villaines-les-Rochers was mentioned in the More Walks section. Wickerwork has been the trade here for many centuries and in many cases is a family business. There are several open workshops in which to admire this particularly high-quality craftsmanship and where you can learn about the growing and cutting of the willow and rushes.

Ste Maure-de-Touraine is a town around the hilltop site of a fortress originally built by Foulques Nerra. There are several buildings worthy of note – the present château, the church, the convent and the covered market. Ste. Maure produces its own AOC (Appellation d'Origine Controllee) goats' cheese – it is possible to taste it at any of the *chèvreries* of the district. To the east is the plateau of Ste. Maure, a region once entirely covered by woodland. The tracts of this that remain are noted for their superb display of wild daffodils in early spring – see the Walk 19 at Sepmes for more information.

## 21. The banks of the Cher at Villandry

The château at Villandry is best known for its magnificent formal gardens. Before or after a visit, escape the crowds and take this pleasant rural ramble leading you out to the confluence of the Cher and the Loire

**Grade:** Easy

**Distance:** 10km (6¼ miles)

**Time:** 3 hours

**Map:** IGN Série Bleue 1822 O and 1823 O

**Start and finish:** The Château of Villandry

**How to get there:** Villandry is on the south bank of the Loire, just west of Tours. Follow signs for the château – there is a large car park with a picnic area and Office de Tourisme just down the road .

**Refreshment:** An assortment of bars and restaurants line the road beside the château – but there is none on the route.

**Notes:** This is an easy walk on reasonable tracks – nevertheless they could be muddy out of season, when you would be best in walking boots. Carry water with you, and, as most of the route is exposed, don't forget the sun cream on a hot day. The walk out along the bank to the confluence is optional but worth taking – it will add a further 20 minutes or so to your time. Short cuts missing out some of the woodland will reduce the distance by a kilometre or two.

**Waymarking:** The route is waymarked in yellow throughout

---

### Introduction

Villandry was the last of the great Renaissance château to be built in the valley of the Loire – in this case, beside the Cher. But magnificent though the building may be, it is for the superb formal gardens that Villandry is renowned. They are the work of the Spanish Carvallo family, who over the last century have restored them to their full Renaissance glory. The gardens are on three levels – the upper water garden with its formal lake provides the irrigation for the other two. The second level includes the famous designs of the Garden of Love and Garden of Music, both of which are best viewed from the terrace behind. On the lowest level, ingenious patterns are achieved with cabbages and the like in the kitchen garden, which is planted twice a year.

The walk around the gardens will take something like an hour, but you may like to visit the château as well. From the top of the medieval keep there is a good view across both the Cher and the Loire. When you have seen and done it all, you will be more than ready to escape the throngs of visitors on this quiet ramble. The route climbs to the plateau behind Villandry, passes an ancient menhir, and then drops again to a wooded path following the old course of the River Cher. More woodland rambling leads you to a raised bank alongside the present-day river, a bank that can be followed to the confluence with the Loire. Here the clean arches of a railway bridge gracefully span the river and on the far side the *pile* of Cinq-Mars-la-Pile pushes its head above the trees. An easy stroll beside the Cher takes you back to Villandry.

*The Château of Villandry*

## The Walk

1. From the parking and picnic area, cross over the main road (D7) and take the D121, heading past the church – you can see the first of the yellow flashes you will be following. At the fork, keep left (SP Druye) and continue climbing. Before reaching the top of the hill, take a turning on the right, signposted to La Joumeraie – the GR with its white on red waymarks joins you here. As you go there are views to the right across the valleys of the Cher and the Loire. The road winds around a bit through some new housing. At its end, turn right and continue on the track along the edge of the field. Just after the last of the houses, turn left on another grassy track between fields and keep ahead to reach a tarmacked road.

2. Turn to the right on this road, and after about 600m (just before a farm), take a wide earthen track on the left – it is well-waymarked. Reaching a patch of woodland on the left, you can divert to see the menhir, the Pierre-aux-Joncs. Turn left on the track through the wood, and after fifty metres or so, turn to the right. Returning through the wood to the main track, continue in the direction in which you were heading. At the fork, keep ahead to arrive at a track junction with a field ahead – and there is not a waymark in sight. Head to the right here, in the direction of a farm. Soon you arrive at a hamlet with a pond and little green. Keep straight ahead on the road (the GR soon leaves you to go right), and at the T-junction, turn left. The road now descends through the wood and passes *Les Caves d'Amont* – evidence of the old tufa quarries from where the stone was taken down to ports on the old Cher.

3. At the main road, turn right and then almost immediately (20m.) left. The road descends and bears left beside the woodland along the old

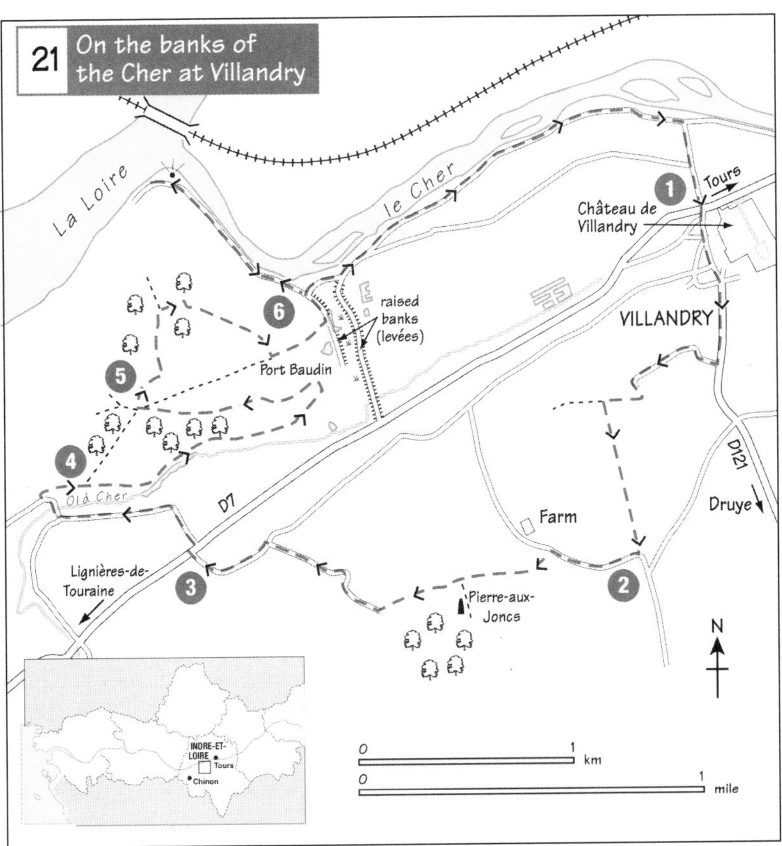


course of the Cher. At the junction turn right to cross the river, and on the far side, take the first track on the right, which follows the Cher on its opposite bank Soon the track forks

**4.** Following the main track downhill to the left will take you quickly to Point 5. But the main walk continues on the grassy track ahead, following the course of the river. The path leaves the wood and crosses open land before reaching an enclosure of cultivated land. On approaching the hamlet of Port Baudin, bear left and then left again. (for another short cut – go into the hamlet and bear left on the dam to Point 6). For the full route, you now have signs for the *Confluence Cher et Loire* to show you the way. After 10 minutes or so walking, a track joins you from the right and you reach a track-junction

**5.** Here bear right (ahead if you have come via the short cut) and in 50 metres or so, keep right again – the wooden signposts keep you on the right track. After about 5 minutes walking, at a track junction in the woods, turn right. The path now goes on to cross a wide field and run along the edge to reach a stone farm. Walk between its buildings, and climb the steps on to the dam. Turning left you reach a road junction

**6** The waymarks direct you on the road to the right – but it is well worth following the bank (*levée*) to the left leading you out to the mouth of the Cher. When you get there, look out for both the château and the 'pile' at Cinq-Mars-la-Pile opposite (see the More Walks section).

Returning to the road junction at Point 6, continue ahead beside the river. Shortly, ignore the road on the right (SP La Tuilerie and waymarked). The more attractive route is the narrow road along the *levée* beside the Cher. Reaching the memorial of the Comtesse d'Hainguerlot, turn right through the avenue of trees to return to the château.

## More Walks in the Area

Just up river, the town of Savonnières is best known for its caves (see Places of Interest). It also has two waymarked circuits – the shorter of them (6km.) climbs the slopes for some fine views of the Loire and the Cher (on a good day you can see the cathedral at Tours). The return is along the banks of the Cher. The Office de Tourisme at Villandry should be able to find you the appropriate leaflet – or you could no doubt get it in Savonnières itself (try the Mairie if the Office de Tourisme is closed out of season).

Ballan-Miré, between Villandry and Tours, is a place full of interest – 12th-century church, château, mill, *commanderie* and ancient Roman road. All are incorporated into a series of walks ranging from 9 to 33km Again the Office de Tourisme at Villandry should have the leaflet.

Crossing to the opposite bank of the Loire, several more circuits are possible. One is at Cinq-Mars-la-Pile – a 14km ramble through woods and a succession of villages, which you could combine with a visit to the château and 'pile'. A little downstream, the village of St Michel-sur-Loire sits high on a bluff above the river (St Michel is the saint of high places). The 7km walk here starts with some fine views as you walk along the cliff, before plunging into a splendid forest of oak and beech. Each of these walks is printed on a leaflet in the *Randonnées Pédestres – Touraine* series and can be found in any local Office de Tourisme, including the one in Tours. The text on these leaflets is in French only, but both the maps and the waymarking on the ground are excellent – you should have no difficulty in following the routes.

Briefly on this walk you followed the route of the GR3, the Grande Randonnée of the Loire Valley. West of Tours it forsakes the Loire in favour of the banks of the Cher. The distance from Pont Saint-Sauveur in Tours to Villandry is around 15km – unfortunately there is no bus service, but the Office de Tourisme will be only too pleased to help you get a taxi in either direction. The route is well-waymarked (Grandes Randonnées always are), but you might be helped by the appropriate Série Bleue map – or by a booklet describing the route of the GR3 through Touraine and obtainable at the desk of the *Comité Touraine de la Randonnée Pédestre* at the Office de Tourisme in Tours. This publication has lots of French text, but the maps, though black and white photocopies, are clear enough. It might also be of use if you are thinking of following the GR3 west of Villandry – Azay-le-Rideau is a mere 13km away, after which you continue through the forest to Chinon.

## Places of Interest Nearby

Les Grottes Pétrifiantes are situated alongside the road between Villandry and Savonnières. These caves were formed naturally in prehistoric times, but in the 12th century were used as quarries. Now the limestone saturated water seeps through the ceiling and has created an eery world of stalactites, lakes and petrified waterfalls. Any object left in these caves will be turned to stone – and there is a museum and shop just full of them. Other attractions include re-creations of prehistoric wildlife. The caves are open every day from February to mid-December (except Thursdays in November and December)

Travelling downstream from Villandry, the first bridge across the river will take you to Langeais. The little town is utterly dwarfed by the superb medieval fortress at its heart. Langeais was built by Louis XI in the 15th century and remarkably has not been altered since. Inside it has been restored with rich furnishings from that period – a chance to get a real glimpse of daily life in a medieval château. The most notable event to take place in this château was the secret marriage of Charles VIII and Anne of Brittany in 1491 – effectively bringing about the union of France and Brittany. The occasion is re-created with waxwork figures in the room in which it actually took place. If possible, visit Langeais when there are few others – its authenticity is most impressive.

Upstream from Langeais is Cinq-Mars-la-Pile. The *Pile* is a slim tower 30m high, dating from Roman times. Its decorated brickwork dates it accurately to the latter half of the 2nd century. The purpose of the *pile* is unknown – possibly it housed a light, an aid to navigation on the Loire, although it is more likely to have been a funerary monument. All that remains of the Château of Cinq-Mars is two rounded towers – the rest was razed by Richelieu in reprisal for its owner's involvement in a conspiracy against him. The parkland and gardens alone are worth a visit.

# 22. Giant Strides around Seuilly

Rabelais set his fantastic satirical tale of Gargantua and the Picrocholine Wars around the area of his birthplace at la Devinière near Seuilly. Display boards unfold the story as you go – but you could simply enjoy an excellent walk for its own sake.

**Grade:** Easy – with one or two very gentle climbs.

**Distance:** 17km (10½ miles)

**Time:** 5 hours

**Map:** IGN Série Bleue 1724 O and 1724 E. But you could save yourself expense by picking up a leaflet entitled *Circuit des Guerres Picrocholines* from Tourist Information. It's designed for car drivers, but it has a perfectly adequate map of the area.

**Start and finish:** la Devinière near Seuilly

**How to get there:** From Chinon, head south on the D759 to Loudun. At the roundabout south of the Vienne, continue ahead (crossing the D751) and in less than 1km, at la Roche-Clermault, turn right on to the D117. La Devinière is on the right in about 1km.

**Refreshment:** None at la Devinière. The nearest is the pleasant little restaurant of les Palmiers in Cinais. At la Roche-Clermault, the smart le Clos overlooks the valley – or you could just settle for light refreshment at the bar near the junction on the main road (Point 8)

**Notes:** This easy walk should be quite suitable for trainers in summer time. It is fairly long, and for much of the time there is no shade, so you should think of protection from the sun on a hot day. Carry lots of fluid – although there are several possibilities for rehydration en route. And allow extra time to read all the information panels telling the tale.

**Waymarking:** The route has been waymarked in blue throughout.

---

## Introduction

Rabelais is one of the most famous sons of the Loire. Born in 1494 at la Devinière (or in a field nearby according to one legend), he spent his childhood in the stone farmhouse on a hillside. He went on to an illustrious career, starting out as a monk, becoming a physician of some repute, and later turning his hand to writing. The texts he created are full of medieval earthiness, satirical, bloodthirsty and often frankly crude, in a prose that is literally crammed with adjectives.

The story of the Picrocholine Wars appears in his book Gargantua, and is set here in the landscape of his childhood. The cause of the war is deliberately trivial – the bakers of Lerné, in the kingdom of Picrochole, refuse to sell their *fouaces* (savoury cakes of flour, eggs, butter and milk) to the shepherds of Seuilly, the subjects of the good King Grandgousier. The shepherds retaliate and the scene moves to the Abbey of Seuilly where the invaders attack the vineyards and are slain by a monk with a cross. Matters progress, and Picrochole having stormed a local château, becomes ambitious and sets his sights on the whole of Europe – while Grandgousier of Seuilly sends for his son, the giant Gargantua. What happens next you will discover as you walk – - a series of five information panels have been set up to spell out the incredible tale in both French and English.

*Bridge at the Gué de Vede*

Aside from all that, this is a pleasant walk in its own right. Starting from la Devinière, you can take time to visit the farmhouse, now a museum of all things Rabelaisian, before you set out. The slopes around Seuilly are scattered with vineyards, and where there are no vines, there are woods. A path through the attractive Bois Chabert brings you down to Lerné, a beautifully preserved old stone village where you can take advantage of the picnic tables in the town square or beside the river. Farther on you pass the ancient Abbey of Seuilly and then follow a little river through its valley to the village of la Roche Clermault – where the château was captured by Picrochole and a large part of his army were drowned when Gargantua's steed answered a call of nature! And that should be quite enough to 'whet' your appetite ...

## The Walk

1. The first information panel is in the car park at la Devinière – it tells of the initial dispute over the *fouaces*. Leaving the car park, turn left up the hill in the direction of Cinais. An occasional blue flash is seen as you continue on the road to the top of the hill. Before reaching the cemetery, take a broad straight track on the left between the fields (no waymarks). Across the valley the Château de Coudray-Montpensier can be seen on its hill. Where the track swings to the right, keep ahead on a grassy track to reach a narrow road.

2. Turn left on this road. Where the road descends and corners left, take a track on the right alongside a wood. Leaving the woodland, the track crosses a field and then arrives at another gravelled road. Continue straight ahead on this road and as it turns to the houses on the left, bear right uphill on a track. The track leads you towards a wood and then bears around to the right in front of it. To the left there is now a vineyard, and the path turns left along its upper edge.

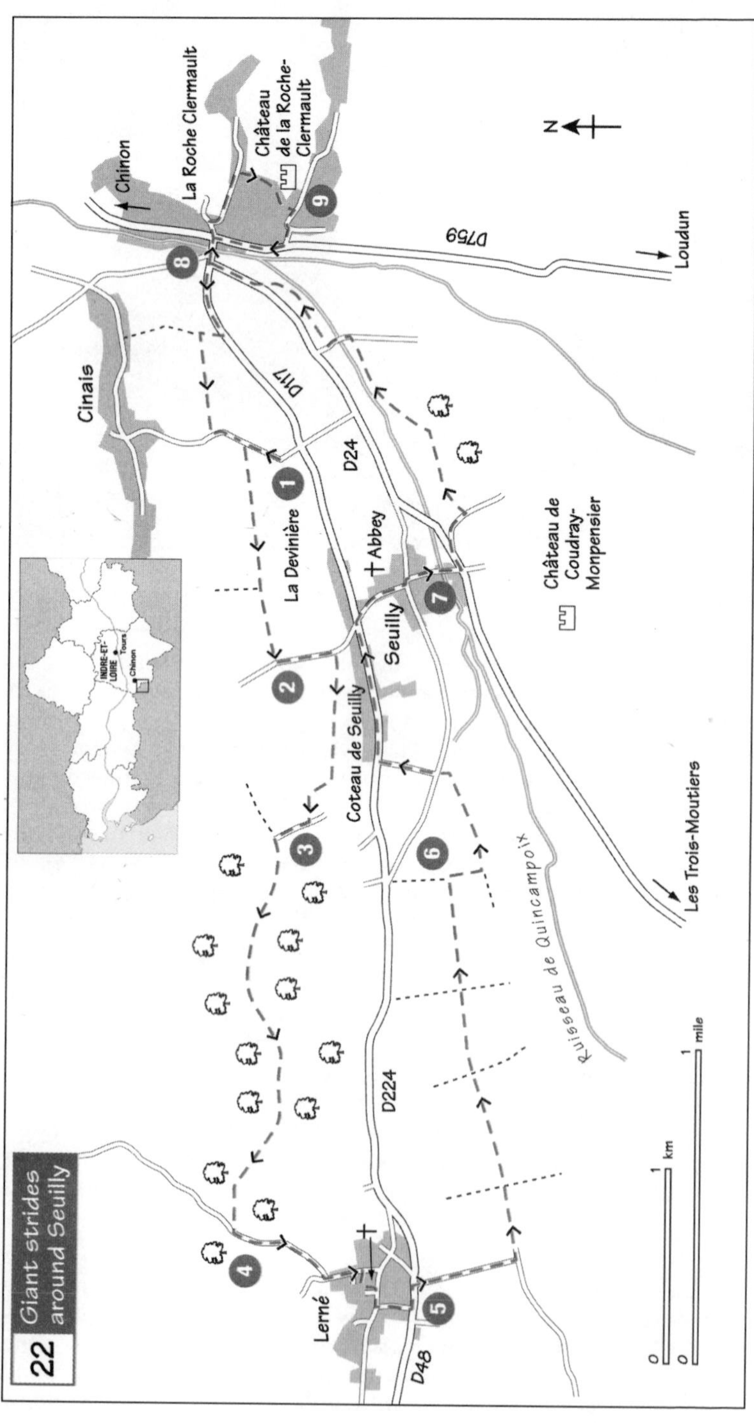
22
Giant strides around Seuilly
Lerné
D48
D224
Coteau de Seuilly
Seuilly
Abbey
La Devinière
Cinais
D117
D24
La Roche Clermault
Château de la Roche-Clermault
Chinon
D759
Loudun
Château de Coudray-Monpensier
Les Trois-Moutiers
Ruisseau de Quincampoix
N
1
2
3
4
5
6
7
8
9
0
1 km
0
1 mile
INDRE-ET-LOIRE
Tours
Chinon

3. Arriving at a tarmacked road, turn right. At the cross-roads in about 250 metres, turn left (a wooden signpost announces *vers Lerné*). Now keep straight ahead on this track, ignoring all rights and lefts. Soon you are heading through pleasant mixed woodland, in springtime dotted with the bright yellow of gorse. A clearing is passed and another sign tells you that you are in the Bois Chabert. Eventually you emerge at a tarmacked road.

4. Turn left and follow the road to Lerné. On reaching the village, turn immediately right on the Rue des Acacias, which leads into the Rue St Martin. Around here there seems to be a profusion of little walking men signs. The odd blue flash is still to be seen, and, following these, you keep straight ahead to descend past a curiously large stone bishop who appears to be watching over the tennis courts. Turn right through a pleasant picnic area (also under the eye of the bishop) and on the far side, turn downhill to reach the square beside the church. The second information panel tells of the destruction wrought in this area by Picrochole and his men. Turn right at the church, and, in about 50 metres, left on the Rue de Portail Blanc (with its walking man sign). Continue ahead to the main road.

5. Turn left on the road (the walking man points the other way), and in about 50 metres, turn right on a tarmacked road heading uphill. At the T-junction at the top of the hill, turn left – the way now stretches before you descending gently. Over to the left you can see the woods and vineyards you crossed earlier. At the next three cross-tracks keep straight ahead.

6. At the fourth cross-tracks there is only a field ahead and you turn to the right and then very shortly to the left. The château is now looking down on you and between is a stream, the Ruisseau de Quincampoix, in its wooded valley. The road swings round to the left (ahead is a spring, the Fontaine de Morin) and comes to a cross-roads. Cross the main road and climb uphill to the place called Coteau de Seuilly. Turn to the right and walk the length of the village street passing some interesting old properties. At its end, bear right to reach the Abbey of Seuilly where Rabelais was educated. Another information panel tells how the destruction of the Abbey's vines was thwarted by the angry Brother John des Entommeures

7. At the main road below the abbey, turn left, and then bear right in Seuilly itself. This road now takes you down over the stream to meet the main road. Turn left on the main road and immediately right on a narrow road heading uphill. After passing the cemetery, take the track on the left. This grassy track parallels the stream for almost a kilometre before meeting a tarmacked road. Here, turn left to cross the stream on a little stone bridge before turning right on the far side. The track soon curves away from the stream to meet the road. Keep ahead on the road to a sort of cross-roads.

8. Keep on the main road, which bends to the right and crosses the stream, now in the village of la Roche-Clermault. At the junction with the D759, cross straight over (the blue waymarks tell you to turn right – ignore them). After crossing the railway, bear right on a road heading uphill. Take the first track on the right – you can see it heading in

the direction of the château on the hill. The track brings you to a road near an entrance to the château. Turn left on the road that runs below the old walls to find the fourth information panel telling how Picrochole took the château and then set his sights on – the rest of the world!

**9.** Retrace your steps to the entrance and now continue on the road downhill. Coming to the main road at the bottom of the hill, an information panel can be seen in the field opposite, not far from a bridge over the stream. Apparently this was the Gué de Vede, the ford where Gargantua's steed relieved itself, thereby drowning a fair proportion of Picrochole's army. Now continue along the main road to the cross-roads you passed earlier (there is a small friendly bar just before it). Turn left to cross the stream again and reach point 8. Now ignore the road to Cinais, and take the next on the right, the D117, signposted to la Devinière. In about 400 metres, take the rough road on the right going uphill, signposted to Cinais. After about 100 metres, take a track on the left, marked with a yellow flash. This track returns you past a windmill to the cemetery you saw at the start of the walk – where you can now turn left on the road to get back to la Devinière.

## More Walks in the Area

Keeping up the Rabelasian connection, there is an excellent 10km walk starting from the village of Panzoult, 12km to the east of Chinon (on the D 21). Panzoult is a wine growing area, but here you climb to the wooded slopes above the vineyards with some splendid views. Descending into the valley of the Coulay, the path arrives at an old mill in a picturesque setting. High on the hillside above you can see a cave, said by Rabelais to be the cave where lived the Sybil, the sorcerer consulted by Gargantua on the subject of his marriage. Unfortunately the cave is now private property with no ready advice available. The valley leads down to the pretty village of la Chauvinière with its *lavoir* and *fontaine*, before a further ramble through the woods. The route of this fairly energetic walk can be found in the leaflet *Sentiers Pédestres – Panzoult* obtainable from the Office de Tourisme in Chinon. The leaflet is in French only, but the maps and waymarking are good so you should have no trouble with route-finding. If you can't get to the Office de Tourisme, the route is shown (in green) on an information panel at the starting point, the playing fields at Panzoult – you could perhaps sketch it before you go.

The Office de Tourisme in Chinon has plenty of other ideas for walks in the region. The leaflet referred to above is one of a series covering the villages of the area around la Devinière. Seuilly, la Roche-Clermault and Cinais each have their own waymarked route and accompanying leaflet.

The GR3 runs through Chinon and can be followed in either direction with the aid of the appropriate IGN Série Bleue maps. To the east, the GR3 wanders through the Forest of Chinon to emerge at Azay-le-Rideau (28km.); to the west, it follows the banks of the Vienne and then turns away to Fontevraud l'Abbaye (17km.). In each case, you would need IGN map 1723 E and another map, either the one to the east or the west of this – an alternative would be to get hold of the booklet describing the whole route of the GR3 through the *département* of Indre-et-Loire, published by the Comité Touraine de la Randonnée Pedéstre (OT at Tours has it in stock). The Grande Randonnée itself is very clearly waymarked with white on red flashes. In summer, it should be possible to travel in either direction on public transport – enquire at the Office de Tourisme in Chinon for times. Otherwise, you could consider a taxi or arrange for a friend to pick you up.

## Places of Interest Nearby

La Devinière, the farmhouse where Rabelais spent his childhood (transformed to the Château de Grandgousier in his book) is open all day from 10am to 7pm between 1st May and 30th September. Outside these months a lunch break is taken – but essentially it is possible to visit it on almost any day of the year. The visit should not take more than an hour and it will set the scene for the walk before you leave.

Merely 5 or 6km away is Chinon, whose 12th-century castle is particularly remembered for one moment in history. It was here that Joan of Arc met – and famously recognised – the Dauphin Charles, and then persuaded him to allow her to lead the French army to relieve the siege of Orléans. It is an incredible story, and in the clock tower it is all spelt out with maps, prints, film and a commentary that you can choose to hear in English. Of the great hall in which the meeting took place, there remains only the fireplace, now exposed on an outside wall. Inside are life-sized tableaux of that historic event. But there is more to the Château de Chinon than just the Joan of Arc saga, and a visit here could easily fill a few hours. On the slopes between the château and the river are the motley buildings of Old Chinon, narrow streets of gabled and turreted half-timbered houses dating from hundreds of years ago. Among them, look out for the Caves Painctes (Painted Cellars – although now without the paint). Here Rabelais himself enjoyed a glass or two of wine – and described it as a frequent haunt of his character, Pantagruel.

A few kilometres west of la Devinière is Fontevraud Abbey. A huge edifice of light tufa stone, it seems stark, cold and uninviting – but it nevertheless attracts swarms of visitors. In the darkened nave of the abbey church lie the painted effigies of some of England's most notable Plantagenets. Henry II, Count of Anjou and King of England, his wife Eleanor of Aquitaine, their son Richard the Lionheart and Isabella of Angoulême (wife of their other son John) are all buried in the crypt beneath. Just to walk around the rest of the abbey will take you the best part of an afternoon – and you may well come out feeling very thankful that you were never a member of a religious community in the Middle Ages.

# 23. Lake and woods at Château-la-Vallière

Château-la-Vallière is at the heart of the *Gâtine Tourangelle*, a vast forested area north of the Loire. Starting from the town's lakeside beach, this woodland wander passes farms, hamlets, a ruined château, a *lavoir* and a string of lakes hidden in the trees.

**Grade:** Easy

**Distance:** 13km (8 miles). Taking the short cut will reduce the distance by about 3km.

**Time:** 3½ hours (2½ hours if taking the short route)

**Map:** IGN Série Bleue 1721 E, 1722 E

**Start and finish:** Beside the Étang du Val Joyeux at Château-la-Vallière.

**How to get there:** Château-la-Vallière is north-west of Tours at the intersection of the D766 and the D959. The lake is just south of the town – look out for signs from the town centre. There is parking along the dam and beside the beach.

**Refreshment:** Château-la-Vallière is a busy town and is well-supplied with bars and restaurants. On the route (after about 5km.), there is a very popular little auberge serving a first-class lunchtime set meal. If you stop here you may get no farther – -

**Notes:** This is an easy walk on good forest tracks and minor roads – there is just a little rough field walking which is cut out by taking the short cut. Trainers are fine in dry weather, otherwise wear boots. The route offers plenty of shade for a hot day, although there is one exposed section along roads. The beach at the Étang du Val Joyeux is supervised for swimming in July and August, so take your bathing costume for the end of the day.

**Waymarking:** The route is patchily waymarked in yellow – but then so are several other local circuits, so don't take too much notice!

---

## Introduction

The *Gâtine Tourangelle* extends from the Loire in the south to le Loir in the north, a vast area that was originally covered by dense forest. The abundance of game and the many natural springs encouraged human settlement, and by the 11th century deforestation had begun. Today all manner of crops are grown here – asparagus, tobacco, maize, sunflower and the rest. But large tracts of forest remain and the splendid oak and pine woodland south of Château-la-Vallière makes a fine setting for this walk.

Château-la-Vallière itself is a busy place at the intersection of two main roads. But barely a stone's throw from the town centre is the Étang du Val Joyeux, a winding tranquil lake created by the damming of the River Fare. You can park your car beside the lovely sandy beach and, in summer, take out a boat or go for a swim. The lake has a perimeter path 6km in length allowing you to wander round to admire the collection of bog plants thriving in its shallow 'tail' and the menhir over 12 ft. high that overlooks it all.

The circuit of the Étang du Val Joyeux makes a pleasant ramble, but for those fancying something more ambitious, the route here heads off into the forest to the hamlet of Vaujours. Here – in addition to the excellent auberge – you will find a *lavoir* beside the river and the extensive ruins of a medieval fortress oddly incorporated into someone's front garden. The château once belonged to Louise de la Vallière, for five years the mistress of the sun-king Louis XIV, and given by him the title Duchess of Vaujours. After Vaujours the route plunges into the forest again – sadly this part of it is fenced and reserved for *la chasse*, being as well-endowed with game as in olden days. But passing the lonely waters of the Étang du Bois, you reach farms and open countryside before a long wander through the forest on the way back to Château-la-Vallière.

## The Walk

1. From the dam, walk towards the town (away from the beach) and take the road to the right climbing uphill parallel to and above the lake. Ignore a waymarked path going downhill on the right and continue to the top of the hill. Here a yellow flash signifies a right turn on to a road that passes the church and goes on to meet the main road. Continue alongside the main road for about 100m, then cross over to walk down the Rue Balzac. At its end bear right on the Rue Réné Baillou and keep ahead on the Chemin de la Noiraie. At the last house, turn right on a broad grassy track with open views.

2. On reaching a tarmacked road – and a very handsome signpost – cross to the track opposite (SP Souvigné/Courcelles and still waymarked yellow). You are now on the tree-lined route of an old railway track. This crosses two roads (take care) and continues through some fine forest. After about 15 minutes walking, you reach another tarmacked road. On the track opposite is the site of the old station, and a few minutes beyond it, the old St Nicolas chapel, once a place of pilgrimage. Divert if you want to take a look, but the route now turns right in the direction of Courcelles. At the bottom of the hill, the auberge sits beside the road.

3. Cross straight over the road – there is an old *lavoir* (washing-place) beside the River Fare. Continue on the road up into the village – the ruins of the Château of Vaujours are on your right as you go. At the bend you can take a closer look at them – but as you will see, they are private and have been incorporated into a front garden. Now you have a choice:

   **For the short cut –**

   continue on this road for about 20 minutes, passing the farm of le Moltron on the right to arrive at Point 5.

   **For the main route –**

   Return to the road and Point 3. Turn right on the road, cross the stream and take the first track on your right almost immediately afterwards. This follows beside private fenced woodland on the left and soon reaches a string of lakes in the valley on the right. After almost half an hour's walking you cross the Étang du Bois on a sort of causeway and emerge at a track and road junction. Ignore the road on your right and keep ahead in the direction of le Houssay. The tarmacked road becomes a track and winds around to reach an attractive farm.

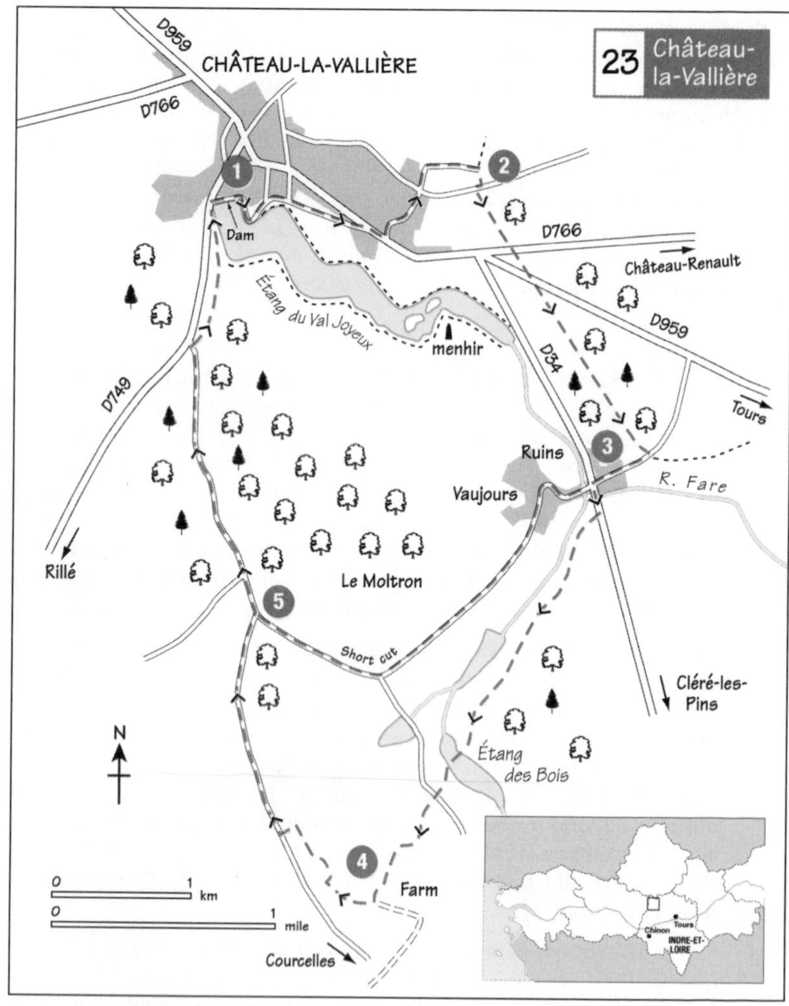


**4.** Just past the farm the gravelled track bends left, but you leave it and turn right here on a broad grassy track. The track becomes less clear and wiggles its way along the edge of several fields. Eventually it enters a patch of trees on the right and arrives at a clear gravelled track with a gate to the right. Turn left here to reach a minor road. Turn right and continue for 10 minutes or so to the road junction.

**5.** Turn left at this junction and continue straight ahead beside the road through the forest. Just before arriving at the main road (D749), take a track on the right dipping down through the trees. This hollowed out track soon opens out with a view across fields to the road below and then plunges into the trees again. With the road just visible about 150 metres ahead, descend some steps on the right to return to the lakeside and the dam.

## More Walks in the Area

An obvious choice – or alternative to this walk – is the 6km circuit of the lake. A bridge takes you across the swamp at the tail end. Take this walk in

*Path through the woods near Château-la-Valière*

the evening at your peril – the shore is apparently haunted by *les Trois Dames Blanches*, three sisters who drowned themselves in the lake some hundreds of years ago after their father murdered their suitors. The local walks leaflet suggests that the closing time of the bars may bear some relationship to these sightings.

The Office de Tourisme (at the *Mairie*) can find you a folder of walks in the canton of Château-la-Vallière. Each leaflet in the folder shows one or more routes that are waymarked – although some are less well done than others, as you have seen. There is plenty of French text on these leaflets, but don't be put off – although the maps are black and white and sketch-like, they are accurate, informative and not difficult to follow on their own. With more than a dozen leaflets in this folder, there is lots of choice, but one of the most attractive spots to visit is the Lac de Pincemaille, near Rillé – see the Places of Interest section. Here six circuits of varying length are waymarked through the forest surrounding the lake – take your pick.

Also contained in the folder (entitled *37 Sentiers de Touraine*) is a map of the *Grand Sentier de Touraine de la Castelvalerie* – basically a circular tour of the canton. The paths of this tour are beautifully waymarked – blue and white are the colours here, and you have already seen some of the admirable signposts on this route. Distances from place to place are given – you have only to arrange your transport. Ask the Office de Tourisme at Château-la-Vallière to help you find a taxi – or do as suggested, stay in the recommended accommodation, and complete the whole circuit in about 10 days. The paths are also suitable for all-terrain bikes, so perhaps you could speed things up a little!

And finally, Le Lude is only 17km away to the north-west – consider taking Walk 24, featuring the valley of the Loir and a Roman amphitheatre.

## *Places of Interest Nearby*

The Lac de Pincemaille just west of Rillé is a very popular spot in high season with its campsite, bathing beach, picnic tables under the trees, pedalos, sailing boats, windsurfers, and the *petit train historique* (a steam train from 1910) puffing its way around it all. Beyond the dyke, the huge lake is home to many wildfowl and waders, their numbers swollen at times by those passing on their annual migrations or winter visitors from the north. Hides have been provided for their observation.

13km due south of Château-la-Vallière is the Château of Champchevrier. Dating from around the 16th century, it became a rather glorified hunting lodge under Louis XIII – and still today you can admire the fine pack of hounds based here. But if hounds and hunting are not your scene, there is still plenty to claim your attention in the grounds, outbuildings, laundry-room and kitchens in addition to the superb Regency furnishings and tapestries in the house itself. The château is open on weekends only in May and June and every day in June, July and September.

# Anjou

*Heading towards the church at Parnay*

# 24. Le Lude and the valley of the Loir

'Le Loir' is just as pretty as its big cousin to the south. Starting from the imposing château at le Lude, this walk takes you to a Roman amphitheatre beside the banks of the river, with some fine views along the way.

**Grade:** Easy / Moderate

**Distance:** 16km (10 miles) A short cut can reduce this to 8km, but the best part of the walk is omitted.

**Time:** 5 hours – allowing time to look around the Roman site.

**Map:** IGN Série Bleue 1721 O and 1721 E

**Start and finish:** The Château of Le Lude

**How to get there:** Le Lude is 45km north-west of Tours on the D306 to La Flèche – the château is off the main road, beside the river. There are two or three small parking areas in the vicinity of the château entrance – should these be full, there is lots of space at the sports ground just off the D307 to the north (see map)

**Refreshment:** There are several bars and restaurants in Le Lude, but none on the route

**Notes:** This longish walk is undemanding apart from one fairly steep climb (and even steeper descent) around the site of the hill-fort. The view is worth the effort. Tracks are good throughout – trainers would be fine in dry summer weather, but otherwise go for boots. The last part of the walk is through low-lying fields, so can be very wet in winter. Carry plenty of water with you, and remember the sun cream on a hot day.

**Waymarking:** About half the walk is on Grande Randonnée, waymarked in white on red. The remaining part is waymarked in yellow.

---

## Introduction

The Château of le Lude is a lesson in architecture. The original building erected here over a thousand years ago was a fortress, solid and square, with a tower at each corner. In the usual way of things, it was assaulted, captured, recaptured and rebuilt. By the 15th century its owners were finding life in the château too sombre and depressing and began by restructuring one wing in the currently-fashionable style of the Italian Renaissance. Subsequent owners continued the transformations, until today the château is said to exhibit a different architectural style on each of its four faces. The impressive edifice is set in open grounds on the banks of the Loir – you may want to take a look before setting out on this walk.

The walk offers plenty more views of the Loir as you follow it upstream before returning through the forest. On the way you pass a couple of mills beside the water and a horse farm rearing and training the famous 'trotters' of the region. A short sharp climb – the only exertion on this walk – will take you to a Gallic hill-fort dating from the 7th century BC, from which there is a splendid view of the valley. But the real gem of the walk is the 1st century Gallo-Roman site in the flat fields beside the river at Cherré. A whole amphitheatre has been uncovered and, beneath it, a necropolis with tombs and artefacts from 400 to 500 years earlier. A little distance away are the remains of thermal baths and a temple. Cherré is thought to have been a sacred place located on a pagan site from a former era – it was abandoned with the arrival of Christianity in the 4th century AD Allow plenty of time to wander around. Your way home from here is a pleasant and uncomplicated ramble in and out of the woods and through the fields of a valley that is said to have been the old course of the Loir.

## The Walk

1. From the château, walk downhill and cross the river. At the road junction, continue ahead on the D305. Opposite the garage (approximately 100m), take a narrow tarmacked road on the right. Here both blue and yellow waymarks tell you that you are following the *Circuit de Malidor*. At the end of the tarmac, the ruined circular building was apparently an equine maternity unit – the stable-hand in the centre would be able to keep an eye on all the mares and intervene as soon as needed. In the field on the right is a memorial to the famous horse, Bougie (1908). Turn left on the grassy track.
2. At the T-junction in front of the house, turn right. This is the manor of Malidor – according to legend, so named after du Guesclin stayed and suffered a bad night's sleep here (*mal-y-dormait*). After about 100m, near an old mill, bear left through a gate into a picnic area and tennis courts. The Loir rushes over a barrage on the right. Cross over a couple of plank bridges and continue alongside the canal heading towards the farm of Malidor. The path turns right, leaving the farm on the left and then continues between fields to reach a tarmacked road beside the river.
3. Turn right here and continue on the road. After about 400m, just beyond la Petite Malfrairie, take the next track on the left heading into the woods– you have now joined the Grande Randonnée and white on red waymarks can be seen along with the yellow.
4. At a fork in the woods, the blue route is seen to go to the left. This is the short cut and by following the waymarks you can arrive at Point 7 on the map – but you will be missing a lot. The yellow route goes right along the edge of the woods and soon arrives at the horse-farm of le Tronchet. In the field on the right horses are schooled in the art of trotting. Keep straight ahead here and follow the track through the woods for about 15 minutes, after which it turns right and descends the slope to meet the road. Turn left on the road. At the junction in about 1 kilometre, keep left (leaving the GR – it goes right here) and continue for a further 5 minutes or so.
5. Turn left on a narrow road signposted to le Vau. Just before reaching the buildings, turn right on a narrow track climbing through the woods to reach the view-point on the hill-fort. It is said that seven spires can be seen – perhaps not a lot by French standards, but at least a countable number. After a pleasant track along the wooded summit you descend steeply to the road again. Turn left and follow the road for about a kilometre, passing first an old paper-mill by the river and then an old hunting lodge on the left.
6. Arriving at the hamlet of la Gravelle, the Loir swings away to the right. On the left, take a sandy track passing between houses and climbing

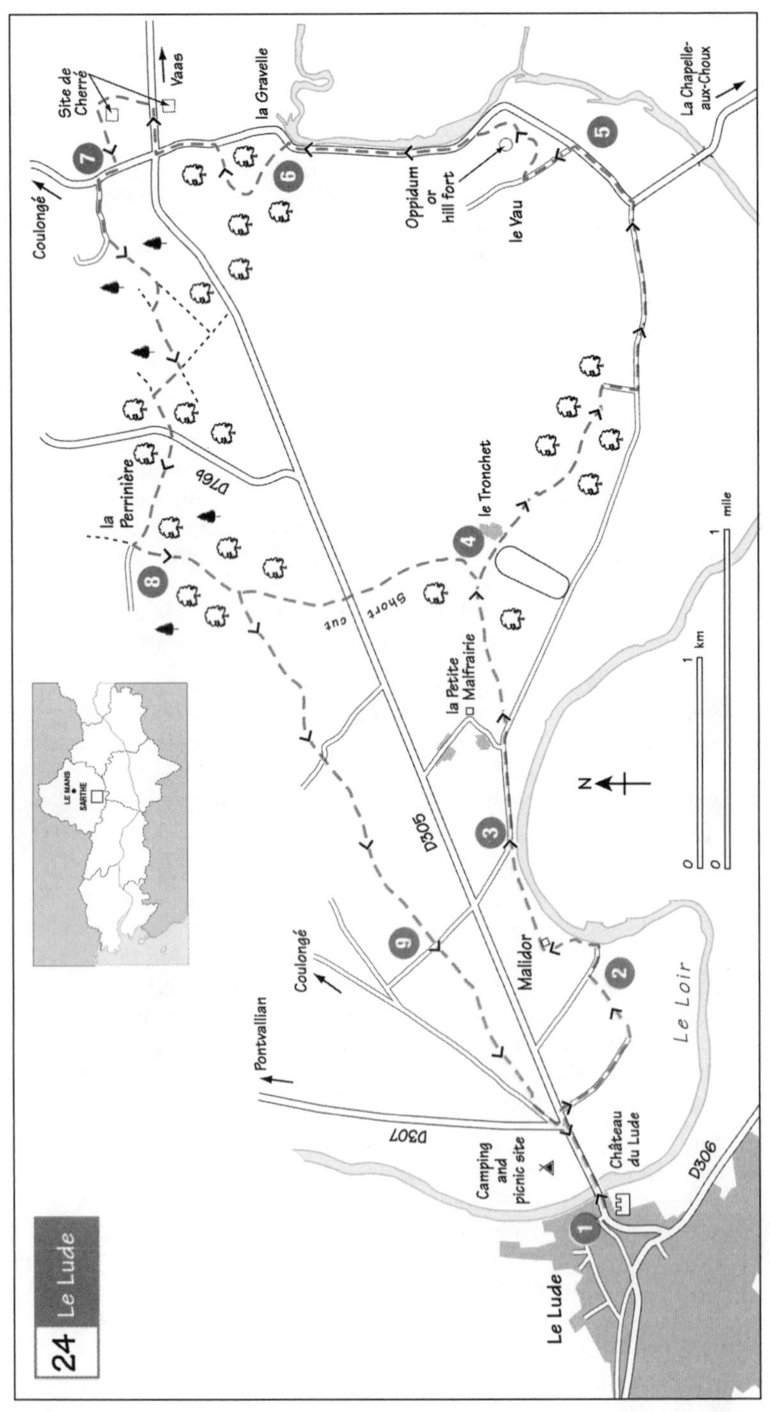
24 Le Lude
Le Lude
Camping and picnic site
Château du Lude
D306
D307
Pontvallian
Coulongé
Malidor
Le Loir
D305
la Petite Malfrairie
Short cut
le Tronchet
la Perrinière
D76
Coulongé
Site de Cherré
Vaas
la Gravelle
Oppidum or hill fort
le Vau
La Chapelle-aux-Choux
0 1 km
0 1 mile
N
LE MANS
SARTHE

Roman amphitheatre at Cherré

the slope – there is a fine view behind you along the Loir valley. The track bends around to the right and descends the hill again – part of the Roman site can be seen in the fields ahead. Reaching the road, turn left, and at the cross-roads, turn right. The entrance to the Roman site is about 200m down the road – the amphitheatre is on your left, the temple and baths on your right. When you have explored it all, walk left past the amphitheatre and alongside the woods. Turn left along the boundary of the site to reach the road again. Turn right on the road for about 100m.

7. Turn left on a tarmacked road, and, after about 200m, where the road bears right, continue ahead on a sandy track into the pine woods. Just into the trees, look out for a sharp right turn – it is waymarked. At the next junction the yellow flashes direct you left, and then, at a cross-tracks, right. At a waymarked T-junction turn left and descend to the road. Cross straight over, heading downhill into the woods.

8. At the hamlet of la Perrinnière, turn left – your route has now been joined by the GR36 (you will follow it all the way back) and there are again white on red waymarks. Continue through the wood – there is only one fork of tracks, and your route is clearly marked to the right. At the edge of the wood there are orchards and the path continues ahead to cross a little road. Keep ahead, now between fields, to reach another minor road crossing

9. Cross almost directly over and continue ahead. The track runs behind hedges to reach another minor road. Turn left and follow this to the junction with the D307 behind the garage. Turn left and follow the road past the D305 junction back into Le Lude.

## More Walks in the Area

If you are staying for some time in this area, the best investment would be the *Topoguide La Vallée du Loir à pied*. 42 walks are described between

Vendôme and Angers, some riverside, some rather more outlying. The Topoguide is published in French only, but the maps are excellent (taken from the IGN Série Bleue) and routes good enough to find their way into a Topoguide are almost always well-waymarked on the ground. You should have no difficulty following them.

Getting away from the river valley, 20km or so north-east of Le Lude the Forêt de Bercé merits some exploration. This forest boasts some magnificent stands of sessile oaks, some of these specimens over 300 years old. One longish (17km.) walk in the forest is described in the Topoguide referred to above, but you can also get details of it (and other walks) from the Office de Tourisme in Château-du-Loir, south of the forest.

Back at le Lude, the Office de Tourisme can find you a collection of relatively local walks grandly entitled *Le Pays du Loir en long, en large et en travers – Le Bassin Ludois*. This collection is well-presented, and most of the routes are waymarked, but you would need a fair knowledge of French to benefit from all the historical and other detail offered. If you want to try a short circuit to see how it works out, go along to the *Mairie* at Chenu (south-east of Le Lude) from where start 3 circuits, each of 5km Of these, the *Circuit du Viaduct* (waymarked in yellow) offers woods, troglodyte dwellings, a railway viaduct by Eiffel and lots of change of contour!

## Places of Interest Nearby

The Château du Lude has some splendid furniture and tapestries and there are formal gardens on two levels above the River Loir. Most exciting is the *Son et Lumière* and firework display held on certain evenings in high season. The château is open every day from April to September, excepting Wednesdays in April, May, June and September. Admission to the grounds is all day (with the usual extended lunch-break) – to view the interior of the château, you would need to take an afternoon guided tour.

At Vaas, upriver from Le Lude, a restored 16th-century water-mill stands by the attractive riverside. The Moulin de Rotrou can be seen in action again every afternoon in high season, and on Sundays and Bank Holidays in April, May, June, September and October. There is also a good film and a museum on the theme 'From Corn to Bread'.

# 25. Along the GR3 to Saumur

From Montsoreau, the Grande Randonnée wanders up and down the slopes, through vineyards, woodlands and quiet villages with troglodyte dwellings – and then makes a dramatic entry into Saumur with some magnificent views of the château and river.

**Grade:** Moderate

**Distance:** 17km (10½ miles). This could be extended to 25km or shortened to 11km.

**Time:** 5 hours

**Map:** IGN Série Bleue 1623 E and 1723 O

**Start and finish:** The station at Saumur. From here you catch a bus to Montsoreau and return on foot.

**How to get there:** The station is on the north side of the Loire. Cross over the river bridge, and turn left where signed to the *Gare*. There is plenty of parking and the bus stop is immediately outside the station.

**Refreshment:** Saumur and Montsoreau are both well endowed with restaurants, etc. En route, it is possible to descend to the D947 at either Parnay or Dampierre-sur-Loire for resuscitation.

**Notes:** A No. 16 bus for Montsoreau leaves the station at Saumur around 8am and again around 1pm. You can check the times at the bus stop, but be very careful – timetables are different during school holidays (*vacances scolaires*). It would probably be best to enquire at the Office de Tourisme (at the south end of the river bridge) where English can be spoken if you prefer. Leave the bus at the road junction beside the river in Montsoreau (the drivers are always helpful). If you prefer to do the trip by taxi, the OT could help you to find one. At Montsoreau, the route climbs immediately to the plateau above the river and from there you will be up and down all day. The tracks are well-surfaced and, at least in summer, there would be no particular need for walking boots – although 16km is a long way to go in trainers. The route is almost entirely exposed, so apply sun cream on a hot day – and despite possible refreshment stops, carry a good supply of water. If you want to extend the walk, get off the same bus at Fontevraud (25km); to reduce it, you could try Parnay (11km). And don't forget the camera – see below.

**Waymarking:** The whole route is on a Grande Randonnée and so is waymarked with flashes of white on red.

---

## Introduction

This walk starts and ends with a classic view of the Loire Valley, the ones you find in every guide book and holiday brochure. At the start it's the view over the vineyards to the gleaming-white Château of Montsoreau beside the Loire; at the end the Château of Saumur is in the frame, looking over the bridges and islands in the river way below. And in between, you have the Grande Randonnée, the GR3, a short but energetic section of that great pedestrian highway that escorts the river all the way from the Massif Central to the Bay of Biscay. Who knows, you may feel inspired to tackle it all when you have a few months to spare.

For some reason it always seems more exciting to follow a linear trail than to take a circular walk. For much of the time, the route here is leading

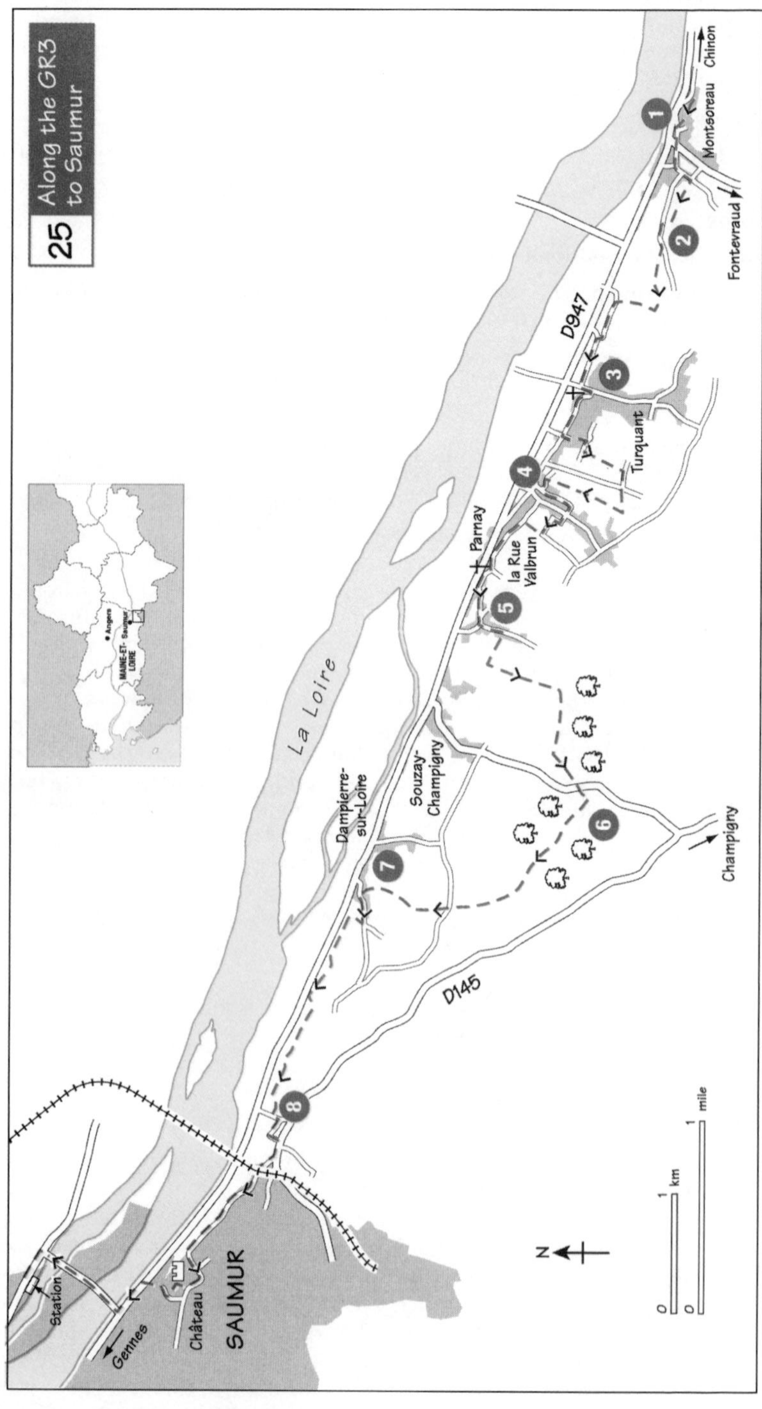
25
Along the GR3 to Saumur
La Loire
D947
D145
Montsoreau
Chinon
Fontevraud
Turquant
Parnay
la Rue Valbrun
Souzay-Champigny
Dampierre-sur-Loire
Champigny
SAUMUR
Château
Station
Gennes
MAINE-ET-LOIRE
Angers
Saumur
N
0 1 km
0 1 mile
1
2
3
4
5
6
7
8

you through extensive vineyards, the source of those fine Saumur wines. Most are family owned and the work in them is still done by hand. The vineyards frequently stretch to the horizon, yet you will often meet just a couple of individuals with a pair of secateurs setting out to tackle them. In fact, the pruning and training of shoots takes up most of the winter, after which there is the weeding and the spraying and finally the harvesting of the crop. Whenever you are walking there should be some activity to observe on these slopes and the distant views are superb. By way of variation, the path from time to time dips to a village in the valley below – Turquant with its white tufa stone church and troglodyte dwellings, and la Rue Valbrun where a *lavoir* hides by a stream. Parnay sits on top of the cliff and from its grey-spired church there is another fine view of the Loire. This is a walk with something of interest all the way – and a magnificent ending as you are led around the walls of the Château of Saumur before returning across the river bridges.

## The Walk

1. At the road junction beside the Loire in Montsoreau, turn your back to the river and walk up the road towards Fontevraud (D147). Crossing a car parking area, you pick up white on red waymarks, and follow them to the right down the Rue de l'Église. At the T-junction at its end, turn left and soon go right on the cobbled Chemin des Bournais. The narrow path climbs quite steeply and comes out in front of a vineyard. Turn right and follow the track to the road

2. To the right you have the superb and well-known view of the Château de Montsoreau beside the water. Your route here turns left along the road, passing the old windmill (Moulin de la Perruche) and heading towards a water-tower. Before reaching it, turn right on a track through the vineyards. The water-tower is now on your left. As you draw level with it, look for a track on the right – the waymarks will guide you. The track goes downhill and does a little twist to the right at the bottom, before swinging to the left again. There are fine views before the path descends steep steps, passes wine cellars and reaches a tarmacked road. Now turn left on the Rue de la Vignole. Continue on this road, passing rock caves, to reach the tufa-stone village of Turquant.

3. Turn left to the church, and then take the Rue de la Mairie, behind it on the right. Now continue on the narrow Rue du Château-Gaillard with its houses sunk into the cliff. At the end turn left and follow the waymarks uphill again. Still going uphill, turn right on the Rue de la Matinière, and 20m or so further on, turn left on a track between vineyards. Coming to a road, turn right, cross another road to a track opposite and finally bear right on a descending track with a village below you in a valley on the left.

4. Reaching the bottom, turn left and begin to ascend again. This is la Rue-Valbrun – look for the tile-roofed *lavoir* beside the stream on the right. Cross over the stream and head up through the village. Look out for an alley between houses on the right taking you up to the plateau once more. Now bear right around the edge of the vineyards and simply follow the waymarks leading you towards a steeple in the dis-

*Château de Saumur*

tance at Parnay – at one point you turn right on a little road and then bear left to reach the church. (To find a restaurant from here, go down the road on the right behind you to reach the main road – there are two restaurants at the bottom.)

5. Pass the church with its views across the valley on your right and walk downhill into the village. Turn left on the Rue Cristal and then look out for a waymarked earthen track on the right, soon climbing between vineyards. At the top bear round to the left (there are views here to the church at Souzay-Champigny) and now continue ahead through the vines, passing a vineyard enclosed by a wall (Père Cristal), crossing a road and heading for the woods. Just before reaching the trees, the route swings to the right, and you have a further 10 minutes or so walking before a sudden left turn allows you to climb to the possibly welcome shade of the woods. Cross the road and continue to the top of the hill.

6. Here your route turns left and then immediately to the right. Looking behind, it seems you can see half-way across France. You are looking east and the smoke you see comes from the nuclear power station near Chinon. Keep straight ahead, crossing tracks in the wood to reach a tarmacked road. Turn left here and then immediately right on another track. After passing through vineyards again, you descend beside a wall to the church at Dampierre. (To find a restaurant from here, continue downhill to the main road. Turn right for about 400m.)

7. At the church, turn left to go uphill again. Reaching a cross-roads, continue straight ahead and after 100m or so, turn right into an alley beside a stone wall. This climbs alongside vineyards once more and there are soon some splendid views along the river. Turn right on a tarmacked road, and, at the iron gates, left. Reaching the corner, ignore the Chemin de la Bonnenquere and continue ahead, parallel to the river. At the bottom of the road turn to the right (where are the waymarks?) and descend steeply. Continue ahead, passing steps descending further on the right, and then turn on the road, uphill between steep banks. Where the road corners left, keep straight ahead on a track beside more vines. Now you can simply follow the waymarks along the track and the views are excellent. After about 20 minutes you descend to a main road, with a water-tower above you on the hill.

8. Cross straight over the road and follow the waymarks. At the end of the alley turn left, and at the main road, go right. Here the GR36 joins you. After about 100m, go right again. Now keep ahead on the scenic Rue des Moulins – before you all the way is that classic view of the Château of Saumur with its many pepper-pot towers, perched high above the town and the graceful bridge over the Loire. The waymarks lead you across the car park and then across the bridge and around the château to the left. Leave through an archway, cross a wooden bridge and a stone bridge and bear round to the right to steps across the grass. Now descend to an alley leading to the town – you can follow the signs to the Office de Tourisme (and the occasional waymark). The pedestrian alleyway leads to an attractive square where you bear to the right. Another alley now leads you to a square with a fountain. Again turn to the right to find the riverside – where you can turn left and then cross the river bridges to reach the station.

## More Walks in the Area

If you are keen to follow the GR3 some more, the no. 16 bus continues beyond Montsoreau to Fontevraud (a further 8km.). Equip yourself with the appropriate IGN map (1723 O) and you should have no difficulty following it. On the way you will pass through Candes-St-Martin, a small town with some splendidly ancient buildings, clinging to the slope above the confluence of the Vienne and the Loire.

In the opposite direction, the GR3 heads for the little town of Gennes, just 7km downriver from Saumur. But it doesn't take the obvious route along the riverside – instead it wanders through a succession of inland villages, passing troglodyte dwellings, wine caves, lakes, churches, a priory, a roman camp and just about every other feature of interest in the area. The total distance is about 22km, and a bus service connects Gennes with Saumur – ask at the Office de Tourisme in either town for details. They can also supply you with an excellent map entitled *Massif de Milly* on which the GR is marked (in black), along with every other waymarked circuit in the area. With the aid of this map, it is easy to shorten the route by substituting sections of other circuits.

For circular walks in this area, the Office de Tourisme stocks a folder of 22 routes – and amazingly an English version is available (entitled *Around Saumur*). But be warned – in France route descriptions are usually very general, more reliance being placed on waymarking. Don't expect too much from the directions (there seem to be some thought-jumps). But the maps are reasonable and (with apologies to fluent French speakers) it can be a pleasure not to have to wrestle with the subtleties of French prose for more information.

For short walks in the area, there is a lovely series of leaflets entitled *Villages et Promenades Botaniques* (the villages are Distré, le Coudray-Macouard, Montreuil-Bellay, Rou-Marson, Louerre and Grezillé). The idea of botanical tours was just being developed in 2001, with the intention that the routes would be marked and flowers and trees labelled. Caves, *lavoirs*, churches, etc. are also described – and English makes an appearance on some of the leaflets. Ask at the Office de Tourisme in Saumur or at the *Mairie* in Distré (or any of the other villages).

## Places of Interest Nearby

There is so much to see and do around Saumur – the Office de Tourisme can find you the booklet *Saumur et sa Région*, an excellent multilingual publication. The château is open throughout the year (not Tuesdays in winter) – and the one at Montsoreau is almost (though not quite) similarly accessible. The following is just a personal selection of all that is on offer:

West of Saumur you are in the heart of troglodyte country and many visits are possible. For the originality of its owner, the underground farm of la Fosse (at Forges, north of Doué-la-Fontaine) is highly recommended. Just north of Doué, the village of Rochemenier is likewise worth a visit – even if you don't take the official tour, you can simply wander and wonder at so many subterranean dwellings. A troglodyte restaurant here specialises in *fouaces* (see Walk 22). At Dénézé-sous-Doué there are underground caves with fantastic carvings said to be more than 400 years old. The nakedness of some of the figures deemed them to be unsuitable for viewing before this current age of liberation. The caves are open daily from April to October.

Caves in the tufa also provide the ideal environment for the growing of mushrooms. Champignons de Paris were once grown in the cellars of the capital – but with the advent of the Métro in 1885, cultivation was transferred to the region around Saumur. Several mushroom caves are open to visitors, but the Musée du Champignon, on the D751 north of Saumur, also exhibits a pickled specimen of just about every known fungus. And you can end the tour in the restaurant, where mushrooms and only mushrooms are the order of the day.

On a different note, this area is also rich in prehistory. Start at the famous Dolmen of Bagneux, said to be the largest dolmen in Europe, on the southern outskirts of Saumur. Signs direct you to it – but unless you realise that this huge dolmen is actually to be found in the garden of a bar you can wander around the back streets for hours (many do!). Not surprisingly, for many years the dolmen was put to good use as a barn, before its greater potential was realised. Even so, the entry fee is minimal and you can always take the opportunity for a drink or a meal on site. The proprietor will also equip you with a photocopied leaflet directing you on a tour of all the many megalithic sites in the area – but concludes that 'even if you cannot find them, you will have seen charming landscapes'. He has a point!

# 26. Prehistory at le Thoureil

The village of le Thoureil has a picturesque setting on the banks of the Loire. In the oak woods above, menhirs and dolmens conceal themselves amid the bracken and heather – and from the heights there are some splendid views of the river.

**Grade:** Easy / moderate

**Distance:** 8km (5 miles). An extension of an extra 800 metres or so each way will allow an additional visit to the Dolmen of Bajoulière – see below.

**Time:** 2 hours walking, but allow time for viewing the megaliths. The extension will take an extra half hour or so.

**Map:** IGN Série Bleue 1622 O

**Start and finish:** The church at le Thoureil.

**How to get there:** Le Thoureil is beside the Loire, 5km north-west of Gennes. There is parking behind the church, and a larger area 100 metres away at the cross-roads.

**Refreshment:** A most attractive auberge overlooks the river at le Thoureil.

**Notes:** This pleasant short walk is largely on woodland tracks – hard-surfaced in summer, but possibly muddy out of season. There is good shade for a hot day, but you should note that the end of the walk is exposed. Finding the megaliths involves a little exploration in the woods beside the track. The Dolmen of Bajoulière is by far the most impressive in the area and it is well worth taking the extension. There are picnic tables at the site.

**Waymarking:** The route is mostly waymarked in yellow with a short section in green – just follow the text.

---

## Introduction

Le Thoureil was once a port on the Loire, a village where bargees made their home, and Dutch merchants settled to export the fine regional wines. Now it is just a quiet stone village in a splendid riverside setting, pretty enough to be named as one of *les plus beaux villages de France*. It would be easy to spend a pleasant hour or two here enjoying a drink outside the little auberge and watching the world go by. But reserve that for the end of the walk – for the moment you are hunting megaliths.

Look at any map of this region south of the Loire and you will see that it is well-sprinkled with the symbol for prehistoric remains – and that the woodland on the plateau above le Thoureil has more than its fair share. This is pleasant country for a ramble – oak, beech, chestnut and holly shade the undergrowth of bracken, heather and broom. With the fine views of the Loire at the beginning and end, you could well enjoy this route for its own sake. But for just a little more effort, there are at least three menhirs and a dolmen to be found on this walk – and that is without the seven menhirs of the Butte aux Houx, a hill where there have been many prehistoric finds, which is unfortunately private land. The extension to the walk will lead you to the remarkable Dolmen de Bijoulière, a huge megalith of around 30 tonnes, with a covering stone more than 7 metres in length. It's an impressive sight. Why did the ancients favour this place? A few thousand years later the Romans did too – they have left abundant

*Dolmen of Bajoulière*

evidence at Gennes and at Chênehutte among other places. If archaeology interests you, this is a fascinating area to explore.

## The Walk

1. From the riverside beside the church, walk up the road with the river behind you (the D156 to Louerre). After just a few metres, take the first turning on the right, a very narrow road going steeply uphill. Turn round for a good view of the Loire as you climb. At the top, bear left through some newish houses to reach a wider road. Turn right and continue climbing, passing orchards on the left and then continuing through the woods.

2. As the road swings right, take a track on the left – it is signed to the *Menhir* and waymarked in yellow. After about 400 metres, look for a rough unmarked track taking you into the woodland on the right. Not too far off the path is the massive Pierre Longue, 4.8 metres high, and curiously orientated due north. When you emerge from the undergrowth, continue along the track to reach a tarmacked road. Turn left on this road, which takes you between the orchards of Marchais-Clair and more fine woodland to the hamlet of St Gondon.

3. Where the road begins to descend in earnest, look for a tarmacked road doubling back around a house on the right. The road soon becomes a grassy track heading into the woods of the Butte aux Houx – appropriately named since there are holly bushes everywhere (*houx* = holly). The seven menhirs are hiding in the chained-off land on your left. After keeping straight ahead on this track for almost a kilometre you will pass another menhir, the Pierre de Nézan, in the undergrowth on your right. This stone nearly 3 metres in length has fallen sideways and is very well-concealed. If you reach a major track junction (Point 4), you have overshot it by about 20 metres.

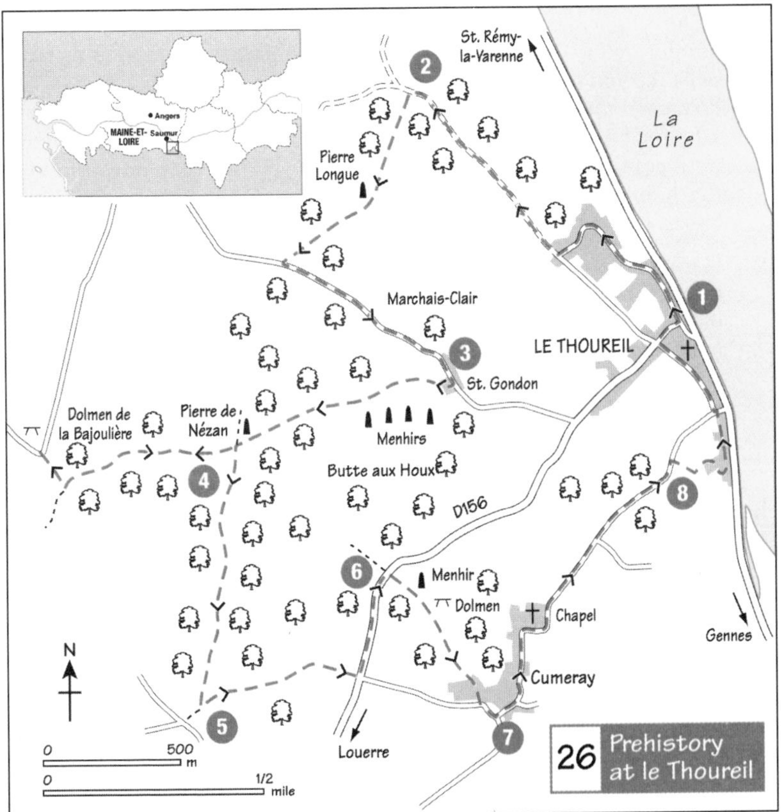


**4.** Here you are at a four-way track junction. From this point it is well worth taking the extension to the Dolmen de la Bajoulière, for which you carry on ahead on a path that soon descends along the edge of the woods. There are green waymarks now. After 10 minutes or so walking, a gravelled track is reached at the bottom of the hill. Turn right here, leave the woods and climb to a wide grassy field at a track junction. The great dolmen is straight ahead of you – and there are picnic tables if you want to take a break here before retracing your steps to the track junction at Point 4.

Arriving at this junction from the Dolmen de la Bajoulière, turn to the right (it would be left if you decided to omit the extension). Again you have a long track through the lovely forest – if you should be here in autumn you will probably meet some of the ubiquitous gatherers of edible fungi. After 15 minutes or so you emerge from the woods and have a view of the open valley ahead.

**5.** Arriving at a cross-track with a road on the right, turn sharply left to head for the trees again. This pleasant track eventually takes you to a junction with the D156. Ignore the waymarks opposite here – you are turning left up the road to seek out more megaliths. Continue up the road to the top of the hill.

**6** Here a track crosses the road. Go to the right on this track (there is the occasional green waymark), once more in woodland. After about 200 m, look for a path into the trees on the left – it leads to another upright menhir. A further 100m or so along the main track, a second side path will take you to a dolmen. This is the Dolmen of Cumeray, somewhat collapsed after the breaking of its main slab. It is said to have been adapted and used for burials as recently as Gallo-Roman times. From here continue on the main track, which will take you downhill into the hamlet of Cumeray. On reaching a tarmacked road, continue ahead to the road junction

7. Here turn left, and at another road junction in about 150 metres, continue ahead, climbing past the houses. In front of you is a chapel dating from the 17th century – it belonged to the older manor house behind. The road bends around it and then continues towards a hill ahead. Keep straight on at the road junction and continue climbing to enter the woods. The reward is at the top of the hill – a long view up the wide valley of the Loire to the suspension bridge between les Rosiers and Gennes and far beyond.

8. Opposite the second house on the left, turn right alongside a hedge and descend on the grassy track. Coming to a house at the bottom, swing left on a grassy track and then for a second time, left on an earthen track running behind the houses above the road and river. The track crosses a small road and continues past the cemetery. Turn right on the Rue des Gabares to return to the church.

## More Walks in the Area

If you want to walk more in this area you must get hold of a truly excellent map entitled *Sentiers de Randonnées – Massif de Milly* – it is on sale at the Office de Tourisme in Gennes (and elsewhere) for just a few francs. On this map are drawn the many waymarked circuits in the area. The map is clear and easy to follow and the circuits are well-waymarked on the ground. On the reverse is just a little French text for each walk, describing the features of interest – if you can manage it, so much the better.

If the prehistory on this walk has appealed to you, the best follow-up is probably the 'yellow circuit' starting from Saugré just outside Dénézé-sous-Doué. On this 10km walk you will visit three more dolmens. Other features are a still-functional *lavoir* and some inhabited troglodyte dwellings reminiscent of a previous age. When you have finished the walk, don't miss the amazing sculptured caves in Dénézé – see Walk 25 at Saumur for details.

Another nearby village worth visiting is Saint-Georges-des-Sept-Voies with its ancient priory church. From here a 10km 'blue circuit' is marked on the *Massif de Milly* map – the route takes you past the well-preserved Dolmen de la Forêt and passes through the village of Sarré with its working water-mill and lavoir still in use. The bonus here is a visit to the very curious *Hélice Terrestre d'Orbière* – just follow the signs into the village. The *hélice* is a huge spiral sculpture in two parts. The 'internal' part is a series of curving, surrealistically-carved and lit tunnels cut into the soft rock; the 'exterior' is open to the sky, a bank of spiral terraces with strange concrete sculptures. The creator of all this is happy to give you his explanation.

## Places of Interest Nearby

If you are still keen to pursue the megaliths, there are two huge dolmens nearby that are compulsory viewing. The first is the Dolmen de la Madeleine, close to the Doué road south of Gennes, a vast sepulchre where a bread oven was installed in the 19th century! Even larger is the 5000-year-old Dolmen de Bagneux, just south of Saumur. The stones here are so gigantic that you wonder how they could possibly be moved –it appears they were rolled in on smaller stones and tipped into deep pits to get them upright. The dolmen is well worth a visit, but it can be a little tricky to find – see Walk 25, Saumur.

Gennes was an important town in Roman times. Close by the Dolmen de la Madeleine is an amphitheatre dating from around the 2nd century AD, once the scene of combats and chariot races. Guided tours are available every day in July and August and on Sundays from April to September. Just upriver at Chênehutte, the site of a Roman camp and a temple can be viewed by arrangement – contact an Office de Tourisme for details. A short red-waymarked circuit of 3 or 4km starting from the riverside at Chênehutte will take you past the site (again, it's on the *Massif du Milly* map)

St Mathurin-sur-Loire (downstream, opposite St Rémy-la-Varenne) is another classical Loire-side village, protected from the caprices of the river by a high bank (*levée*). The old station here is currently being converted into *La Maison de la Loire* where you will be able to learn all about the river and the history of this region

## From the Source to the Sea

Continuing downstream from le Thoureil, you have initially a riverside drive, followed by the villages of St Rémy-la-Varenne and Blaison-Gohier on the slopes. Cross the river to Angers at your peril – it's big and busy, the sort of place where you find yourself always in the wrong lane or wanting to go in the opposite direction but unable to turn. The château is striking with its alternating bands of stone, but it is relatively empty inside apart from the long dimly-lit hall containing the 14th-century Tapestry of the Apocalypse. Across the river is a contrasting museum of contemporary tapestry (Musée Jean-Lurçat). If you forego these delights and stay south of the river it is easy to remain on the D751. At Rochefort-sur-Loire you are on the edge of the *Corniche Angevine*, where a ridge of hills with spectacular views divides the valley of the Layon from that of the Loire. If you have time, stop and take Walk 28 – or at very least, divert into the Layon valley with its pretty villages and sample the rich local wine. Continuing along the Corniche road, you will pass the memorial and viewpoint at La Haie Longue before arriving at Chalonnes beside the river again. As you reach the town, it's worth taking a sharp left turn beside the lake and driving to the top of the hill for the panorama (walk up a short track on the right at the top).

It is always a matter of opinion, but the stretch from here to Nantes is quite possibly the prettiest and most interesting part of the Loire Valley since you were in the mountains. Montjean-sur-Loire has a lovely church and square overlooking the river – and, down on the quay, the classic square-sailed Montjeannaise, waits to take visitors out among the islands of the Loire. A riverside road takes you on to St Florent-le-Veil – from the old abbey church on its bluff above the river you can enjoy more fine views. The D751 now turns inland. A scenic and winding road, it will bring you to the fascinating town of Champtoceaux for the penultimate walk in this series.

# 27. A château in the valley of the Sarthe

Crossed by three rivers, the low-lying region north of Angers is particularly attractive and is well-known for its bird population and wild flowers. A good starting point for exploration is this easy ramble from the picturesque riverside at Cheffes, passing the fairy-tale château of Plessis-Bourré.

**Grade:** Easy

**Distance:** 12.5km (7¾ miles)

**Time:** 3½ hours

**Map:** IGN Série Bleue 1521 O and 1521 E

**Start and finish:** The church at Cheffes-sur-Sarthe.

**How to get there:** From Angers, take the D52 north to Tiercé, then turn west across the River Sarthe to Cheffes. There is parking beside the church.

**Refreshment:** There are one or two bar/cafés in Cheffes, but nothing on the route (apart from a seasonal kiosk selling ice-creams and drinks beside the lake at la Grande Maison).

**Notes:** This is a very easy route on good tracks – but note that this countryside is subject to flooding and the tracks can be muddy, especially out of season. There is little shade, so take suitable precautions on a hot day. The Château du Plessis-Bourré is open to visitors most afternoons of the year – see below.

**Waymarking:** The route is waymarked in mauve throughout – not the most prominent of colours.

---

## Introduction

North of Angers is a unique area known as the *Basses Vallées Angevines* – the Low Valleys of Anjou. This is a land of rivers – here the Loir flows into the Sarthe and the Sarthe joins the Mayenne to form the short River Maine, itself soon emptying into the Loire. This is a land that knows the rhythm of the seasons. With the first rains of winter the rivers begin to swell and spill across the fields; by the end of that season, the whole wide valley may be 'white' with water. Just how much land disappears under the water varies from year to year – and is said to be at the behest of the 'spirit of the water', personified in pagan times by a dragon. Several churches in the area are dedicated to St George. In spring the waters recede and the pastures that have been covered for several months become rich grassland, speckled with many-coloured wild flowers. Several rare species are found in the *basses vallées* – and the fields of pink fritillaries are a famous sight. With the flowers come the insects, and with them the birds – some just passing on migration, some to nest here. In July the grass is cut, and the pastures are given over to grazing cattle and horses for the autumn before the rains return. This fascinating area is not exactly on the tourist trail, but it does have its own Grande Randonnée, a path of 80km, wandering along the banks and visiting most of the lovely riverside villages. A handful of circular walks also offer a chance to explore.

The route of this walk is unusual in that it is said to be passable all year round. Even so, in the floods of 1995, the village of Cheffes, where the walk starts, became an island in a huge lake – choose your time carefully.

*Beside the Sarthe at Cheffes*

The route is simply a wander along the lanes and tracks between the low-lying fields. The highlight is undoubtedly the shining-white turreted Château of Plessis-Bourré with its moat and draw-bridges, but you can also enjoy the lovely riverside at Cheffes, the manor of les Grandines with its dovecote, the lake at le Grand Maison and the elegant horses at the stud of la Rousselière.

## The Walk

1. Facing the church at Cheffes, go through an archway on the right and turn left on an alleyway leading down to the riverside. Continue on the path along the grassy banks of the river until you reach the water-purifying station. Turn right on to the track that runs alongside, and then meeting the gravelled track, turn left. There are waymarks of a GRP here (yellow on red). Follow the track around the manor of Les Grandines where a splendid chêne-vert (holm-oak) shades the path and a circular dovecote stands in the field opposite. Continue to the main road, at a cross-roads known as the Croix-Mahé.

2. Here join the road ahead to maintain the same direction. In about 200m, the road bends to the left – look here for a broad track on the right (it is waymarked in mauve on the metal fender – but now you will see the problems of using this particular colour!) Keeping on this track for a few minutes, you meet the D74. Cross straight over and continue as far as the second electricity post. Turning left here, you will see a bank in front of you – either go to the left or keep ahead over the bank to reach the lakeside. You are now in the grounds of La Grande Maison, a camping site and water-sports centre in summer. Walk along beside the attractive lake, passing the farm and the buildings of the centre. A little farther along, you reach a parking area and, through it, a tarmacked road

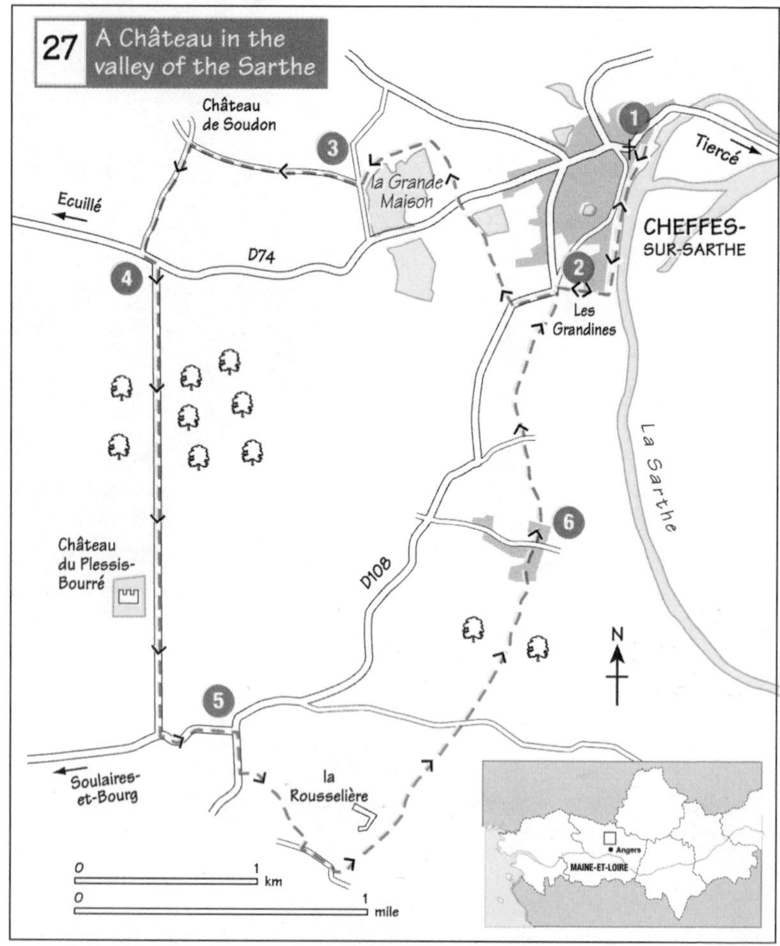


3. Cross over this road to a narrow road virtually opposite and continue on this for about 15 minutes, with views to the Château of Soudon on the hill on your right. If you were thinking this route is not well waymarked, you are in for a surprise – at a T-junction before a gate to the château, you have an impressive signpost. Turn left here in the direction of Ecuillé and continue to the main road.

4. Turn left on this road and then take the first road on the right, signposted to the Château du Plessis-Bourré. This long straight road soon enters woodland, and after about 20 minutes walking, you arrive at the gate to the château. There is an excellent view of it from the road – moat, towers, turrets and drawbridges. Continue to the end of the road where there is another fine signpost – turn left on the mauve route. In a few minutes you arrive at a road junction

5. Turn right here, signposted to la Rousselière. After about 200m, take a track on the left running between hedges. Coming out to a road junction beside a farm, turn to the left across the front of the house. As the road bears right, take a broad grassy track on the left – you have now joined the GRP again and the waymarks are yellow on red. Passing la Rousselière on the left you can admire the thoroughbreds in the

fields around. Continue across a narrow tarmacked road, after which the track becomes muddy as it passes a residence with a huge pond on the left. The track narrows as it passes through the woods and soon arrives at a cross-roads in a hamlet.

6. Cross straight over. At the next cross-road, go left and then immediately right on a grassy track. There are glimpses of a distant lake on the right as the track bends and soon arrives again at the cross-roads of la Croix-Mahé. Turn sharp right here to retrace your steps to the riverside at Cheffes.

## More Walks in the Area

The key to walking in this area is a Topoguide entitled *Les Basses Vallées Angevines à pied (Ref. P492)*. To quote the *Mairie* in Cheffes, 'if you have that, you have everything'. What you will have is a comprehensive description of the 80km Randonnée du Pays (it would take about 4 days – there are suggestions for lodging, eating, etc.) and maps and directions (in French) for 21 waymarked circular walks. The route here is one of them, and has the merit of being passable virtually throughout the year. Others have limitations in this respect but are nevertheless excellent rambles.

One of the most popular hikes is the 16km 'green route' that follows the right bank of the Sarthe from Briollay to Cheffes and then returns on the other side. There is plenty of opportunity to view the wildfowl on the marshes – but of course the path is subject to flooding in winter.

Cantenay-Epinard has a most attractive riverfront, this time on the Mayenne. Three routes are described from here, each starting at the car park beside the river. If you just have a short time to spare, take the 7km route that circles the higher ground between the Sarthe and the Mayenne. The flood meadows are always alongside you – and a splendid wooden hide has been built in the woods to enable you to watch the bird-life. Take your binoculars – and a bird book in English.

The Topoguide starts with a walk at Bouchemaine, a place aptly named since it sits at the confluence of the Maine and the Loire. The starting point of the route is actually just south of Bouchemaine at the little old village of la Pointe, once a port on the river. This is a most attractive spot, very popular with the population of Angers for their Sunday morning strolls. The walk described is 14km in length, initially on the GR3 along the riverside, and then rambling home across country.

If it is the riverside section of this latter walk that appeals most to you, consider something different. Leave your car at Savennières, downstream of Bouchemaine – from here you can catch a train to Angers (OT at Bouchemaine or Angers should be able to help you with times). At Angers, the station is not far from the riverside. Cross the river bridge (the Topoguide walk no. 3 will show you a route) and pick up the white on red waymarks of the GR3E. You have only to follow it beside first the Maine and then the Loire to return to Savennières – a total distance of 13km.

## Places of Interest Nearby

The Basses Vallées Angevines is an exceptional bird-watching site. The logo of the area is a corncrake, of which there are generally around 300 breeding pairs in season. More information on excursions, hides etc. can be obtained from the Ligue pour la Protection des Oiseaux, 84, Rue Blaise-Pascal, Angers. And if you would simply like to cruise the rivers at your leisure, a trip boat offers excursions of various lengths (summer only) between Angers and the Abbey of Solemnes – ask at an Office de Tourisme for details

Angers is renowned for its château, its tapestries and its Cointreau (with apologies to everything else). The huge 13th-century château with its prominent bands of grey schist and white limestone dominates all else – the walk around its walls is almost a kilometre and there are splendid views of the river. The château is home to the 14th-century Apocalypse Tapestries. 103 metres of woven cloth once used for anything from carpets to horse blankets, the intricate tapestries are now rescued and preserved for posterity in a darkened dust-free room with a more than eerie air about it. The Apocalypse Tapestries were first seen by the artist Jean Lurçat back in the 1930s, and were the inspiration for his almost-but-not-quite-as-long *Chant du Monde* tapestry. This magnificent piece of work is housed in the Musée Jean Lurçat (an old hospital) across the river, and depicts modern scenes from the holocaust to space travel.

As for the Cointreau, the recipe for this orange liqueur was found (or invented) by the family of that name who lived in Angers in the middle of the 19th century. The present *Espace Cointreau* is located in the St Barthélémy district, north-east of Angers. You can take guided tours of the distillery all the year round (check with OT for times) and, yes, you get to taste the product.

Finally, back to the Château du Plessis-Bourré. Jean Bourré, who built the beautiful but fortress-like château in the 15th century, was a favourite minister of Louis XI. He was also a passionate alchemist, and had the ceiling of the *Salle des Gardes* painted with a series of symbolic, mysterious and sometimes humorous scenes – they may be the most memorable part of the visit. The château is open throughout the year with the exception of December and January – check times with an Office de Tourisme. You can opt for a guided tour or simply a wander through the grounds.

# 28. The Corniche Angevine

A long ridge of vine-clad hills separates the valley of the Layon from that of the Loire. Old villages, windmills and splendid views are with you all the way on this walk – but for a touch of extra magic, go along in autumn when the vines of the Coteau du Layon blaze colours of red and gold.

**Grade:** Moderate

**Distance:** 15km (9½ miles)

**Time:** 5 hours

**Map:** The walk crosses several IGN Série Bleue maps. As an alternative, get hold of a free walkers' map of the area, *Les Randonnées autour de la Corniche Angevine,* available at the Office de Tourisme in Chalonnes (and elsewhere). It hasn't the detail, but it's all you need for the walk.

**Start and finish:** The church at Rochefort-sur-Loire. From here you catch a bus to Chalonnes-sur-Loire and return on foot.

**How to get there:** Rochefort is about 15km west of Angers and south of the Loire on the D751. The church is in a square just south of the main road, where there is plenty of parking space. The bus stop is right beside the church.

**Refreshment:** Both Rochefort and Challones are well-supplied with bars and restaurants. There is also an attractive auberge at La Haie Longue, near the mid-point of the route.

**Notes:** This walk is reasonably energetic by Loire standards, although there is only one real climb (to the Moulins d'Ardenay) and all the tracks are good and exceptionally well waymarked. Nevertheless, you would probably appreciate stout footwear. The route is almost entirely exposed (hence the views), and you would be foolish to attempt it without a hat and sun-cream on a hot summer's day. In winter, the part of the route beside the Layon could be flooded – as an alternative, follow the road (and the GR) between Points 2 and 3. The bus stop for the start of this walk is right against the church at Rochefort and there is usually an early morning bus and another around midday – you would need to check at an Office de Tourisme or on the bus stop for details, and watch out for variations at times of vacances scolaires (school holidays). Leave the bus in the square at Chalonnes.

**Waymarking:** All the walking routes in the Corniche Angevine are waymarked in yellow. To avoid confusion, there is also a signpost at every intersection of routes – very impressive.

---

## Introduction

This walk starts with a bus ride that is a treat in itself – the bus takes the back road through the valley of the Layon passing through the lovely villages of St Aubin-de-Luigné and Chaudefonds-sur-Layon. On the way you will get a first glimpse of the vineyards that yield the smooth sweet wines of the *Coteau du Layon*. Rochefort is the centre of this wine-growing region, and produces three wines of note – Rochefort, Chaume and the superior Quarts de Chaume. They are said to be at their best served chilled as an aperitif and apparently make the perfect accompaniment to paté de foie gras. One curious feature you may notice – from the bus and

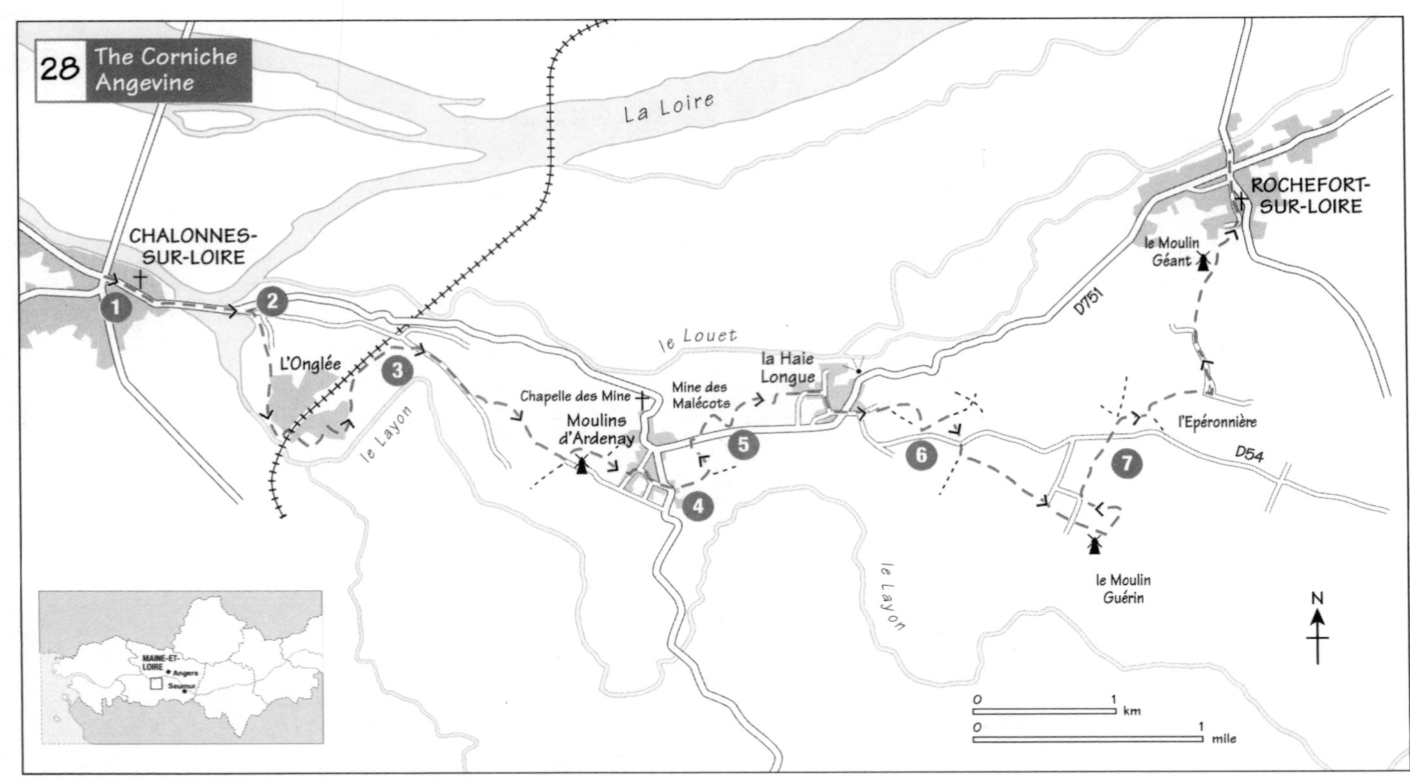
28
The Corniche Angevine
La Loire
CHALONNES-SUR-LOIRE
ROCHEFORT-SUR-LOIRE
le Moulin Géant
D751
le Louet
L'Onglée
la Haie Longue
Mine des Malécots
Chapelle des Mine
Moulins d'Ardenay
le Layon
l'Epéronnière
D54
le Layon
le Moulin Guérin
1
2
3
4
5
6
7
N
0 1 km
0 1 mile
MAINE-ET-LOIRE
Angers
Saumur

again when walking – is the custom of planting an occasional rose at the end of a row of vines. This is a tradition all over France, but is particularly upheld here. Its origins have been lost in time, but a practical suggestion is that mildew on the rose warned the vine-grower to spray his crop (although, in fact, the vines would probably have got the mildew first).

Arriving in Chalonnes, you are ready to walk back along the Corniche Angevine, the ridge of hills that separates the Loire and Layon valleys. These hills seem to have been overlaid with a patchwork carpet of vineyards that covers their every undulation. In autumn, around the time of the harvest, the colours are stunning. Although the highest point here has an altitude of less than 100 metres, there are splendid views into the wide valley of the Loire and the more intimate one of the Layon. The hills are capped by windmills – Ardenay, Géant and notably, the Moulin Guérin, whose top floor is now graced with a fine ceramic *table d'orientation*. At another viewpoint there is a memorial to an early aviator, René Gasnier, who in 1908 flew 500 metres, 5 metres in the air above the prairie below. Tucked into the folds of the hills, the old stone villages provide a contrast to the vineyards – and the auberge at la Haie Longue could offer a welcome break.

The paths of the Corniche Angevine are exceptionally well waymarked and there are several trails across the hills and through both river valleys. If you enjoy this walk, there are plenty more to choose from.

## The Walk

1. The bus will drop you in the square at Chalonnes. Walk down to the bottom right-hand corner (passing the *Mairie*) and leave on the Rue Fleury. At the main road, turn right and continue alongside the road, which soon reaches the Loire and then crosses the bridge over the mouth of the Layon. Immediately after this bridge, take the road on the right beside a lake.

2. The road continues ahead uphill, but you keep right and follow a yellow-waymarked path around the edge of the lake. Soon you will reach the first signpost beside the track – at this moment you want to follow the direction of route no. 2, the Vallée du Layon. The track follows the river and then passes under a railway bridge on the right. Turn immediately right here, and then left between the fields to reach the village of l'Onglée. With the bus shelter in front of you, turn right. Coming to the riverside again, bear left on the Rue de l'Écluse and follow the path, which now has a pleasant view of the water meadows with their grazing Charolais cattle. Reaching a plantation of poplars, you join a tarmacked road.

3. Turn right here, picking up the white on red waymarks of the GR3. After a line of pollarded oaks and ashes, look for a path on the left, soon heading uphill – it is well waymarked. Continue to climb past the vineyard towards some old windmills, the Moulins d'Ardenay at the top of the hill. Reaching the signpost, continue ahead, now following the *liaison* to the *Corniche Angevine* route. There are views of both the Loire and the Layon valleys at this point. The track bears left and then right across the front of the mills. Coming up to the village, you reach another of those signposts – from here on you will always follow the direction of *Corniche Angevine* to Rochefort. At a tarmacked

road, turn left and then continue to follow the excellent waymarking through the lovely old village. At its end you descend to the main road, where a sign tells you the altitude here is 75 metres.

**4.** Turn right here, and in about 40 m, turn sharp left on the Rue de la Richardière. Continue down the broad gravelled track through the vineyards. In a couple of minutes, at the bottom of a descent, take a waymarked track on the left (leaving the GR to go ahead). This soon brings you to the main road, where you turn right for 20 metres or so and then find a track on the left. Here you are above an old coal mine and to the left you can see the elaborate Chapelle des Mines, built in the 19th century to serve the new mining community. Now just a few spoil heaps remain. At a wall, the track turns back – but you could first glance over for a view of the valley below.

**5.** Reaching the main road, do not join it but again turn left on a waymarked track through the vineyards which brings you to the village of La Haie Longue. At the second signpost, turn to the right on the Rue René Gasnier (views of his monument across the valley) and follow the waymarks to the main road and the Auberge de la Corniche. Now you can see the Gasnier monument and its viewpoint along the road on your left – it's worth going along for the view over the Louet, one of the *boires* of the Loire. Return to the road junction and now turn to the left (straight over if you didn't go along to the monument). At the fork in about 100m, go left on the Chemin des Essarts. At a track junction go straight on and at the next junction, turn to the right – it's all clearly waymarked.

**6.** Just before reaching the main road, take a track on the left. Now you have your one chance to get lost on this walk – don't take it. Ahead of you are some woods and just before them, a waymarked post directs you to turn right. You may well wonder where. The track you want is actually about 15 metres behind you, going uphill between vineyards. Reaching the main road, cross to a road opposite. At a cross-tracks in about 150m, turn left. The path winds around the edge of a vineyard and continues alongside the hedge. Continue following the waymarks straight ahead at every junction to reach the Moulin Guérin. On its top floor is a splendid ceramic *table d'orientation* – you can see the route you have followed across the Corniche and far beyond. The path you now want goes on past the Moulin and then turns to the left. At another splendid signpost, you turn left again and continue through the vines to a farm. Here you turn to the right, after which the excellent waymarks will lead you ahead beside and through more vineyards to the D54.

**7.** Cross the D54 to a gravelled road opposite, and at the junction past the farm, turn right. Here the Loire is ahead of you, with Angers on the horizon. At the next junction, turn right towards the manor house of l'Éperonnière, and then continue following the waymarks to reach it. Turn left and follow a gravelled track to a tarmacked road, where there is again a signpost. Turn left here and walk downhill to the bend in the road. Here go right then left to maintain your direction through the vineyards, still aiming for the Moulin Géant on the hill ahead. Nearing the bottom of the hill, leave the vines for a grassy path on the left, taking you over the stream on a stepping stone. Climbing again, you come up to the Moulin Géant and there is a fine view of the church in Rochefort. The path swings right and brings you to a tarmacked road. Follow the waymarks right, and then down an alley on the left, to reach a road descending to the church.

*Church and vineyards at Rochefort*

## *More Walks in the Area*

If you have the map *Les Randonnées autour de la Corniche Angevine* (see above) you will see that there are 12 suggested – and very well waymarked – routes in this area, along with liaison paths joining them together. There are several circuits that might interest you – the two short walks from the very pretty village of St Aubin-de-Luigné, or perhaps one of the routes on the water meadows between the Loire and the Louet. The map could also be used to shorten this walk – you could leave the bus at either St Aubin-de-Luigné or Chaudefonds-sur-Layon and connect with this route.

A few kilometres up the valley from St Aubin-de-Luigné is another delightful village, Beaulieu-sur-Layon. This is the starting point for a fairly dramatic walk by the standards of this region, a 10km route that takes in forest, vineyards and the steep-sided river valley. It is the descent into the latter that provides the excitement. This valley was the scene of one of the bloodiest battles of the Vendéen War – a plaque on the old bridge, the Pont Barré, commemorates the defeat of 25,000 republican troops by a mere 3,000 Vendéen rebels in September 1793. You can find the route of this walk (and around 30 more circuits) on a map with the title *Sentiers de Randonnées Pédestres – Boucle 'Coteaux et villages en Layon'*. The Office de Tourisme at Beaulieu (at the western end of the main road) should have it in stock.

Thinking of another linear walk, the GR 3D winds its way up the Layon valley – on the map *Sentiers de Randonnées Pédestres* referred to above, it is shown as a black line. Its course between Beaulieu and Thouarcé (approx.15km.) would make an interesting day's ramble, passing through

Rablay-sur-Layon and Faye-d'Anjou for resuscitation en route. Grande Randonnées are reliably well-waymarked, and always take you to the most interesting features of an area – this one passes *lavoirs* and windmills, a château, a cave and many viewpoints. A bus service connects Beaulieu and Thouarcé – the Office de Tourisme at Beaulieu should be able to help you with times.

## Places of Interest Nearby

After all those vineyards, you will probably want to find out more about the production of wine. The *Musée de la Vigne et du Vin d'Anjou* at St Lambert-du-Lattay should provide some of the answers – a printed text (available in English) will guide you round rooms of old tools and wine-presses and tell you some of the history of viticulture in this region before bringing you to the present day. An added extra is the humorous *Salle de l'Imaginaire du Vin*, where, among other diversions, you can take a smell test to assess your potential as a wine-expert.

Back beside the Loire, go downstream a little to the old town of Montjean. Here, in summer, you can choose either a trip boat or (on Sunday afternoons only) the Montjeannaise, a traditional *gabare* under sail, for an excursion on the river. Not far from the quay, the *Écomusée de la Loire Angevine* recounts the history of navigation on the Loire, when boats like the Montjeannaise brought stone, slate, wine and hemp down the river.

It is worth exploring the villages of the Layon valley – Chaudefonds has a fine old *lavoir* and a warm spring, the *fontaine de la Madeleine*. At St Aubin-de-Luigné, the *Mairie* is housed in a presbytery dating from the 16th century – and you can take boats out on the river. Rochefort-sur-Loire has a very pleasant riverside beach where bathing is supervised in July and August – you might like to take your costume to cool off at the end of the day.

# 29. From the Evre to the Loire at St Florent-le-Vieil

At St Florent de Vieil, the abbey church sits high on a cliff with splendid views. This walk descends to a pretty path beside the River Evre and returns on the Grande Randonnée along the banks of the Loire.

**Grade:** Easy

**Distance:** 15km (9½ miles)

**Time:** 4 hours

**Map:** IGN Série Bleue 1322 E and 1422 O

**Start and finish:** The abbey church at St Florent-le-Vieil.

**How to get there:** St Florent-le-Vieil is on the D751 south of the Loire, about mid-way between Angers and Nantes. Follow signs uphill to the Office de Tourisme – the abbey church is close by and there is some parking in the square. Should it be full, there is a huge car park at the nearby Ferme des Coteaux – follow the signs.

**Refreshment:** There are bars and restaurants at St Florent, but none on the route – although you could divert to a restaurant at Marillais, a few hundred metres off the route.

**Notes:** This is an easy walk through fairly flat low-lying countryside south of the Loire. For much of the walk you are on a riverside path, either beside the River Evre or beside the Loire itself. Note that both paths could be muddy and possibly flooded in winter. In high summer, the ground is dry and you could probably get away with trainers on your feet. What you will need then is sun-cream – most of this route is exposed to the elements.

**Waymarking:** The route is waymarked in blue throughout. The path beside the Loire is on the GR3 and so is also waymarked in white on red.

---

## Introduction

At St Florent-le-Vieil, the old houses cling to the slopes of Mont-Glonne, a bluff rising 45 metres above the Loire. In the 8th century a Benedictine monastery was established on its summit. Later, the Vikings came, and made the island of Batailleuse in the river below the base for their raids upstream. The monks retreated – but their monastery remained and survived through the years. The abbey church you see today dates from the 18th century.

From the tree-shaded square before the church there is a fine panorama over the valley of the Loire. This square played its part in the tragic story of the Vendéen Uprising – it was here in March 1793 that the Vendéen peasants first gathered in mass rebellion against the new Republic's execution of the king, its persecution of Catholic priests and finally its demands for conscription. They enlisted as one of their leaders a nobleman by the name of Bonchamps. In the resulting battle the Republicans were driven from St Florent, and over the long summer, most of the Vendée as far as Angers and Saumur changed hands. In October the Vendéens were defeated at Cholet. They retreated to St Florent to cross the Loire – and thought to execute 5000 Republican prisoners held in the abbey church there. Bonchamps had been wounded at Cholet and was

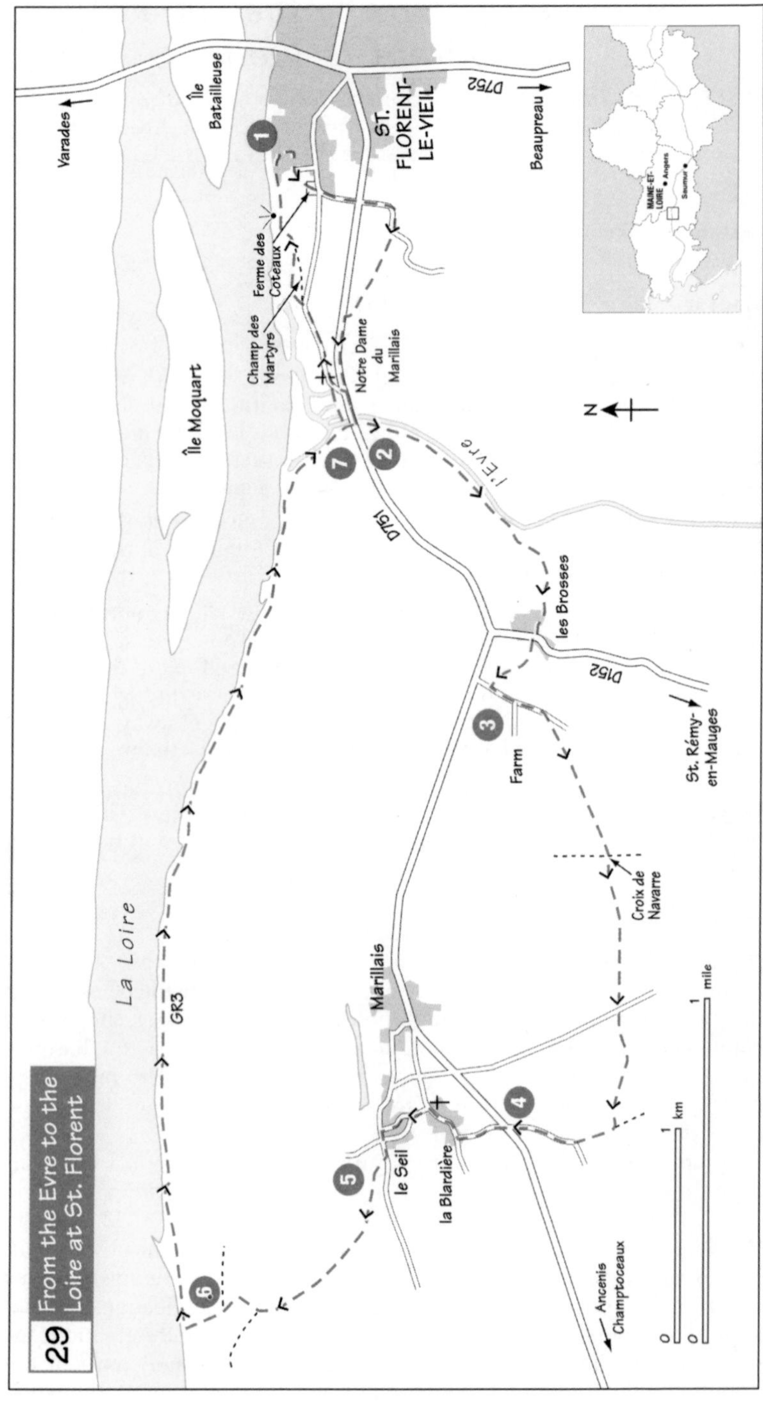
29
From the Evre to the Loire at St. Florent
Varades
Île Batailleuse
Île Moquart
La Loire
GR3
ST. FLORENT-LE-VIEIL
D752
Beaupreau
Ferme des Coteaux
Champ des Martyrs
Notre Dame du Marillais
l'Evre
D751
les Brosses
D152
St. Rémy-en-Mauges
Farm
Croix de Navarre
Marillais
le Seil
la Blardière
Ancenis
Champtoceaux
N
0
1 km
0
1 mile
MAINE-ET-LOIRE
Angers
Saumur
1
2
3
4
5
6
7

dying – but, hearing of the intention, almost with his last breath asked for the prisoners to be spared. Among them was the father of the sculptor David d'Angers. In gratitude for this act of clemency he later fashioned a marble figure with raised hand for Bonchamps tomb – it can be seen in a side chapel of the church. The Republicans went on to punish the Vendéen 'whites' without mercy. In December of the same year they held 2000 Vendéen prisoners in the same church – they were given no reprieve, but rather led out to be shot in a field now known as the Champ des Martyrs. You will pass the site with its memorial on your walk.

This has been a long story, but it would be a pity to walk at St Florent without knowing some of its history, and you may well want to take a look at Bonchamps tomb or visit the nearby Museum of the Vendéen War before leaving the town. The walk you are taking from St Florent is a very pleasant and undemanding rural ramble. It sets out along the banks of the Evre, a slow-flowing and shallow river on its way to join the Loire. Flat-bottomed punts and rowing boats line the banks and can be hired in summer. From here, paths through the low-lying countryside bring you to the Loire itself. The GR3 follows it closely and you have a long stretch in which to admire the river. In summer there are sandy banks and islands – and curious long breakwaters reaching into the flow from either shore. These are the *épis*, a feature of this lower part of the river – they were set up in the early part of last century with the purpose of stabilising the banks and encouraging the deposit of sand. The walk ends with views of Mont-Glonne from the river, stepping stones across the Evre – and the tale of a donkey.

## The Walk

1. From the abbey church, follow the signs beside the *Mairie* to the *Ferme des Coteaux*. Cross the car park, walk through the courtyard of the farm (behind the toilets) and leave through the archway to reach the Rue des Coteaux. Walk downhill beside the wall and at the bottom, cross the D751 to a road opposite. Follow this as far as a left-hand bend – here you keep straight ahead on a gravelled track. In front of you is the lovely chapel of Notre Dame du Marillais, a place of pilgrimage. Keep right of a wall to meet the main road again. Turn left along the pavement to pass the chapel and cross the bridge over the Evre.

2. Having crossed the bridge, turn left immediately to a track alongside the Evre. Pleasantly shaded by poplars, the riverside path becomes narrower and less well surfaced. After about 20 minutes walking, the track bends away to the right and climbs a bank to reach the village of les Brosses. The blue waymarks lead you across the D152 to a grassy track almost opposite.

3. Reaching another narrow road, the main road is on your right, but you turn left towards a big farm. Pass the farm on your right, and immediately, at the fork, go right. You are now on a wide track between fields. Continue ahead to the Croix de Navarre, where a tree is surrounded by huge rocks. Here a path crosses, but you keep to the main track and soon cross directly over a narrow road to the village on your right. After another 20 minutes or so, the track bears right and joins a minor road. Keep right here to meet the main road

4. Cross straight over the main road and continue ahead into the village of la Blardière. Go right at the T-junction and, coming up to a little chapel, left on the Rue des Gabelous (Road of the Customs Officers). Walk downhill on this, now in the village of le Seil. Where the road swings left, keep straight ahead to meet a wider road at a T-junction. Turn left.

5. Pass the cross-roads and after about 100 metres, take a narrow road on the right. Its surface soon becomes gravelled as it heads down towards the Loire. At a prominent fork with lots of confusing waymarks, go right. Where this track now bends right, go ahead between the poplars to reach the banks of the Loire.

6. Turn right on the riverside path and now pick up the white on red waymarks of the GR3 which will accompany you all the way back to St Florent. The riverside path is pleasant and obvious, allowing you to enjoy views of villages across the water, gulls and cormorants on the islands and *épis* and finally the *abbatiale* on its cliff high above the river. After about an hour, the path bends inland beside the Evre.

7. At the barrage you have a choice determined by the height of the river – continue ahead, cross the river bridge and turn left, or at low water, turn left across the barrage and continue on the stepping stones to reach the same point. Pass the chapel of Notre Dame du Marillais on your right and continue for a further 200 metres or so. Here turn left – the Champs des Martyrs is on your right with its monument topped by a Sacred Heart, the emblem of the Vendéens. You can walk through the field or around it to continue on the riverside path. Now you are almost home and a display board tells you the story of the donkey. Barnum played his part in the building of the *épis*, for which the stone was cut from a nearby quarry – his life's work was to return the empty trucks. Continue past Barnum's hut, and then past a track leading up the slope on your right. Take the second such uphill path – it is waymarked white on red – and will return you to the abbey church at the top of the hill.

## More Walks in the Area

The area from the Loire as far south as Cholet and beyond is known as the *Mauges* – an ancient term referring to the metals that were once found here, iron and gold. The countryside is gently undulating farmland with woods and sunken lanes such as you might find in Normandy. In 2001 the local tourist board began the production of five walking books of the region, each with its own particular theme – history, the countryside and religion were the themes of the first three, published by the end of that year. These are excellent books with thick shiny paper, good maps, plenty of photos and interesting text (unfortunately French only). Each has 20 – 30 walks and as far as it is possible to ascertain, the waymarking on the ground is of the same quality as the books. These publications are relatively expensive (although not for what you get) so you probably wouldn't want to purchase all 5 – but where to start? If you go for the countryside book *Loire et Bocage*, there are several routes not too far from St Florent exploring the *boires* of the Loire – those peculiar backwaters and arms apparent when the river is low in summer. To the west, the commune of Bouzillé has two such routes, and farther on, near Drain, there is an excel-

*The chapel of Notre Dame du Marillais*

lent circuit of 6.2km taking you across the low-lying land between several *boires*. A couple of picnic sites and a discovery trail with display boards are to be found on the route – which, as you would expect, is under water in winter.

Pursuing the story of the Vendéen War, a major victory for the 'Whites' (named from the white flag of the monarchy) was gained at the Battle of Torfou (west of Cholet) in the summer of 1793. A walking circuit of 9.3km starts from *la Colonne*, the monument erected in commemoration of this event. The route includes a stretch along the banks of the Sèvre-Nantaise and passes the site of Blue-Beard's château. This walk appears in the *Loire et Bocage* volume of the Mauges series – others relating to the Vendéen War appear in the volume entitled *Les Chemins de l'Histoire*.

On a completely different note, le Fuilet, south of St Florent, is a village of potters (see below). The pottery was once exported down the Loire from the port of Marillais. Following that route, a 27km waymarked *Chemin des Potiers* takes you from the le Fuilet to the Loire at St Florent and is described in the Topoguide *L'Anjou à pied*. It will also be included in the fourth book of the *Les Mauges en Marche* series, entitled *À la rencontre de savoir-faire: Potiers, Meuniers et Mariniers* to be published in 2002. There is no public transport between St Florent and le Fuilet, so you would need two cars or a taxi. The Office de Tourisme at St Florent would be able to advise you.

## Places of Interest Nearby

The *Musée d'Histoire Locale et des Guerres de Vendée* is housed in a 17th-century chapel not far from the abbey church. It's a bit of a mixture as its name implies, but you can see weapons and uniforms from the Vendéen War along with some interesting snippets about the Loire etc. The museum is open every day in high season and otherwise at weekends between Easter and November.

The *Ferme des Coteaux* is again open only in summer, when there are exhibitions of all kinds. There is also an aquarium of aquatic life from the Loire.

South of St Florent, le Fuilet and its surrounding villages stand on good clay soil and have been home to generations of potters. Follow the signs to *La Maison du Potier* at les Recoins south-west of le Fuilet – the *Maison* is an exhibition centre set in pleasant gardens with picnic tables. In the neighbouring roads, many pottery workshops and display rooms invite you to browse – it's hard to leave without a souvenir.

At la Chapelle-St Florent, the Moulin d'Épinay is a working windmill producing buckwheat flour – the miller will take you on tour. Both the Maison du Potier and the Moulin d'Épinay are open every day in July and August (not Saturday, Sunday or Monday mornings) – for other times check at the Office de Tourisme

# 30. The long history of Champtoceaux

From its wooded bluff above the Loire, the medieval town of Champtoceaux enjoys a commanding view. Far below, the houses of its old port still sleep in the sun and the grey stone arches of the toll bridge on the river have survived eight hundred years. This short walk is packed with interest all the way.

**Grade:** Moderate

**Distance:** 8km (5 miles). The route can be split into two circuits of 4 and 5km – if you only have time for one, it's a difficult choice.

**Time:** 2½ hours

**Map:** Champtoceaux is on the corner of 4 maps (1322 O and E, 1323 O and E). The route is very well used and waymarked – but if you would like more than the sketch map in this book to guide you, the two halves of the walk appear in two different books (Loire et Bocage and Les Chemins de l'Histoire) in the series Les Mauges en Marche.

**Start and finish:** The church at Champtoceaux

**How to get there:** Champtoceaux is situated on the south bank of the Loire about 25km east of Nantes. Arriving on the D751, climb up the hill and head for the centre of the town to find the church. The Office de Tourisme is behind it and there is plenty of parking in the same area.

**Refreshment:** Champtoceaux is well supplied with bars and restaurants and there is also a restaurant beside the river near the toll bridge.

**Notes:** This excellent walk combines two circuits, both involving some climbing and descending on the slopes beside the Loire, but nothing too serious. The riverside sections are at times a little rough and can be muddy out of season – stout footwear would be preferable. This is only a short walk and there is plenty of shade, but on a hot day it would be sensible at least to carry fluid with you. It is easy to opt for just one circuit or the other if you want a shorter walk. The second circuit can be started at Point 5.

**Waymarking:** The first circuit is waymarked in a sort of beige colour (*fauve*) and the second in red. Parts of both circuits are on the GR3 and so are additionally waymarked in white on red.

---

## Introduction

Perched on a granite outcrop high above the Loire, Champtoceaux was once the site of a Gallic hill fort, later taken over by the Romans and fortified again in the Middle Ages. Its stronghold known as *La Citadelle* was well placed to keep an eye on any comings and goings on the river below. The fortress was finally demolished by the Duke of Brittany in 1420 – you will see the remains of it on this walk.

On the riverside below *La Citadelle* stands another witness to life here in the Middle Ages. Two grey stone arches are the remains of the *péage fortifié*, a 13th-century fortified toll booth, one of only two surviving in France. A barrage was built across the river, compelling all river traffic to pass through. Various commodities were taxed, but the most important was salt, whose price inland was perhaps twenty times that in Brittany.

*Toll Bridge on the Loire*

The banks here saw many skirmishes between 'smugglers' and customs officers. By the 19th century goods were moving freely up and down the Loire. Not far from the *péage*, Port Hamelin was built to handle the wine, tufa stone, slate, lime and more that arrived on the flat-bottomed boats that plied the shallow river. Now Port Hamelin has been renamed la Patache and the once-busy quay is lined with fishing boats.

The walk at Champtoceaux really is a gem. It starts out promisingly enough, crossing the gardens of the 'Champalud' and descending through the trees to the *Coulée de la Luce* – a path spiralling around a stream in a steep grassy valley that is said to be a pagan site. The Loire and la Patache follow, and then, in the second part of the walk, the *Citadelle* and the *péage* are visited before a final climb past the old ramparts. Champtoceaux is justly proud of its history – recently the tourist board has erected twelve fine ceramic display boards to tell the tale in English as well as French. If you complete this walk you will have learned a lot.

## The Walk

1. Facing the church, take the path along its left-hand side, and continue past the Office de Tourisme and the gardens of the Champalud. On the edge of the precipice is a *table d'orientation* with a fine view up and down stream. Take the path that leaves on the right and soon follow signs to the *Coulée de la Luce* (ignore a path descending steeply to the road). Your path bends around to the right and eventually reaches a tunnel under the road. On the far side is the *Coulée de la Luce* – a curving path following the course of a spring to the Loire below. The spring at its summit is precisely orientated to sunrise at the summer solstice – this site and perhaps Champtoceaux itself may have been involved with early man's worship of the sun. Display boards will tell you all about it as you descend.

2. Reaching the Loire, turn right on the riverside path and continue to the quiet hamlet of la Patache. Keep to the path past the boats along

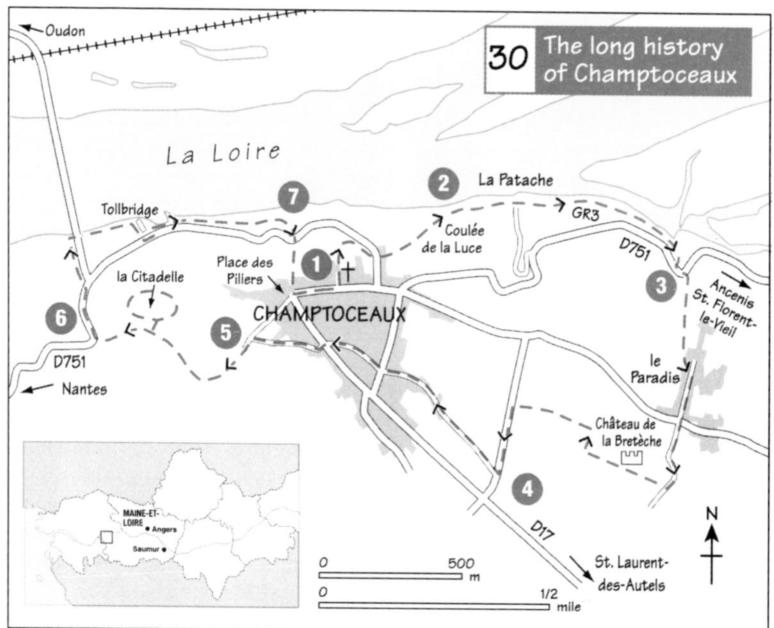


the riverside (waymarked in white on red and occasionally in *fauve*) – at one point a raised wooden walkway takes you around an outcrop of rock. Soon you reach a path cross-roads. To the left is the remains of an old lock on the arm of the river – the GR goes that way. The path you want is the one straight ahead – the narrowest of the three. This rather unlikely-looking track shortly brings you up to the main road.

3. Cross the road to a track directly opposite climbing uphill under the chestnut trees to arrive at the hamlet of le Paradis. The track joins a tarmacked road bringing you to a cross-roads with a Calvary. Keep ahead here and after about 200 metres, just after a right-hand bend, find an earthen track on the right. This pleasant path runs under the trees along the wall of the Château de la Bretèche and at one point offers you a good view of the building. The path bend right around the corner of the château grounds and then heads off towards houses on the left. Reaching a road in an estate of new houses, turn to the left.

4. With the stadium on your left, turn right down the Rue du Champ de Bataille, heading in the direction of the church, and soon passing an old windmill. At the cross-roads, go straight ahead on the Rue du Petit-Saint-Jean to reach the main road, the D17. Cross it directly and continue on the Chemin du Voinard, passing the school. At its end you arrive at the Chemin des Remparts.

5. This is the end of the first circuit and you can choose to return swiftly to the church – turn right on the Chemin des Remparts to reach the Place des Piliers with its medieval gateway, and then go right along the main street.

   For those continuing, the walk has now reached the second circuit, and the waymarks are red. Turn downhill on the Chemin des Remparts, which descends into a deep valley beside a stream. The path swings to the right beneath rocks and after further descent, you reach a signed path on the right climbing sharply through the woods to the Citadelle. The mossy ivy-clad walls invite you to use your imagination – and to help, a ceramic plaque shows Champtoceaux as it was in 1400. When you have explored all the nooks and crannies, and taken in the view across the river to Oudon, return to the track at the bottom of the hill and continue to meet the main road

6. Follow the road (with care) to the right for about 200 metres. Just before reaching the bridge, take a path on the left. Follow this almost to the Loire, and then turn right, walking under the main part of the bridge. The narrow track now leads you on alongside the river to the ancient toll bridge, where you should be able to look around (unfortunately it was under repair in 2001). To continue from the toll bridge, take a narrow track above it on the right. This sinuous path climbs and descends along the wooded bank of the river (an easier option would be the main road). The path bears waymarks from time to time, but there seem to be more flashes of yellow on red than red alone. Eventually (10 – 15 minutes) coming to a T-junction with a wider track, turn right (red and yellow on red) and continue winding uphill away from the river to reach the main road.

7. Cross the road slightly left to a track climbing up the hill on the opposite side. This track leads you under the ramparts (if it's midnight look out for the ghost of a monk – if it isn't, at least you can read about it!) and arrives at the Place des Piliers with its towers, the impressive remains of the one-time gateway to the town. Turn to the left along the main street to return to the church.

## More Walks in the Area

A board outside the Office de Tourisme will give you a quick glimpse of the waymarked walks in the immediate vicinity of Champtoceaux. Inside it should be possible to get more details in the form of a Topoguide entitled Balades en Pays de Champtoceaux. The same walks and many, many more are included in the 5 splendid books of the *Les Mauges en Marche* series – see Walk 29 at St Florent-le-Vieil for the details.

For those who enjoy following a linear trail, the railway running along the north bank of the Loire makes it possible to pursue a Grande Randonnée in three directions from Champtoceaux. To the east, the GR3 runs along the south bank of the river before diverting inland near Drain. It returns to the banks for a long stretch leading to St Florent-le-Vieil – see Walk 29. The total distance from Champtoceaux to St Florent is around 20km and in each town you would need to cross the bridge over the Loire to find the station. Heading west from Champtoceaux, the GR3 itself crosses the Loire to Oudon and then follows the north bank into Nantes. There are rail stations on the route – Mauves (around 10km from Oudon) and Thouaré (around 15km.). The GR3E heads east from Oudon, following closely the north bank of the Loire. Ancenis is less than 10km away and you could explore the lovely old town and ruined château before returning. For each of these routes you could seek out the appropriate IGN Série Bleue maps (on which they are marked) at a local newsagent or at the Office de Tourisme. Grandes Randonnées are always well waymarked on the ground, so you should have no difficulty following your chosen route.

## *Places of Interest Nearby*

If you have taken this walk, you will already have seen the tall tower of the medieval keep at Oudon. On the site of an earlier castle, the present keep dates from around 1400 and is open to visitors in the summer months. Not unexpectedly, there is a fine view along the Loire Valley from the top.

Again on the other side of the river, the old town of Ancenis was once thought of as the 'gateway to Brittany'. Now the centre of a wine-growing region (Coteaux d'Ancenis), you can taste the local wines at the Maison des Vins d'Ancenis and at Les Vignerons de la Noëlle. You can also take a guided tour of the old town and ruined château – or visit the canoe centre where an excursion on the Loire can be tailored to meet your needs.

You may or may not feel like entering the hustle and bustle of Nantes, the ancient capital of Brittany. It is in some ways a city in two parts – to the east is the old town where you will find the cathedral, the Château des Ducs de Bretagne and the Musée des Beaux Arts, to the west is the fashionable Quartier Graslin, built over the last two hundred years, with its centrepiece the neo-classical colonnaded theatre. Between the two is a 20th-century skyscraper known as the Tour de Bretagne – don't miss the (free) panorama at its summit.

## *From the Source to the Sea*

Leaving Champtoceaux, you can continue on the scenic D751 alongside the Loire as far as the junction with the ring-road around Nantes. If you decide to visit the city, cross the river here and follow the signs. To continue to the coast, take the ring-road to the south and leave where St Brévin-les-Pins is signed. Keep following the signs to St Brévin – and if you remain on the D723 you will first pass through the fascinating old port of Paimboeuf. It's worth stopping to take a walk along the quayside. From here the road parallels the river and there are views of the bridge to St Nazaire, the longest bridge in France and the last crossing of the Loire, as you approach journey's end at St Brévin-les-Pins.

# Loire-Atlantique

*Port de Tréhé in the Brière*

# 31. Windmills and wine at Monnières

Here you are in the heart of the Muscadet region. From the old village of Monnières on the banks of the Sèvre, take this ramble in the vine-clad hills – and at their summit, climb to the top of a windmill for a splendid view.

**Grade:** Easy / moderate

**Distance:** 10km (6¼ miles)

**Time:** 3 hours

**Map:** IGN Série Bleue 1324 O

**Start and finish:** The church at Monnières

**How to get there:** Monnières is just south of the N249 (E62) a few kilometres east of Nantes and is signed from that road. There is parking beside the church in the centre of the village.

**Refreshment:** Monnières has a couple of bar/cafés, but there is no refreshment on the route. There are picnic tables beside the Étang de la Tuilerie, about two-thirds of the way around, and another at the Moulin de la Minière

**Notes:** This walk is entirely on good tracks and quiet minor roads – trainers would be quite suitable footwear in summer. Out of season, the riverside tracks in particular could be muddy. All climbing is gentle. There is little shade on this route, so include the hat and sun-cream and carry plenty of fluid when the weather is warm. And take binoculars for the views – particularly if you want to count the spires from the Moulin de la Minière.

**Waymarking:** The riverside path is a Grande Randonnée du Pays and so is waymarked in yellow on red. Elsewhere, the waymarking is blue.

---

## Introduction

This is a surprisingly delightful walk in an area little-known to visitors. South-east of Nantes, the low rounded hills are cut through by two rivers whose names have become almost synonymous with this region's *raison d'être* – Muscadet. The Sèvre and the Maine wind their way through a landscape of vineyards that has changed little in two thousand years – the first vines were planted here by the Romans. Those early vineyards were destroyed by the Vikings of the 10th century, who had settled on the island of Noirmoutier. Subsequently replanted, the vineyards encountered other problems over the years. The bitterly cold winter of 1709 killed all the vines, except for one variety that had recently been brought in from Burgundy. Its grape was known as the *Melon de Bourgogne* – the Muscadet grape – and it was thereafter planted throughout the region. Worse was to befall in 1881, when the vine roots were attacked by a beetle from America known as phylloxera. Despite insecticides and the removing of infected plants, all the vines in Europe were destroyed. Only in America were there vines with a resistant root – but good French wine could never come from American grapes! The solution was to graft French vines on to the transatlantic rootstock – and so the *Melon de Bourgogne* lived on and the famous Muscadet is still produced here.

When the vineyards were replanted after the phylloxera crisis, the vines were set in rows to give easier access for horses pulling ploughs and harrows. You wont see the horses now, but much of the work is still

Moulin de la Minière

manual. The pruning is entirely done by hand and is incredibly time-consuming – as you walk, imagine setting out with a pair of secateurs to reduce each vine in those vast acres to just one shoot. The process takes all the winter months. Harvesting is becoming more mechanised, with tractors pulling a sort of 'threshing machine' that fits over each row of vines – but 40% of grapes are still picked by hand. The story of the vineyards and of the production of Muscadet is told in the *Musée du Vignoble Nantais* at nearby le Pallet – a visit would complement this walk.

Having said all that, the ramble here has more to offer than the charms of the vineyards. It sets out on a lovely riverside path leading to a *Grottes de Lourdes* pilgrimage site, a cave in the rocks. Farther on, the route passes an estate where fallow deer run in freedom and climbs to a windmill on a hill with fine views back over the little town of Monnières. A path through vineyards and woodland brings you to the peaceful Étang de la Tuilerie – and a final gentle climb leads to another windmill, the Moulin de la Minière, where you can mount the old staircase, survey the rolling landscape, and attempt to count the 23 spires said to be visible from this point. At the end of the day, the route returns through the oldest part of Monnières with its alleyways, stone houses and well-preserved communal bakehouse.

## The Walk

1. Walk downhill past the church in the direction of Saint-Fiacre. As the road swings left, go down an alleyway on the right heading between houses and agricultural buildings to a vineyard. Here turn left and then immediately right through the middle of the vineyard. Continue ahead past a road and then, with a wall on your right, turn left on a broad track between the vines – yellow on red waymarks can be found on the occasional stone. Over to the right you can now see the houses of Port Domino, the old wine port across the Sèvre. Keep straight ahead at a cross-tracks and then cross a wooden footbridge.

The path now bears right alongside the stream and then swings round along the riverside in front of the football pitch and stadium.

2. Turn left to leave the river and cross between the two playing fields. Behind the pavilion building a road leaves to climb steeply up the slope. At its lower end, take a track on the right into the woods – there are still the yellow on red waymarks of the GRP. Soon you arrive at the *Grotte de Lourdes* in the cliffside – it was established here as recently as 1957. Continue down steps and along the riverside until, after passing a plantation of poplars, the track reaches a tarmacked road

3. Turn left here (the GRP goes right). The road climbs past a field with a stream and a lake – look out for fallow deer here. A road joins from the right and you continue to climb above the stream. At the top of the hill keep left and then, at a cross-tracks, take a track on the right doubling back a little and winding through the vines. After about 150 metres or so, find a blue-waymarked track on the left leading up to the windmill, the Moulin de la Justice, at the top of the hill. There is a good view of Monnières in its valley ahead.

4. The track swings right in front of the windmill and descends to meet a broad track. You are now in a vast vineyard and following blue waymarks – turn right on the broad track and very shortly, with the windmill virtually opposite on the right, look out for a track on the left. This descends through the vines to a tarmacked road. Turn left here and continue for about 5 minutes, until the road is climbing again after the dip. Now take a waymarked track on the right, once more heading into a vineyard. Keep straight ahead on a well-waymarked track with a windmill and a wood ahead of you to the left. The track bends sharp left to meet the D7.

5. Cross this road (with care) to a track about 20 metres to the left on the opposite side. A couple of minutes walking on this brings you to a T-junction, at which you go right. Soon you are in a fine wood with chestnuts, beech and holly. The track passes right through and continues to meet another tarmacked road. Turn right here to reach the D59. Cross to the road opposite, and after about 300 metres, turn left on a gravely road (SP Étang de la Tuilerie). The lake and its pleasant picnic site are now before you.

6. If you take the path around the lake shore in an anti-clockwise direction, you will reach another exit just before the point at which you arrived. Leave here on another gravelled road and cross the D59 to a track opposite. This climbs gently and crosses a little tarmacked road almost directly as it continues to the windmill (the Moulin de la Minière) at its summit. Here is another picnic table, and you can climb the steps inside for more views and spire-counting. Away behind the mill a statue of Notre-Dame looks across the sweeping vineyards – the crop is at the mercy of the weather and needs her blessing. When you are ready to move on, continue straight ahead down the broad track for about a kilometre to reach the D76.

7. Cross to the track directly opposite. At the major cross-tracks, continue ahead – you have now picked up the yellow on red waymarks of the GRP again. At the road junction, turn to the right towards the

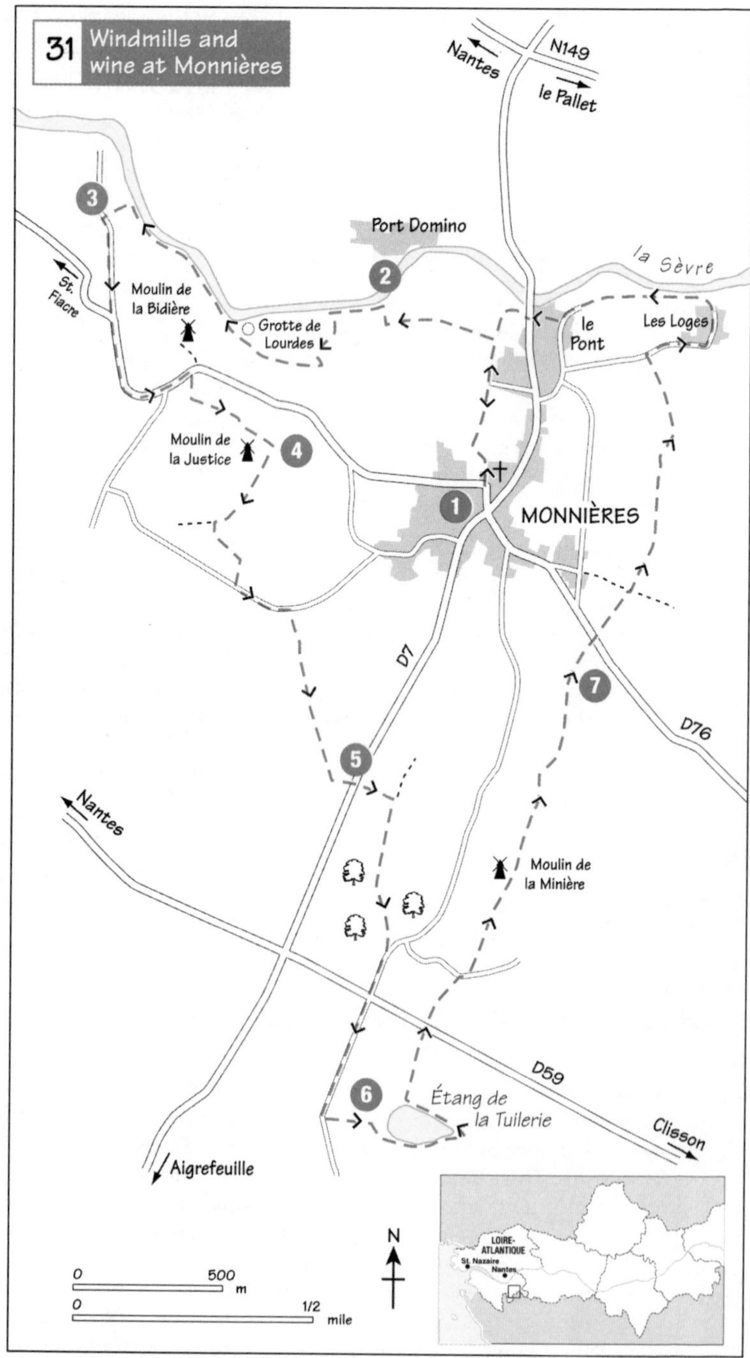


hamlet of Les Loges and follow the road now bending downhill to the left. Continuing ahead, you arrive at a path junction, and turn right to gain the wooded track along the riverside. The path arrives at the hamlet of le Pont – bear left on an alley between the stone buildings and keep ahead to reach the old square with its *four banal* (communal bakehouse). Retrace your steps along the alley, and now turn left (before the river), following the waymarks. Fine old stone residences line your route as you make your way to the main road (D7) and the bridge over the Sèvre. Now finally you have a choice. You can always turn left and walk up the main road to return to the cross-roads beside the church. But if the river is not high, you might like to walk under the bridge and continue alongside the river until the path is blocked by a wall. Turn left up the bank and keep ahead beside the stone wall to reach the junction in the vineyard passed in Point 1 – from where you can retrace your steps to the church.

## *More Walks in the Area*

The local tourist board's book of walks in this region is not surprisingly entitled *Randonnées – Détours en Vignoble*. Inside, however, it seems there's more to life than vineyards, and the first-class maps and colour photographs are an invitation to explore further. 46 walks in all are described. The text is, as usual, only in French, but the waymarking on the ground should help you round. Another publication that will serve your needs if you are staying around here is the Topoguide *La Sèvre Nantaise à pied* – the selection has been narrowed to 22 walks this time, but the maps are just as clear. The Topoguide also includes the routes of the three Grandes Randonnées du Pays (GRPs) of this region, one of which (the *Boucle de Vignoble*) you met on this walk. This particular GRP starts in Nantes and follows the Sèvre south as far as Clisson, returning along the valley of the Maine. The total distance is around 90km, possibly 5 days' gentle walking – if you are interested, get hold of the Topoguide and write to the Office de Tourisme in Nantes or Clisson for help with accommodation, taxis etc.

One local walk that appears in both the above publications is the 7km orange-waymarked *Circuit de la Sanguèze* at le Pallet, just north-east of Monnières. The circuit officially starts from the Chapelle St Michel in le Pallet, but as the *Musée du Vignoble Nantaise* is on the route, it could equally start from there if you are visiting. The Sanguèze is a tributary of the Sèvre and the walk takes you above and through its steep-sided valley.

Another walk from le Pallet is the 8km *Circuit de la Sèvre* – again with lots of wine-related interest. The route passes through Port Domino (once the port where wine was loaded into flat-bottomed boats to be taken into Nantes) and goes on to Le Pé-de-Sèvre, a typical wine-growers' village where the old stone houses have their external staircases (you may have seen them also at le Pont on this walk)

## *Places of Interest Nearby*

The *Musée du Vignoble Nantais* is at the southern end of village of le Pallet – cross the river bridge in Monnières and in 1km turn right on the N149. The museum sits above the valley of the Sanguèze and on the slopes around the building many vines of old varieties have been planted. Inside you can view past and present equipment of viticulture along with the presses, barrels, bottles etc. used in the wine-making process. An English text is offered to take you round. An unexpected twist appears at the end of the visit – the museum is run by the Pierre Abélard foundation (the great philosopher and theologian was born in le Pallet in the 11th century) and a room is reserved for the showing of a film relating to his life and his tragic love affair with Héloise. And after all that, you are invited to sample the wine. The Musée du Vignoble Nantais is open every day from 1st April to 10th November

Carrying on down the N149 from le Pallet will bring you to the remarkable town of Clisson, perched on high cliffs on both sides of the Sèvre. Destroyed in the turmoil of the Vendée uprising, the town was later rebuilt in Tuscan style according to the whim of three men who had recently returned from Italy. One of them, Frédéric Lemot, was a sculptor, and you can walk through the grounds of his country home (Parc de la Garenne-Lemot) with its columns, statues, grottoes and all the trimmings of Italy. The town also boasts a fortress-château dating from the 12th century and a Renaissance covered market. To be sure of seeing all there is to see in this unusual town, the Office de Tourisme can find you the route of a 7km walk, *Circuit au Coeur de Clisson*

One other nearby château deserves a mention – the Château de Goulaine, about 10km north of Monnières. In some ways this is the 'last' of the Loire châteaux – although there is,, of course the Château des Ducs de Bretagne in Nantes. Goulaine is a stone slate-roofed château that has belonged to the same family for over a thousand years. The present incumbent is not short of ideas to attract visitors – in addition to the lavishly furnished apartments there is a greenhouse of tropical butterflies and an exhibition relating to the history of the LU biscuit company. You can also purchase the local estate Muscadet – whose label bears a butterfly logo.

# 32. St Brévin-les-Pins – estuary and ocean

After a journey of more than 1000km, the Loire reaches the sea between the industrial port of St Nazaire and the little holiday resort of St Brévin-les-Pins. Follow the river to its very end, and then head south along the pine-fringed beaches of the Atlantic coast.

**Grade:** Easy

**Distance:** 14km (8¾ miles). A short cut will give you a circuit of only 7.5km (4¾ miles).

**Time:** 3½ hours for full circuit. The shorter route will take less than 2 hours.

**Map:** IGN Top 25 1123 OT – but the best map, with all the road names, is in the tourist brochure of St Brévin-les-Pins, obtainable from the Office de Tourisme.

**Start and finish:** The *Ancre de Marine* (a large ship's anchor) on the sea front at St Brévin-les-Pins.

**How to get there:** St Brévin-les-Pins is south of St Nazaire across the estuary of the Loire. Head for the town centre (not St Brévin l'Océan) and from there take a road to the sea front where the anchor is obvious. There is parking along the sea-front and on other roadsides.

**Refreshment:** There are plenty of restaurants and bars around the centre of St Brévin. On the walk you will also pass a couple of restaurants beside the estuary.

**Notes:** This is a very easy walk for everyone on good tracks and minor roads all the way. There is little shade, so if the sun is shining, remember the sun-cream and carry plenty of water. If you choose the shorter route, you will be missing the country lanes and hamlets – and, more importantly, the estuary with its fishing shacks (but you could drive back there in the car later).

**Waymarking:** The route is first waymarked in yellow, then sporadically in blue. There is then no waymarking until you reach the Grande Randonnée du Pays along the estuary (yellow on red). Just follow the text.

## Introduction

Here you are at the mouth of the mighty river, more than 600 miles from its source on the slopes of the Gerbier de Jonc high in the Cévennes. The Loire slips silently into the sea between contrasting banks – to the north, the docks and oil tankers of St Nazaire and to the south, the holiday promenades of St Brévin-les-Pins. Between the two sweeps a bridge of certain French elegance – opened in 1975, the Pont de St Nazaire is, at 3356m, the longest bridge in France.

The walk here takes you through country lanes and holiday hamlets to reach the estuary. If you have seen any tourist information from St Brévin-les-Pins, you will have seen that its logo appears to be a silhouette of a shack on stilts supporting something like the skeleton of a four-ribbed umbrella. Here you can see the real thing – a long row of fishing huts, each raised above the water on what look like the most rickety of stands. From each 'umbrella' hangs a square net – it is simply lowered into the water to

*Fishing huts in the estuary*

catch the fish. Some of the shacks are painted in bright colours creating a photogenic scene with the grey waters of the estuary and the bridge to St Nazaire in the background. The route from here follows a rough track alongside the estuary – the tourist board has yet to realise the potential of this one. After a diversion inland, you return to the estuary – and now the scene has changed. The bridge is behind you and seats under the trees look out on a harbour of fishing boats, and the activities of the jet-ski club. The promenade continues to the point, where an old fort, now the *Musée de la Marine*, hides from the Atlantic breeze behind a high wall. You can climb to the viewpoint with its *table d'orientation* and say farewell to the river as it slides imperceptibly into the ocean – from where it will only be born again.

Once you turn the corner, you are definitely in the Vendée. There are wide golden beaches and tall pines that are the first of those that fringe these western shores all the way to Spain. This is a pleasant place to finish a voyage – and if you are fortunate enough to have time to spend here, you may be surprised to find that this 'journey's end' is one of the most fascinating regions of the Loire Valley.

## The Walk

1. From the *Ancre de Marine*, cross to the Rue de l'Église opposite and walk up into the town, passing the Office de Tourisme on the right. Maintain the same direction leaving the Place de la Victoire and then continue across the main road and past the parking area (you may not get any further than this on a Thursday or a Sunday – the street market is irresistible). Now continue on the Rue Albert Chassagne – there is the occasional yellow waymark. At the end of this road is a statue of

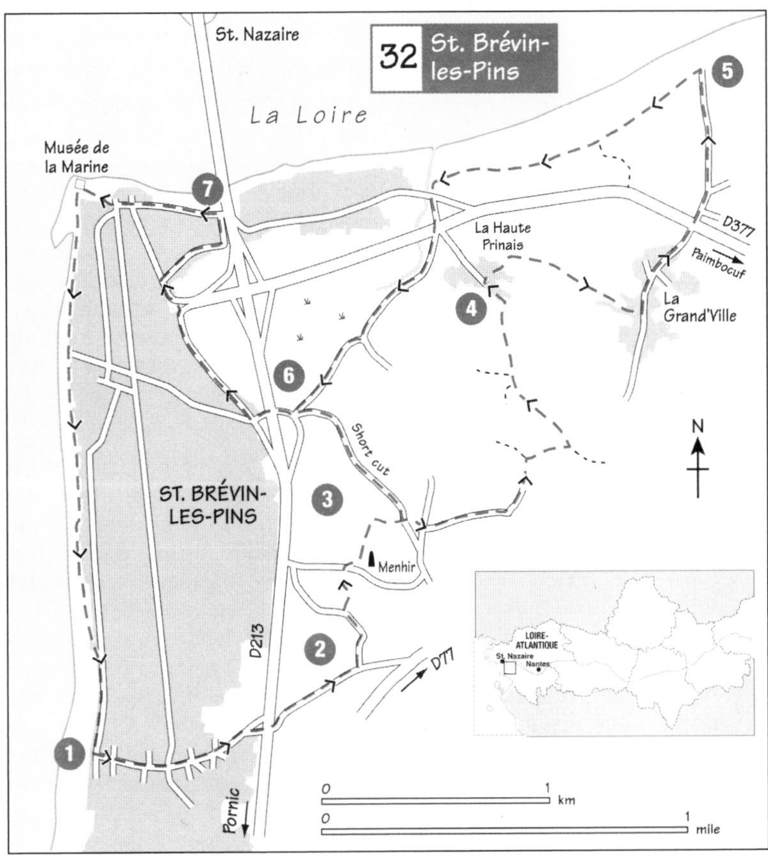


the Virgin Mary, erected in fulfilment a vow made by the inhabitants of St Brévin during the terrible Second World War bombings of the Loire estuary. From here, your route dips under the fast road and continues gently uphill for about 500m

2. Turn left on a road that is waymarked in both blue and yellow, the Chemin du Grand Ruau. After passing a narrow road on the right, take a track on the same side, heading in the direction of the water tower – the waymarking is blue. Passing the tower, you reach a tarmacked road. Turn right and then left on to a track, which itself soon swings round to the right – in the field ahead is a menhir, the *Pierre du Plessis-Gamat*. The track continues to the top of the field and then to the right to meet a tarmacked road.

3. Here you could choose to take the short cut to Point 6. For this, turn left here and continue along the road for approximately 800m to a road junction. Turn left and walk under the fast road.

   To continue with the longer walk, cross this tarmacked road and then immediately another and continue ahead on the Chemin des Rochaffais. Passing a German *Blockhaus* on the left, the road corners left. Continue ahead now until you come to a T-junction. Turn right here, still on the Chemin des Rochaffais, and, coming soon to another junction, turn left on the Chemin des Grinchais. Of course, all the waymarking seems to have disappeared just when you need it – but at least the tracks are named. Continue ahead (passing a track going off on the left) to meet a tarmacked road in the hamlet of la Haute Prinais.

4. Turn left into the village and, after about 100m, turn right on a track alongside a white garage. The track becomes tarmacked as you approach the village of la Grand' Ville. Reaching the 'main' road, turn left and continue past the bee farm, (Ferme des Abeilles) – some of the houses are very Vendéen with whitewashed walls, red roofs and powder-blue painted shutters. At the centre of the village there is a pretty pond with picnic tables shaded by tall pine trees. Here the blue waymarked route turns right, but you keep straight on through the village to meet the D377, and cross it to the road opposite. Continue ahead on this road to meet the banks of the estuary beside a factory building. Walk down on to the sandy shore to get a good view of the fishing huts and the St Nazaire bridge.

5. When ready to go on, continue on the road behind the factory (boat hulls are made here). The road becomes a sandy lane and after about 500m, bears round to the left. Turn off to the right here and take the rough unmarked track that continues parallel to the estuary. The terrain now looks a bit uncared for, but you have fine views of the bridge to divert you. 10 minutes of walking will bring you again to a tarmacked road, where you turn left. (Turning right here looks like a short cut, but it takes you through the extensive campus of a hospital for the handicapped. The intended 'blue route' diverts as this one does). Continue ahead to meet the main road. Cross with care, and take the road opposite, bearing round to the right. Continue ahead for about 15 minutes, passing marshes on your right, to reach the road junction.

6. Bear right and walk under the fast road. At the road junction on the far side, turn right in the direction of Mindin and keep to this road for 10 minutes or so, passing the junction with the road to Paimboeuf. Take the next road on the right after this junction, the Avenue des Fosses, which at its end bears left to meet a road.

   Cross this road to a footpath running up to the carriageway of the fast road. You could walk across to St Nazaire – but instead, turn left before you reach the road and drop down above the beach.

7. This is now a pleasant promenade taking you out to the point and the Musée de la Marine, housed in a fort that was built by Vauban in 1754. From this promontory you have your last view of the Loire – take your photographs and say goodbye. Your route now turns south and there are no more difficulties with navigation. Simply keep to the path above the beach to reach the road along the sea-front and the *Ancre de Marine*.

## More Walks in the Area

The promontory of land south of the mouth of the Loire is known as the Pays de Retz. Its local tourist board has produced one of the finest collections of walking leaflets to be found anywhere along the length of the Loire – *Pays de Retz Atlantique – Randonnées*. The individual leaflets are available free from each local Office de Tourisme or you can buy the whole collection containing 56 circular walks and the route of the Grande

Randonnée du Pays. The best Office de Tourisme in which to find this collection is undoubtedly the one on the harbour at Paimboeuf – it is one of those tiny offices that somehow manage to stock tourist information from all over France. Sadly the waymarking on the ground is not in every case up to the standard of the leaflets themselves – you saw how the blue waymarks disappeared on this walk at St Brévin. Nevertheless, the maps are excellent and you might like to try the yellow route at St Brévin-les-Pins or one of the routes at St Brévin l'Océan.

South of St Brévin, the coast curves out to the westernmost point of the Retz, the Pointe St Gildas. Starting just north at the little town of La Plaine-sur-Mer, a 'blue' circuit of 15km will take you right around the point with some very attractive coastline. The route is included in the collection mentioned above – and it is well waymarked. More coastal walks are to be found all along the south of the Retz peninsula – don't miss the superb seascapes around Pornic.

The walk here at St Brévin ended with a section on the Grande Randonnée du Pays (GRP) along the coast. That GRP continues along the coast past St Brévin l'Océan, heads inland around St Michel-Chef-Chef and returns to the sea at la Plaine-sur-Mer – a total distance of 24km (15 miles), a very suitable length for a day walk. Unfortunately there are no good bus connections, so unless you have two cars in your party, you would have to get a taxi one way – the Office de Tourisme at St Brévin should be able to help you. The route is to be found in the collection *Pays de Retz Atlantique – Randonnées*.

For walking of quite a different sort (and strictly confined to the summer months), head north across the bridge to the atmospheric marshland of the Parc Naturel Regional de Brière (see Places of Interest). Here you can walk on raised paths between reedy swamps and peaty canals alive with wildfowl. The Maison du Tourisme de Brière (see below) can offer you various routes. One of the most attractive spots is the Port de Bréca on the west side of the marshes. Two routes start from here – if you want just a taster, take the 4km 'blue' route passing the picturesque Port de Tréhé.

## Places of Interest Nearby

St Brévin-les-Pins is an unsophisticated holiday resort with a long safe sandy bathing beach (supervised in summer) and a first-class traditional market spilling through the streets twice weekly. Festivals, fetes and fireworks are added in July and August. The Musée de la Marine is open from June to September, and houses maps, models of ships and other maritime objects.

To the south is the Pays de Retz where the Côte de Jade extends around the Pointe St Gildas and on along the wild coast to the picturesque and fashionable pleasure port of Pornic. Back beside the Loire, Paimboeuf was, until the 18th century, the first port on the Loire. You can wander along the old quay where there are sometimes exhibitions and, in July or August, enjoy a cruise on the estuary as far as St Nazaire. Just to the east of Paimboeuf is the entrance to the Canal de la Martinière, built at the end of the 19th century to carry large shipping to the port of Nantes. Abandoned only 18 years later, you can walk and picnic beside it and wonder at the size of those huge locks. Between Paimboeuf and St Brévin, the village of Corsept surprisingly has murals by Corot in the Maison de

Pasquiau. Ask at the Office de Tourisme in Paimboeuf if you would like to see.

North of the Loire, do not miss a drive along the peninsula to la Croisic – and then continue on the narrow road across the salt flats where egrets stand silently in the shallows and you may spot modern day *paludiers* (salt workers) plying their trade. If the latter has interested you, turn in to the village of Saillé and visit the *Maison des Paludiers*, where they will tell you that there are about 300 salt workers in this bay and they are training more each year. A film (in English if you are lucky) will tell you all about it – and, of course, you can buy the salt.

And last, but not at all least, the Parc Naturel Regional de Brière is more than worth a visit. The Brière is a low-lying marshy area cut by canals created by early peat diggings. Around the marsh are several 'ports' where you can hire one of the traditional flat-bottomed boats and punt off into the reeds – or, since it's not that easy, opt for a guided trip instead. In summer when the water is low it is possible to walk out on designated paths – in winter, the marshes are flooded and in the long evening light the vast expanse of wetland is perhaps at its most beautiful. Other attractions here are the well-preserved old villages and many houses thatched with local reeds. The *Maison du Tourisme de Brière* at la Chapelle-des-Marais can give you all the information you want on this magical region.

## From the Source to the Sea

If you have made this journey all the way from the Cévennes, it's now high time for a celebration. Find a restaurant to suit the occasion, perhaps overlooking the sea or estuary, and order with your meal a bottle or so of your favourite wine – which will naturally come from the Loire Valley. This is the moment to raise your glass to the Royal River – and to those who, like you, have completed this voyage from the Source to the Sea.*

*If you have completed and enjoyed this journey, the author and publisher would be very pleased to hear from you with regard to future publications. Please write (with any comments you may have) to Sigma Press – the address is on the back cover.